THE
MADNESS
OF JULY

THE
MADNESS
OF JULY

James Naughtie

The Overlook Press
New York, NY

For Ellie

This edition first published in hardcover in the United States in 2014 by
The Overlook Press, Peter Mayer Publishers, Inc.

141 Wooster Street
New York, NY 10012
www.overlookpress.com
For bulk and special sales please email sales@overlookny.com,
or write us at the above address.

First published in the UK in 2014 by Head of Zeus Ltd

Cataloging-in-Publication Data is available from the Library of Congress.

Manufactured in the United States of America

ISBN: 978-1-4683-0882-2

1 3 5 7 9 8 6 4 2

'... I was unjustly accused of being a politician, because I was privy to the secret griefs of wild, unknown men.'

F. Scott Fitzgerald, *The Great Gatsby*

The characters in this story, like their governments,
are imaginary. Only the cities and the highlands
of Scotland are real.

People

The British
Will Flemyng, minister in the Foreign and Commonwealth Office,
   London
Francesca Flemyng, his wife
Mungo Flemyng, historian, his brother
Lucy Padstowe, civil servant, his private secretary
Paul Jenner, secretary to the cabinet and head of the civil service
Jonathan Ruskin, cabinet minister in charge of government
   coordination
Janus Forbes, defence minister
Harry Sorley, secretary of state for education
Tom Brieve, foreign affairs adviser to the prime minister, 10
   Downing Street
Gwilym Crombie, private secretary to the government chief whip
Jeffrey Sparger, Elias McIvor, ministers
Chief Inspector Jarrod Osterley, metropolitan police special branch
George Denbigh, clerk, House of Commons
Sam Malachy, officer in the secret intelligence service, MI6
Arthur 'Babble' Babb, the Flemyngs' caretaker at Altnabuie,
   Perthshire
Aeneas MacNeil, a priest
Archie Chester, a doctor

The Americans
Abel Grauber, diplomat, US mission, United Nations, New York
Hannah Grauber, his wife
Maria Cooney, chief of a department of US intelligence, Washington
Zak Annan, Barney Eustace, her assistants
Joe Manson, an operative for Maria
Guy Sassi, CIA officer
Jackson Wherry, US embassy, London
Bill Bendo, liaison, US mission, West Berlin

THURSDAY

ONE

Will Flemyng took cover. The falling willow branches shielded him from view and he watched Lucy weave through the encampments of deckchairs in the park, passing him unawares. He was close enough to hear her humming a tune as she steered a course towards the office, beyond the trees. But Flemyng stood rock-still in his hideaway and stayed calm. His life had so often involved the deception of friends.

When she had gone, he slipped from the fountain of greenery that protected him, and a few steps took him over the little bridge and away. No one stirred in the crowd around the lake and not a single duck rose from the water. He left them slumbering into the deep afternoon, turned his back on Whitehall and let London swallow him up.

Sam would be punctual, reaching their rendezvous at the appointed minute and moving on if Flemyng didn't appear. He had in mind the last scribbled words on the postcard he had destroyed in the early hours of the morning: 'Don't dawdle.' They were playing their old game.

That meant there was danger, and his second encounter came less than three minutes after Lucy disappeared.

He had crossed the Mall and climbed the steps at the other side, eagerness lengthening his stride and speeding him up. As he turned the corner, a government car slowed down alongside him, pulled up and parked a few yards ahead. He couldn't turn back without risking a scramble. Knowing the back of that head and the cut of the spade beard, he prepared himself and felt a flicker of fear that surprised him. The passenger heaved his bulk out of the rear seat, spotting Flemyng as he straightened up, and pushed a government red box out of sight.

'Will!' Jay Forbes could always summon up cheeriness from the depths. He steadied himself on the pavement with one hand against the car, and boomed, 'Whither?'

'Hi, Jay. Lunching, I assume?' Flemyng smiled and raised a hand in greeting. He swung his jacket over one shoulder.

'Not going for a swim, that's for sure.' Forbes grinned. 'On patrol. You know me.'

He took a step forward and leaned closer. 'Ball-crushing cabinet committee. I was called in. Jonathan Ruskin chaired it – God knows why – but at least he gave your Foreign Office lot a bollocking. Defence sails on, thanks to the Russians playing around. Nothing like having a frisky enemy. Hardly had to say a word.'

He laughed and his eyes gave Flemyng a slinky scan from top to toe, unblinking. He seemed to balance his weight on one foot in an ugly pirouette, drops of sweat springing from his broad brow. His cream shirt was too heavy for the heat, and he wore a purple brocade tie. 'What brings you out in the sun?' he said, and didn't wait for an answer. Swinging round, he gave a merry wave and steadily climbed the steps to his club. There was a rattle of glass from the tall door as it closed behind him.

Flemyng took a moment to get back into his stride, caught between on-and-off affection for an old friend and alarm. He concentrated on breathing regularly, and crossed the street to stay his course without looking back. By the time he reached the next corner he had found a rhythm, and was a picture of calm. His rich blue linen suit seemed to brighten with the sun and his polished black shoes caught the light. He was tanned and slim. A man of style and purpose, on the move.

Summer crowds swarmed and chattered around him, yet for Flemyng the winding down of the dog days brought claustrophobia, and the contrary suspicion that he was adrift on a wide sea with a spreading horizon, maybe lost. Despite the status he had achieved and the famous confidence that was his shadow, he felt creeping over him the fear that Sam had stirred up.

Striking across Soho, he wondered if he'd be recognized. Strangers were fine; friends worried him more. His route steered him away from places where they might be lunching, or spilling out from a familiar bar. He had plotted a course around obvious dangers, trying to turn the city's byways and surprising angles to his own purpose and safety. It had to be a walk. Government cars turned a few heads, and ministerial drivers were the princely chatterers of Whitehall, alert to the slightest trembling in the web, and reading the political runes with a deadly eye. Their ears picked up in an instant the enticing beat of a private crisis. He thought of Forbes's man watching their encounter on the pavement from the car, his eyes turning to the mirror and away again.

Will Flemyng savoured his rivalry with Forbes, his opposite number at Defence, each of them climbing the ministerial ladder at the same pace, with a seat in cabinet the prize for the first to haul himself up to the next rung. Although he carried the weight of his name – Janus Forbes had borne the two-faced jokes on his back since schooldays – he could lighten a room with his high-octane bonhomie. And for Jonathan Ruskin, of an age with them in his mid-forties but already in cabinet and entrusted with the right to roam in the corridors of every government department, he felt less jealousy than an outsider might have expected. The secret friendships of politics persisted, and it was helpful to be close to the minister who was the first to carry Ruskin's dread but alluring label, the Co-ordinator. 'I'm the pioneer,' Joanthan had said on the night he was appointed in a chaotic ministerial reshuffle the previous year, 'but I won't be the last to do this job.'

In the street, Flemyng checked his watch. He was now at the game he and Sam had learned together, when they walked the same frontier – checking faces, watching for the one that turned away too quickly, remembering the old rule that when you sensed the absence of the normal, there was trouble round the next corner. With an actor's ease he established a comfortable pace and pressed on. Lifting his head, for a moment he thought a woman coming towards him might have clocked him as her eyes came up to meet his. Elegant, distracted. He broke his step, and cursed silently. She slid past him with no more expression than a ghost's.

Then the touch of a dream, like a whisper of silk. The passer-by had a hint of his mother's spirit – something about the walk? For a moment or two, in the Soho steam enveloping him, Flemyng felt the whisper of a breeze from home, coming down from the hills and up from the burn that cascaded past the woods on its way towards the loch. A happy picture flashed in his mind's eye, of his mother in contentment, perched at her easel in the wide first-floor window on the southern gable of the house to catch the last of the sun, her shadow fading gradually into the dusk of an early-autumn day. Mungo and Abel were with him, and they walked three abreast up the rise from the loch towards Altnabuie, where a flicker on the bow window of the drawing room told them that Babble was lighting the fire. Soon they would be together in their favourite room and could draw the evening around them. They would sit down at the old orrery, setting off its mechanism and watching the brass planets and moons weave their courses in perpetual peace.

The bright idyll faded as quickly as it had appeared.

'Happy days,' he said, and realized that he had spoken louder than he'd meant to. A barrow boy on the corner laughed, unbuttoning his shirt and scratching himself in the heat. Flemyng raised a hand in friendly farewell and hurried across Oxford Street, which he disliked more than any other in London, striking westwards for a few minutes. He looked at the sign on the corner. Harley Street, Sam's choice. Just in case, Flemyng carried on to the next turning, where his discipline faltered for a moment. At the last, when he should be keeping on the move, he paused.

Fame and privacy clustered together at the door of every mansion block around him, each with its ladder of shining brass plates bearing a list of the doctors busy inside, the top men, whose names were whispered among the desperate rich and the lonely, and accorded by them an intimate celebrity. The greatest secrets were so often the greatest boasts.

'Lost?'

A friendly voice, welcome in any other circumstances. No one he knew, and no one who knew him, because there was no giveaway smile. A guy on the street in helpful mood, no more. An innocent.

'No, but thanks. On my way, that's all. Just enjoying the warmth.' Flemyng pulled a dark blue handkerchief from his breast pocket and wiped his brow.

'Aren't we all? Ta-ta,' came the reply.

The ships passed in the night and Flemyng watched him sail off towards the happy tables of the Cock and Lion on the next corner, jacket slung off and trailing on the ground, unseasonal pin-stripes sliding dangerously down his rump, an arm waving high in the direction of a friend who had appeared through the doorway of the pub, two foaming glasses raised in silent salute. Flemyng envied them.

Nearly there. First, the phone box on the next corner. He made a pile of coins and dialled, thinking of Mungo making his way to the hall at Altnabuie, maybe having slipped down the iron spiral staircase from his library or come in from the garden with the dogs running ahead and capering at his feet. The line clicked, and his brother's soft voice said, 'Flemyng speaking.'

'Mungo, it's me. We're well, I hope.'

'We are, I'm glad to say, little brother. And all the better for hearing you.' His voice was reassuring. The sun was on the hill, the bees in the lavender. All calm. They spoke for a minute about the heat, stifling London and the cooling shimmer on the loch at home, before Mungo said, 'You are still coming north, aren't you?' His change of tone betrayed a suspicion that something had gone wrong.

'It's why I rang. I may be delayed a little. The weekend should work out, but I can't be sure. You know what it's like here in summer. Politics goes haywire; a little daft. So I'm afraid I can't promise.'

'Please come. I've got all those papers and we do need to talk. They're ready for you.' Mungo was speaking more quickly.

'I will try. Be sure of it.' There was a brief silence, then Flemyng said, lightly, 'One thing… I wondered if you've heard from Abel.'

'Nothing back yet.' Flemyng could hear his brother moving, perhaps sitting down. He was conscious of the echo from the hall. 'I'm sure he'll be in touch.'

Flemyng said, 'Of course he will. And I'll be coming home…
when I can.' The phone gave three beeps. He looked at his
watch, slid another coin in the slot. 'Soon. Try not to worry.'

He spent a few seconds more in the box, oblivious to its
rancid smells, before he pushed open the door and turned
back along the street.

Just as the bells on two nearby churches began to sound a
ragged sequence on the hour he reached the opening to
Mansfield Mews and Sam appeared from behind him. He
had the knack of materializing from nothingness. A hand on
Flemyng's shoulder and they were moving towards the shadowy side of the street. Sam was broad and beefy these days,
shorter than his old friend, his curled russet hair grown
longer. He wore black jeans and carried a cracked leather
jerkin that made him look as if he was on the run. At first
sight he was threatening, but had soft liquid brown eyes.
Flemyng believed that most secret servants came in two
guises: the silk-smoothies who were quiet and always listening, or the unbuttoned wild boys who were always talking.
Each to his own, but sometimes he wished he had been more
like Sam.

'Trouble?' he said, without preliminary.

'Of course,' said Sam, giving his toothy smile. Flemyng
absorbed his presence, rolling some scenes across his mind
like the rerun of a favourite film with chance meetings and
scrapes on the battlefield, remembered days of despair and
the sound of the tunes of glory they'd sung, long into the
night. He thought of Berlin and Helsinki, a freezing border
post in the dark, chilly interrogation rooms, and nights on the
street. The endless waiting.

He was touching the scar that ran from his neck across his
chest.

'The war wound?' said Sam, who could remember when it hadn't been there.

Flemyng had picked it up in Vienna, of all places, where the spies enjoyed opera and Sachertorte as well as thrills in the street. The Stygian darkness of an underground bar after midnight, a botched handover and a fight springing up from nowhere that left him bleeding and crawling back to the embassy with the thought that he might die before he'd got through his thirties.

'Cherish it. We've all got our mementoes,' said Sam. His were a broken marriage and a dry-out that had left him hollow for a year. With a touch of embarrassment, Flemyng took his hand away from his neck and leaned back against the railings behind him, looking directly at his friend. His own face was cast half in shadow, which emphasized his sharp profile and turned his longish dark hair to jet black. The deep hollow clefts on his cheeks were like two extra scars. The light cast the two friends differently – Flemyng's sharp edges giving him a clear profile, Sam's outline a construction of curves and wobbly lines.

'So?'

'First,' said Sam, 'I know my Will. Worried?'

Flemyng sighed. 'I've found out something, old friend, and I wish I hadn't. That's all.'

Sam tried a joke. 'That's a change for you.' But there was no response from Flemyng. Sam's shoulders rose as he pressed on. 'If you're wondering why I summoned you to these parts, I have an appointment across the street with a quack of a certain kind. But I don't think I'm going to be keeping it, do you?' He pushed Flemyng's shoulder to turn him slightly, and nodded up the street. He saw a government car. Not a numberplate he recognized, so a driver pulled from the ministerial pool with an anonymous vehicle for a one-off run. No passenger inside. 'Who?'

Sam shook his head. 'I'd like to find out – I daresay I will – but we don't want to be seen, do we?' Flemyng dipped his head and Sam led the way quickly round the corner. Before he turned, Flemyng glanced back at the black door of number six in the mews, where the car was parked. No one to be seen. He thought there was a hint of movement at a net curtain on the second floor, then nothing.

Head down, he fell into step with Sam, gesturing towards a pub in a side street that looked at first glance like a dead end, but had a narrow lane at the far end if it was needed for a fast exit. He had used it before. 'Let's have a quick one.'

Flemyng was alert for signs of fear in Sam but he seemed unrattled, relieved to see his old colleague. 'I'll fill you in quickly. Sorry for pulling you out, but I had to. Walls have ears.' He spoke in a rich northern voice that had never picked up the speech of the south, of any class. The tone was flat, but in compensation Sam's language always danced. 'What's the buzz on the Rialto? In the salons. Hear anything intriguing, anything odd?' He paused. 'Because I do.'

They sat down by a window without drinks, but the barman took no notice. Flemyng shook his head. 'About whom?'

Sam's smile flashed at him. 'Can't say. But somebody's in trouble.' Our kind of trouble, he might have said. His sunny expression disappeared.

'Out with it,' said Flemyng.

'Something unusual, strange – a watch on somebody, and here's the thing. It's on your side of the fence and not mine, just for once. There's a minister in the middle of this. Breaks all the rules, of course.' He laughed. 'Will, I can't get a handle on it. I'm not sure why, and that's the truth.'

Flemyng kept his voice low. 'Leaks? Dirty work?'

Sam's head was almost touching his. 'I haven't a clue, old cock. The place is tight as a drum. Hardly a whisper. Scary.'

As so often when they had walked the line together, wrestling the Great Bear as Sam used to put it, Flemyng's mind cleared as if it had been cooled and refreshed by a passing shower. Concentrating hard, he gave Sam the question he wanted. 'Why me? What can I do?'

Sam's voice was almost inaudible now, and Flemyng could feel his breath. 'This time, for once, I'm not taking from you. I'm giving. OK?'

Flemyng waited.

'I heard something yesterday. Just a word muttered in the undergrowth. That's why I scrambled you overnight; got you here fast. Sorry about that.'

'Give it to me, Sam.'

'It could be you.' His hand was on Flemyng's arm. 'The one they're after.'

TWO

Lucy Padstowe, twenty-nine and a woman of steely confidence, was shaking as she put down the phone. Melancholy visited her from time to time; but genuine alarm, the kind that penetrated to the core, was rare. Her habitual calm had been strengthened by two years in charge of the private office, riding the excitements and ploughing through the weary troughs, so the cabinet secretary's words had brought on a tremor of unease that was unfamiliar to her. She closed the door to the inner office and sat behind Flemyng's desk.

The window was shut despite the heat, and long white net drapes kept out the glare of the sun. She arranged his papers, embarrassed herself by trying the top drawer of his desk and finding it locked, and started trying to track him down. She'd turn to his network, which was hers as well as Flemyng's, the gift of her ministerial patron to his closest civil servant which shaped her days and coloured both their lives. She took to its byways to try to find him.

Ringing Jonathan Ruskin's office on the other side of Downing Street was a natural start. The Co-ordinator sat in an island mid-stream and events flowed towards him. Colleagues thronged at his door, with favours to trade. Although he was a graceful bird of passage in government and a master of the soothing phone call, the barons of Whitehall had a natural

12

resistance to his existence. With the power to break the territorial rules by which officials lived, Ruskin was a constant irritant. For gossip, however, he was always reliable. And around the watering holes of Westminster, he was fun.

She rang his office first: 'Lucy in Will Flemyng's office. Has my man dropped in?' – but she got nothing, tried Jay Forbes's private secretary next and felt the tinge of frost that came with Defence, even gave Sparger's people at the Home Office a call despite their minister's serpentine ways, and talked to Harry Sorley's bag-carrier at Education, although she was sure Flemyng would avoid that quarter for the moment. There were two or three others, and a disingenuous call to the press people downstairs just in case. No news. His constituency secretary knew nothing, but begged for a quick word in the afternoon; Flemyng's chairman was agitated.

Lucy was lost.

She considered her options and after a few moments rang the cabinet secretary's office, aware of her nerves. 'Is Paul around? Lucy Padstowe again. Sorry to come back so quickly, but I need him if he's there.'

The line went quiet, a red light winking every two seconds on Flemyng's phone as she waited. Then Paul Jenner himself. 'Have you spoken to Will?'

'I'm sorry, no. I'm sure he'll be here soon. But I'm afraid I have to confess something that I didn't say earlier. I don't know where he's been, or why.' She added, by way of defence, 'Does this sound odd?'

'Not in the least,' said Paul. 'What are you suggesting?'

'Nothing. I'm just saying.'

She found herself continuing without waiting for an answer. 'It's natural that I'm a bit worried, given what you said a few minutes ago. Unusual things have been happening.' Her voice was speeding up. 'He's been distracted. Off-kilter. No fun around the office, and you know what he's like.' She rushed on. 'I'm sorry, I know this is a little embarrassing. Private secretaries shouldn't blab.'

'I wish more of them did. Let me know when Will's back. I'll need him here. He's just away from his phone. Some day we'll find a way of tracking them everywhere – can't come soon enough for me – but there's nothing we can do for now. Try not to worry.'

The conversation was over. Having wound herself up, the words tumbling out, Lucy felt a heaviness in the room as if time was slowing down around her, forcing her to think. She'd suspected from his voice that Paul Jenner, spider at the centre of her web, was trying to suppress a tremor of his own, which surprised her because his command appeared effortless and the power of his writ was unquestioned, running through every channel of government, from its sacred places to the last secret corner. Nothing bypassed Paul. She pictured him at his vast desk, looking to the high bow window that gave on to the park, his perfectly round grey eyes unblinking while he concentrated. Flemyng said that when he was in that mood it looked like the onset of *petit mal*; but Paul never lost control.

Back to her minister. One of her assistants had seen Flemyng leave the office about an hour earlier, and told Lucy that nothing seemed out of the ordinary. Jacket over his shoulder, he had traded smiles with her in the corridor as he turned towards the broad staircase to take him down, gesturing to the sunshine outside. His tie was loose, the collar of his pink shirt open.

He had told the office that he would need no driver, so Lawrence could have a quiet lunchtime with no fear of a summons. The weather was up and there were personal errands to run, no more than that. The word was a welcome breeze in the private office. 'He'll be buying a birthday present,' someone said. 'No,' said Lucy. 'Covent Garden for lunch, I'd say.' But she wondered why he hadn't told her.

In his absence, a lazy air settled on the three rooms that protected Flemyng's own; the tea trolley squeaked to a stop in the corridor, and a little queue formed; leisurely gossip flowed through ministerial offices, each protecting its own oasis. Everyone was trying to enforce the calm, driven on by the heat. Meetings were cancelled across Whitehall, as if to hurry summer along.

Little Simon, than whom no one was more junior, was putting together pen portraits of backbenchers due for end-of-term drinks on Monday, writing in loopy longhand because the new electric typewriters ran away with him – and because it was a shirt-sleeve day and lunchtime, with the minister not at his desk, he pushed the boat out, rowing with schoolboy gusto, stripping the guests of their last shreds of dignity. Wife trouble, new boyfriend, money worries, love affairs with the booze… all the chatter he'd heard. It would be filleted and cleaned up in the afternoon, the list rendered acceptable for Flemyng's overnight red box, but no one took Simon aside for a heavy word of advice, which was a symptom of the season, because in sharper, cooler times he'd have been pressed against the wall and filleted himself for his foolishness. But it was hot, and rules were suspended.

Summer had come and parliament would rise in a few days. Relief, and everyone felt the beguiling touch of an unexpectedly balmy time. From the office they could sniff the atmosphere beyond the long windows, see the greenery through the scaffolding that had gripped the building for a year and more. Layers of soot and grime were being scraped away and carted off in processions of wagons that left black trails along Whitehall; the inner courtyard held a ring of iron skips filled with decades of pigeon droppings from the roof, and an acrid reminder lingered in every hallway. Some day, they were told, their Victorian palace would shine again, a painting with its bloodless colours restored and cracks healed. But not yet.

Lucy wondered how she would explain to Flemyng why Paul wanted to see him. Peering through her window, streaked with dust, she sensed the warmth outside.

Taking to the corridor to steady herself, she set off on a clockwise circumnavigation of the building. It echoed to scraping and banging from the courtyard. They were carrying off the skips again.

It would have been no reassurance to her as she walked out of the office if she had known that at that moment Flemyng had been lost to the world for a minute or two in the fetid heat of a phone box near Oxford Circus. A hand banged on the door. 'Get on with it!' Then banged again. Flemyng, who had not entirely lost his capacity for embarrassment, burst from the box without ringing Lucy as he'd meant to, and walked quickly to a bus stop with his head down. She would have to wait. He ignored a taxi rank, climbed on the platform of a bus that was crawling towards the traffic lights, and swung through a crowd of Dutch schoolchildren on the bottom deck. It would be a slow haul down Regent Street, and the more welcome for that.

The man next to him leaned across.

'I know who you are.'

Flemyng's head snapped back.

'Sorry, but I saw you on TV the other night. You weren't bad. Better than the bird in the red dress anyway. A bimbo, that one.'

Flemyng said, 'Well, we try our best.'

'Mind you, I can't remember your name. Sorry about that.'

'Flemyng.'

'That's it. I've always had you down as one of the posh ones. Top drawer. I'm surprised to see you on the bus, Mr Flemyng. Nice, though. You working today?'

'There you are, you see. Taking the bus, taxpayers' interests at heart. Just out for a few minutes.' Flemyng smiled and leaned towards his companion. 'Good to meet you.' They had reached Pall Mall. He took his leave, crossed the street and headed for the park. From the top of the Wellington steps he could see the window of his own office through the trees, three along from the foreign secretary's corner lair. Five minutes away at a gentle pace.

Behind the window, Lucy was back at her desk and making another call. 'Francesca, it's me.'

'Hi. What's up?'

'Have you got my wandering minister with you?'

'Wandering?'

'I need him.'

'No. Don't you know where he is?' Flemyng's wife laughed. 'That's a change.'

'Just out, that's all.'

She knew Francesca would be alerted by the oddness of the word. Lucy was precise about where her man was, day and night, the dog who was never off his leash. 'Out' carried no conviction.

'Any ideas?'

Francesca wondered aloud whether he might be present-hunting for her birthday the next month, then they shared their puzzlement in a moment of silence.

'Probably a quick walk in the park,' Lucy said, unconvincingly.

She could sense Francesca treading water. Her voice was deep and smooth. and Flemyng often spoke about its hypnotic effect, her style being elegant and unhurried. She was two years older than him, although she had looked the younger at their wedding the previous summer, and Lucy had concluded early in her time with him that it was from Francesca he absorbed some of the free spirit that enlivened their office. She often thought that in Flemyng's character, gaiety and darkness were always struggling with each other. Without Francesca there might have been more frenzy.

Now Francesca said, 'Well, he needs to be back for the opera,' changing the tempo. In her professional role as social manager at Covent Garden – queen bee of the opera party, Flemyng called her – she had become the famed impresario of the interval encounter, and a simple supper she had planned for the private room was getting bigger by the hour. 'The cabinet secretary's office has been on,' she said. 'There are two Americans coming from somewhere, and now it's going to be Paul Jenner himself and two other ministers on top of that. I still don't know who. His office have put it together. All of a sudden it's turned quite... political. They're laying on lobster – the works. Can you warn Will?'

'Americans?' said Lucy.

'Yup. But from where I don't know, if you see what I mean. I expect you've noticed he's been a bit distracted in the last week or two. I don't know how much he's told you.' No response from Lucy, so Francesca plunged on. 'There's a thing going on in his family that seems to be awkward. News to you?'

Lucy said that organizing his life in government was difficult enough without families getting in the way, and avoided the point.

The conversation made a quiet and quick gear change, without warning, as if they had pushed open a door together. 'Can I be frank?' said Francesca.

'Please.'

'Something else has knocked him sideways, and I'm not sure what it is. You know how much Will enjoys his politics. Now it all seems to be turning sour for him, and quickly. That's what troubles me.'

Lucy didn't hesitate, aware that a pause would produce awkwardness. 'I've noticed. Don't know anything about family matters, of course.' By unspoken agreement, as if the conversation needed to be wrapped up before it took on too many complications, they were quick to wind things up.

Francesca asked, 'Anything on your desk that might have caused all this, if you're allowed to tell me?'

'Nothing that comes to mind. Pretty routine right now.'

Then an offer from Francesca. 'Lunch next week, OK?'

'Please.'

Francesca said, 'I'm glad. I'll fix it.'

The two women spoke of a sultry weekend, and the unreliability of men who didn't say where they were going, and made cheerful farewells because neither wanted the conversation to drift. Lucy closed the outer door again to get some quiet, ignoring a thick file that she saw being placed on her desk. There was too much uncertainty. Americans turning up, names unknown, to sit with him and two other ministers for a whole evening, and at the bidding of the cabinet secretary. Paul should have told her. She shifted in her chair. Coincidences, Flemyng always said, were never what they seemed.

*

At the Royal Opera House, Francesca was feeling a ripple that disturbed the heaviness settling over everything with the rising heat. She didn't believe the birthday-present story that she'd concocted for reassurance, knowing Flemyng to be a last-minute merchant, but she had needed to confide in Lucy. She leaned out of her window near the top of the building, put both elbows on the ledge, and found a faint stream of fresh air. The crowds of high summer were down below, around the old vegetable market, now empty and a place of bare stone since the last traders had been shunted south of the river to their new home. A place of memories and sweet echoes. Murmurs from the holidaymakers rose towards her. She looked over the rooftop landscape towards the river. It was just an unusual day. Her man had wanted to be out of the office, get some air, have a break. That was all.

But Lucy was off balance, which broke the pattern on which they all depended. Francesca let her eyes scan the heads of the crowd below, an anonymous throng, close and yet unaware of her gaze. A singer was practising in a dressing room one floor below, window open, and Francesca listened for a few minutes. The voice was Russian, melancholic, lonely.

The phone on her desk was just behind her, and its ringing shook her out of her mood. A secretary from Paul Jenner's office.

'I have the names. They're all looking forward to it. We're so glad Will can make it, and we're sorry to be in such a rush. You know how it goes.'

'That's just how we like it,' Francesca said. 'It's opening-night panic here.'

In Whitehall, the pavements were thick with gangs of visitors, the curious and the lost. Crackling commentaries spilled from the open-topped tour buses and a few words floated through the window in Flemyng's inner office that Lucy had decided she must open at last.

She was still at the desk, fiddling with a heavy black pen but writing nothing. She didn't know he had arrived back until the door opened and he was standing in front of her. She noticed sweat stains on his pink shirt, and a hint of wildness in his hair. But he smiled.

'Where have you been?'

'I went for walk. I'm allowed to, don't you think?' He was still smiling, hanging his jacket on the coatstand, undoing another shirt button. Looking away as he spoke, he said, 'Anything up? An exciting telegram maybe?' He busied himself with an open red box on the corner of the desk, and she saw the nervousness in his shuffling with the files inside. He closed it and turned the lock with the tiny brass key that went back into his pocket.

Lucy was ready. Her tremble had gone, and she was alert to every change in his expression. He was relaxing, but she spotted the effort in masking the tiredness. Lucy said he should sit down, and even gestured to his chair as she stood up from it, in charge again.

She took his place in the doorway, turning away to close the door quietly. Spinning round, strands of light red hair sweeping across her face, she sensed that they were both reluctant to break the deep silence. His eyes were fixed on her, and she realized that his concentration had kicked in.

'You're going to have to get to Paul's office quickly,' she said.

'Paul? Quickly?'

She watched him lean back and slip one hand into his shirt, touching the scar.

'When you were out...' and she added with a deliberate hint of the cruelty that intimates understand '... wherever you were...'

21

He was utterly still.

'… I heard some strange tidings from Paul. And bad, however you look at it.'

His hands were back on the desk and she saw that he was trying to hold them still.

'There's a dead American. And he has your phone number in his pocket.'

THREE

Half a world away, at the moment when Flemyng got his summons to Paul Jenner's office, the clock on Grauber's kitchen wall in New York was showing eight-fifteen. He set coffee on the hob and quickly took the four steps outside the house for a walk to the bakery three blocks away.

Hannah would be up when he got back, kids too, and there would be time together before he headed uptown to the mission and his desk. He wanted to lift his mood after a broken night, and the auguries were good. A storm had powered down the Hudson Valley in the evening and was safely out to sea, leaving a layer of lightness on the city. The skyline sparkled in gratitude, the weight of the last week gone and the air on the move. The freshness encouraged Grauber to find a spring in his step, despite the day ahead.

He was above medium height, though not tall enough to stand out, and slim. Against the fashion his hair was cut close to the skull, almost to stubble, and that often gave him a serious look whether he liked it or not. He had the advantage that when he smiled, a dimple on his chin gave him an air of cheerfulness that even suggested frivolity. His outward appearance could change in an instant. But most of the time his jet black eyes under shadowed lids, and lips that were heavier than his finely boned face might have promised, seemed to veer towards

23

gloom. This was misleading but helped at work, where he carried serious burdens.

The United States Mission to the United Nations, squatting on the corner of 45th and First Avenue, was heavy duty. On his floor, never visited by outsiders, he led a working life that forced him every day to balance flurries of excitement and exhilaration against the weary conviction that conflict would never end. He worried above all about Berlin and points east, and believed he always would; moving pieces on a board which seemed to stretch to infinity. He'd come to believe that the slow-motion struggle in which his life had been subsumed would roll on beyond him and carry him off in its wake. A few cold warriors on the other side would doff their fur hats to him as he disappeared, as he might do for them; that was how it went. There was little he could reveal of such thoughts to anyone except the few who passed through the third-floor doors with him each morning, and from time to time to Hannah, who had been introduced to some, but only some, of the intimacies of his trade. Yet against the grain of his time Grauber seemed to his friends an optimistic man, with a priestly air of calm. He knew that it was misleading, because his hopes were laced with melancholy more often than he would have wished.

And as he stepped along East 20th Street his upbeat morning mood was tested. Not particularly by the shadow of a National Day celebration in the East 80s in the evening at which he was to be the senior American alongside his ambassador, although that would be a trial, but by the planned meeting with an old comrade-in-arms for lunch in one of the faded city watering holes that he treasured: the Oyster Bar in the depths of Grand Central Station. In the night he had spent two silent hours at his study desk worrying over the encounter while Hannah slept upstairs, the dog bundled at his feet and a friendly glass of whisky in hand, from a bottle he seldom opened, playing war games with the conversation they might have. The drink was almost untouched when he slipped into bed.

Now as he crossed Irving Place, the memory of the previous night's ball game took hold. The Yankees had been obliterated in a double-header at Cleveland. He knew what awaited him, and he loved the tangy flavour of old New York that it represented, always taking trouble to let the city play to its strengths. There were surprises and turnabouts enough at work; he wanted this place to stay as he loved it, although he would remain an interloper. He got to Lehman's corner, and the guy who always sat at the top of the subway steps caught his eye. 'Go Mets!' Grauber acknowledged the taunt with a grin.

Inside the shop, bakery on one side and the small deli on the other, connected by a swinging glass door that allowed husband and wife to rule their own domains, Lehman was more sympathetic because he shared Grauber's commitment. 'Mr Grauber,' he said, the formality an endearment, 'that pitcher!'

An unknown voice came through the half-open door to the deli. 'He pitched like my granddad… dead five years.' A rumpled grey head followed the voice. 'World Series, my ass! Forget about it. Excuse me, Mrs Lehman.'

No one disagreed and Grauber took the chance to ask for his bread. A round rye as usual, and a long sourdough, which would see them through the next day or two. Then through the door to the deli, where the pickles glistened in their jars and the air was sharp with sauerkraut. Husband and wife swapped places each day, Monday to Saturday, bakery one day and deli the next, which gave their lives a nice symmetry, and pleased their customers who liked the atmosphere of a shop where something was always happening. He asked Mrs Lehman for a particular salami, tied up in its red string bag, which they'd work through in the course of a week.

'Things good?' said Mr Lehman as he passed back through the bakery.

Grauber raised a friendly fist. 'Can't complain. Better times coming. Seattle here Friday. Whole new ball game.' The baker inclined his head, and smiled after him when Grauber stepped into the street.

He was back on 20th in a few moments, thinking of the box of work he'd locked in his office safe the night before. Nothing too troublesome, although there was a rumour which might be productive about a Czech, new-blown into town, and the mission was alarmed about a secretariat appointment in the wind: the Australian was a disaster, too prone to vodka parties with the wrong gang, and had to be stopped. It was in hand, and a French friend might help. But that could wait, and in the office it would be an easy, catch-up day. Lunch was everything.

As he turned the last corner, he almost collided with a neighbour whom he knew by sight. He seemed to be Spanish, though whitewashed by the pallor brought on by a high life that was nearly over. He was accompanied by a tiny dog, decorated with a jewelled collar and trotting fast behind him. The matchstick piston legs reminded Grauber of happy days in Paris when just such a precious animal, the only love of the ambassador's wife, was suffocated on a sofa at the end of a memorable embassy party with one heave of the mighty buttocks of the Norwegian chargé d'affaires, who was never told what she had done. The beast was buried the next day under the magnolia tree in the residence garden, after a night of tears. Grauber smiled. Old times.

But Bill Bendo was in town, and Grauber couldn't escape the consequences. By the time he'd crossed the street towards the front door, his brown bakery bag in one hand and the salami swinging from the other, his smile had gone.

In a minute he was in the hall of their narrow townhouse. 'Maria called,' said Hannah from the kitchen.

Washington.

And if it was Maria at that hour, as Hannah well knew, it could be London too. She hadn't waited for him to reach the office. He felt a familiar, welcome prickle of excitement. 'She'd like you to call. Quickly, I guess.' Hannah smiled at him, and nodded. He placed the bread and the salami on the table, and went to the door. 'Back in five. Ten, maybe.' He never called Maria from home.

The routine suited Hannah too, because there were parts of his life that could never be shared. He went along the block to Gramercy Park where he had a key to the private gardens, a privilege that came with membership of the National Arts Club across the square, one of his quiet places. He would often spend time in the first-floor sitting room there, under a painting hung near the window. It was calming at bad moments, and in darker times had been a solace to him, bringing the family to mind. He felt the energy and tranquillity of his distant home in all its deep colours and the boldness of the long, familiar brushstrokes.

There was a payphone at the corner of the garden where he could safely make a call, but only if it was brief. 'What's up?'

'I need you here.' No preamble; no names.

'It's the lunch today.'

'Don't I know it,' she said. 'But straight after. We have troubles of another kind.'

So no panic flight, no helicopter scramble from the East Side pad. Grauber would keep his date with Bill Bendo, just rolled in from Berlin. 'I'll get the four o'clock shuttle,' he said. No more.

'Perfect. Dinner at home. Just show up.'

They rang off.

A game was afoot. Must be. He was now relishing the day, for all its promised difficulty, and the prospect of Washington always lifted him a little higher, Maria's troubles notwithstanding. As he turned east along 20th, the low morning sun was brightening the sidewalk. It signalled a clear and warm day, the sky a duck-egg blue and a breeze of perfect strength freshening the streets. The pretzel seller on the next corner was manoeuvring his metal cart into position and it sent out silver flashes in the sunshine. Grauber speeded up as he reached his own steps and pushed through the door to find Aaron and Michaela up and about, full of summer camp talk, getting their bikes and tennis things and their hiking gear in order.

'There's sailing. Canoes.' Departure was two days away. 'Dad, are you sure we have to take our clarinets?' He would certainly – surely – be back from Washington by the next night, so he could drive them to camp at Kiamesha Lake, a couple of hours north-west of the city. 'Will there be bears?'

He drank a quick coffee and gave everyone his news. A short trip. Hannah hugged him. She whispered in his ear, 'Only Washington?' He nodded, taking care to add a little shrug, and grabbed his coat, picked up the overnight bag that he kept ready in the closet, and said he'd take the subway at 23rd to the mission. ''Bye, babe. 'Bye, kids.' He gave them a joint squeeze. 'Think about those bears.'

He was at the avenue in less than a minute and, taking in the sunshine again, he changed his mind about the subway, waiting for an uptown bus instead. The traffic was flowing well towards the gentle slope of Murray Hill, and he'd be there by nine. He'd picked up a *Times* at the bus stop and skimmed the front page, then digested the paper, watching the horizon for any change in the pattern, the cloud no bigger than a man's hand that might yet spread to fill the sky. No puzzle this morning that couldn't wait. He left the bus at 44th and walked a block to the mission, its frontage on First Avenue dappled with sunshine.

There was a new pair of security guards when he passed through the door. 'Sir,' one of them said, glancing at his pass, and that was all. Sometimes he had to open his shoulder bag, but not today. The other guard nodded in silence, an efficient and sober exchange, stripped of small talk. Grauber got into the elevator and went to the part of the mission on the third floor where he and his immediate colleagues worked and gossiped undisturbed, without the artifice they practised on the other side of the heavy door.

'Hey! Seen a pitcher lately?' The water cooler was host to a town meeting on the Cleveland disaster. But he wanted to see if there was another message from Maria and slipped away.

There was, securely transmitted and left for him to decipher alone after it had chattered out of the printer and a marine brought it to his desk in a square green file, flagged with a yellow tag. 'Priority, sir.'

It was a paragraph only. He was not going to London – a relief, because he'd make it to summer camp – but something required his attention and advice, now. There was enough in the message to convince Grauber that Maria, the coolest of cats, was rattled. And, because she knew how to do it, she had dropped in a magnetic word: 'Joe.'

At their section meeting, his mind wandered. There was time to take the morning slowly. With the arrival of high summer, the tourists were overwhelming the diplomats. Missions winding down, restive bureaucrats fanning out in the heat to find some shady places. Even for lives governed by the whispers that were his daily bread, the pace was slackening. No one rushed.

Scanning the list of meetings for the day, he checked for Brits, from habit, and found none, noting that Her Majesty's permanent representative, his ambassador's opposite number and sailing friend, had left already for a long annual leave, involving a week in Maine (this from a dinner at the ambassador's residence two nights before, duly logged by one of Grauber's assistants along with a sharp account of the conversation) and then three weeks in London and Devon, where he would be forgetting New York.

One of Grauber's equivalents in the British mission two blocks north of the Americans, nominally a cultural attaché, was in temporary charge. He was a friend with whom Grauber transacted a good deal of business between their agencies at least once a week. Neither ambassador, perched above them, knew everything. Grauber wore his extra skins with ease. It was like having a second name and gave him a special pleasure. He worked with many who had obligations of secrecy but few enjoyed the extra twists and complications that shaped his life. He cherished the mystery, and in the jumble of intelligence outfits that had been mangled and juggled in rolling reorganizations through the years of scandal it was more difficult than ever to work out where the power lines lay. A question that would once have been laughed out of court – 'who exactly do you work for?' – was apposite again. Byzantium reborn.

The more people gave up on trying to work out the lines of communication, the happier he was. He doubted if there was anyone in the mission who knew Maria, where she worked or what she did. 'I enjoy being the second string to your bow,' she would say, with a dirty laugh. 'Or third?' he'd say. Washington churned, and he loved it.

He had no worries about his own ambassador, with whom he had a placid relationship, though it was devoid of warmth. Underneath it lay the certainty that the boss, whose white mane gave him a Falstaffian presence but whose diplomatic horsepower was puny, would always be limping miles behind. Grauber preferred the company of those on the other side of the veil.

He had no cause to inform the ambassador that he was going to Washington, and every reason not to. He passed a routine morning, telling his secretary that he would be out of town for twenty-four hours, and otherwise saying little. No other details were offered and there was nothing odd about that.

He arranged for a colleague to deputize for him at the National Day party in the evening, and fixed a lunch with his British friend for the following Monday – they'd head off-piste to an uptown German restaurant they enjoyed, both of them having done *Mitteleuropa* time, where there would be no other diplomats. He would need to tune in. There was some reading to catch up with and personnel files to scan, because of a reshuffle near the top of the mission. He'd have views. Then it was time to walk the five blocks to Grand Central to indulge in a lightning shoeshine before he pushed open the heavy doors from the street.

He'd contributed to the public campaign to save the old station from the wrecker's ball two years before and longed for an end to its strung-out, dingy decline. The aged Oyster Bar had begun to recover something of the spirit of great days, and he liked to think it would encourage the rest of the building to throw off its despair. He had another reason for choosing it: he would see no friends there, only Bendo.

He walked down the ramp from the concourse, the whistle for a departing train sounding at his back, and prepared for a mad city scramble.

The garish tiles on the vaulted roof reflected a riot every lunchtime. Diners were buffeted in a storm of instructions and demands, their compensation the feeling of being cast adrift in a city at play – they were seafarers in a speakeasy, sluicing and dredging through Bloody Marys and coast-to-coast all-year-round oysters, cherrystones and little-neck clams, Long Island steamers and striped bass and sturgeon; sinking old-style martinis in frosted glasses; shouting at each other across the room; moaning at children and parents; hurling imprecations at the mayor for letting the city go bust; bawling news bulletins about the Yankees or the Mets, and listening to a pink-haired regular, her face limed with chalk-white powder, imprisoned in a dialogue with herself about awful happenings in the street far above. They poured their energy into the communal cacophony, then sucked it back. Their lifeblood.

He had come early to grab a couple of seats at the end of the long bar, just on the rounded corner, where they could put their heads together and exchange words under the canopy of noise produced by the crowd. There would be no fear of silence, no danger of isolation. They were pebbles on a stony beach, secret whisperers in Bedlam.

He passed on the Bloody Marys because it would be a long day, but set up a mound of clams and a jug of water. A man next to him was working his way with care into a lobster, poking at the leg cavities with a set of thin blades and spikes. He cracked the claws with a flourish and a happy grunt, sending a hailstorm of shell fragments across the bar. The waiters shouted at each other, made maracas noises with their cock-tail shakers.

'Dozen Wainoo, half Moonstone, half Tamagouche. Razors on seven!' The swing doors to the kitchen banged back and forth. 'Gotta go, fourteen! Folks in line.' Then a cry from the door.

'Grauber!'

'Bendo!' Grauber had prepared for the expected show of enthusiasm – their usual locker-room greeting, followed by a bear-hug. Appearances mattered, even now. Bendo was wide and tall with curly blond hair, of Grauber's own age, born and bred in the city. He had four children and a wife called Nancy from Poughkeepsie and had never let a party down in his life. They sat together, clinked glasses, Bendo wheezing and succumbing without protest to a Bloody Mary, ordered their food without discussion and caught up. Summer camp talk, wifely updates. They got through it quickly.

Grauber opened gently, though without a smile, giving some reassurance to his friend, but not too much. There must be no mistake. 'We may have a deal. If you're willing.'

Bendo pulled a bowl of chowder towards him, carefully. 'So we're wasting no time. Right?'

'Right.'

'But here?'

'Why not?' said Grauber. 'Kind of place we like. Thought we might remember better times. Fellow soldiers for Uncle Sam, all that. That's my question. Willing?'

'To talk?'

'Of course,' Grauber said.

Bendo picked up, responding to the pace that had been set. 'Will it help me?'

'More payback for us,' said Grauber. 'Something of value. I guess that helps you. A little, anyway.'

'But not much,' said Bendo. 'We know that.' He was chewing a salt cracker, and dropping his voice as he spoke. 'I'm done.' In a few moments they had travelled a long way.

'Yeah,' said Grauber. 'It's over for you, old friend. The game's up. We've both been waiting for this moment, and it's come.'

Bendo waited for more. It was a question from Grauber. 'When they fixed this… encounter, did they leave it to you to work out why?'

Bendo spread out both hands. 'They knew I was ready. I'd run out of road. Never thought it would be like this, though. Us. Here.'

'But you knew it would come.'

'The confession? Sure,' said Bendo. 'Just couldn't tell how it would feel.'

'And?' said Grauber, hoping Bendo wouldn't flag. 'Relief?'

But he tried a joke, asking if Grauber had brought handcuffs in his bag. Neither of them laughed. 'It's easy to stray,' he said. 'Even when you know there's no way back. We wanted a thrill when we started in this game. We were in love with the danger – me, you too – and we never lose that feeling. It beats away underneath. Always there, promising another adventure. I can hear it now.'

With that appeal, Bendo placed a hand on Grauber's arm. He got nothing in return. As his voice had softened, Grauber's had taken on a sharper tone and he shook his head. 'It's going to be easier if we don't play it like that when we have to sit together in some damned room, wherever it turns out to be. You didn't drift, you changed sides, old buddy.'

Faced with the fact, they fell silent for a moment.

Grauber picked up first. 'And the question why isn't the important one for me – you know that – it's the beginning. Who, how, when? The timeline. All the stuff that's going to help us in other places, with other people. The ones after you who'll come along. They always do.' It was the first cruel jab. Bendo was no longer the guy who'd slipped through the same streets as Grauber, a secret gunner in the same army, but an emblem of betrayal. A miserable statistic, and a wraith of a spy.

But he hadn't yet given up asking questions. 'You say we've been waiting. I guess I have. But you – how long?'

Grauber looked him in the eye and said, 'No dice'.

He listened to Bendo setting off on a detour, trying to steer the conversation up a siding as neatly as he could manage. It was absurd. For a few minutes there was a pretence that their conversation hadn't taken place. Bendo spoke of another audit of European stations going on with the Langley bean-counters in charge, and London was in a sulk. 'Really pissed.' Berlin might scrape through, the island in the east that was still the bulwark and therefore protected to the last. Bendo might have been bred for its charms and demands. He flitted between the soldiers and the diplomats, happy to be neither one nor the other. 'Liaison!' he'd sometimes cry to friends. 'I'm the whore who visits every bedroom, the highest and the lowest. Everyone knows, and they never give it a name. Just let me work the street.'

His ambassador in Bonn, with whom he exchanged messages from his Berlin satellite, because that was the propriety that they observed for form's sake, was a diplomatic bird of passage who'd worked clandestinely in an earlier life, and that helped. Knew some useful levers in Washington that he could jerk, a few old debts to call in. 'You? How's Santa Claus?' Grauber shook his head with a thespian's sigh, and he spoke inconsequentially about his own ambassador for a minute.

But the atmosphere cooled quickly; Bendo was forced back to earth.

'My time's up. OK. Still have my uses, though, even if I'm going to miss out on all the shit in Poland. That's coming, I promise you, and soon. Got some good lines in there, believe me. Just like us, in the old days. Never again.' Grauber listened to him doggedly treading water, and was touched by the gentle, lingering boastfulness of the boulevardier spy. 'I'll miss it. The city that never changes.'

He looked up. 'Going across?' he asked Grauber, playing with the leafy celery stick growing out of his cocktail. 'London?'

'No plans. No reason right now.' Grauber was hunched over the bar, dealing with a softshell crab, his voice almost a whisper. They created their own pool of silence in the crowd. Bendo and he had shared so many secrets since their paths first ran together in Saigon in the full bloom of the war nearly a decade before, and taken them from the heat to the chill of the western front. History between them, ancient and modern.

Bendo said, 'I'm a loyal man.'

Grauber spoke as if he hadn't heard, the appeal dismissed. 'You're ready for everything that…' he had unwittingly picked up Bendo's fear, and stumbled over the words '… has to happen, whether or not we want it? It'll take time to tell the whole story. Long days.'

Bendo, however, wanted to complete his thought and wouldn't leave his script. 'I still think you can bring good out of bad. Always believed that. Keeps me going.'

But the answering silence obliged him to answer Grauber. He raised the glass to his lips and said, 'You'll get what you need. Promise.'

Grauber replied, 'Names, places, times. I'm trying to make this work for everyone. That's a promise, too.'

Bendo looked sideways with eyes that had yellowed since they'd last been together in Berlin, when they'd walked for two hours in the Tiergarten. Grauber waited for a question, maybe a plea, and put his hand on Bendo's for encouragement, the first time he had reached across since they sat down.

Then Bendo said, 'Sorry, of course.'

'Me too,' said Grauber.

Their eyes met, and Grauber winced a little as if he was wondering whether Bendo might cry. Then, before fear turned to self-pity, Bendo shook his glass of iced water like a bell and in an improbable riff steered things away as best he could to baseball and summer camps. Two of his brood were already upstate for the summer, having a rough time in the Adirondacks. He was a Syracuse graduate, knew the mountains, and they agreed that the families might try to get up to their cabin on Saranac Lake before the fall. Grauber went along with it, for friendship's sake, knowing that Bendo's reserves would soon be depleted, and admired the effort.

Spinning a gossamer web of normality, aware of the self-deception, they went through some stories of days long gone, remembered a few dead warriors who'd been friends, joked about a promotion that had just junked an A-star under-secretary at State with a hack who was a five-star Pentagon nark to boot, and concluded that nothing changed. 'Whatever,' said Bendo flapping a hand in a gesture of faux-aimlessness. You toiled uphill, and hoped there was only a gentle slope on the other side. That's how it went. They carried on, whatever, and rolled home in the end. Grauber could hardly bear it.

'We keep things hanging together,' said Bendo. 'Always been the same. Can't ask for more.' His hand was shaking as he reached for his glass.

Grauber said quietly, 'And we look after our friends when we can.'

Bendo accepted that he had to meet his eyes again. 'Please,' he said. The restaurant seemed to dance around them, the noise rising, but they were still. 'Maria?'

Grauber shrugged. 'She's sad.'

'Friends,' Bendo said, as if he hadn't heard, and raised his glass. Grauber waited. Nothing more. Bendo was the first to turn away, and finished his drink. They tidied up, and Grauber paid. Bendo thanked him, and his eyes moistened again.

They were in the street a minute later. 'Ready,' said Bendo, without turning towards Grauber, his voice rising unexpectedly. 'That's all. We'll talk. They know where I am. Now they'll be watching.'

'Sure,' said his friend, falling into step. 'But it will be me who sits with you. That's a promise. Hope you're glad.' There was no answer.

Together they strolled up to the concourse. Bendo was at the Algonquin so they slipped through to 44th and Grauber joined him in the lobby to say hi to the cat he'd known for years. The two friends shook hands as if their last bear-hug was already behind them, and parted. 'Soon,' said Grauber as Bendo pulled open the door for him, giving him a bow and looking for a moment like an oversized bell-boy. They said no more and Grauber turned away to the street.

A gentle ten-minute walk, good thinking time, found him at Third Avenue where he pulled over a cab and headed for the mid-town tunnel and La Guardia.

Berlin was in his mind, nights with Bendo and the melancholy music of the streets, and the moment when Maria told him what she knew and what had to be done.

The Thursday tide was starting to run through the airport, and he speeded up to beat the crowd. Fifteen minutes, but they would still let him buy a ticket at the gate. Long might it last.

The clerk whizzed his roller across his credit card for an imprint. Grauber scribbled a signature on the carbon copy and the ticket was in his hand. Less than a minute later he was stowing his backpack in the rack and looking for a seat where he might sit alone. He thought there was a chance on the right side, halfway back, and settled in.

For a few minutes, he thought he might survive. There was lawyer talk from the seats behind, a mother and child across the aisle, but still an empty seat beside him, where he'd placed a book and a *New Yorker* as a discouragement. He looked away as a wide, swaying figure began to move towards him from the front of the plane, and feared that he wouldn't find peace. The man flopped down beside him, handing him his book and his magazine, then dug around for his seatbelt.

'The shuttle. That's America. Roll up, and you're on. No crap.'

'Yeah,' said Grauber. He smiled a welcome, turned away as if to snooze, and as the plane left the gate he settled in his favourite zone, just under the surface of full consciousness, where he could think with bracing clarity and shut out the world.

Maria had tapped him on the shoulder. He wasn't going to be sent away, as he had been so often in the past, but his knowledge was needed. The benefit of the state he had attained on the plane – a *dwam* his mother would have called it, from her rattlebag of words – was that he could assemble his options before he rolled up at Maria's. In his seven years at her side, he had done a job that was sensitive enough but which concealed more secrets underneath. Thinking about her message, he guessed that Maria was back on his special territory, maybe in the town where he had worked his own network on the embassy posting that had ended five years before. It had often been unhappy despite the benefits it bestowed on him, but had been the making of him. As he told Hannah, when she worried about the glooms that had visited him regularly in London and sometimes returned, contradictions were his business.

He made a list in his head. Maria had discovered something that only he would understand, and it had blown up quickly. Otherwise there would have been noise: meetings, secure memos, a call for papers, a cry of 'Heave-to' running through the ranks. The boys would have jumped. Fat Zak Annan would have phoned in a whisper from Fort Meade, and Barney Eustace, a beanpole farm boy from Tennessee, whose joy was boozing and schmoozing on the embassy listening circuit and bringing home scuttlebutt for Maria, would have been sending messages in his own near-indecipherable code. But none of this had happened. Grauber drew two conclusions.

First, whatever information she had received had arrived in the last day or two. It was Thursday. He'd take a punt and say that it concerned something that had occurred – or changed, or *been* changed – since the weekend. Then there was Joe, whose name Maria had slipped into her message.

Joseph O'Connell Manson was up to something, had to be. They had last met a few months ago, Joe having returned to his natural territory in Miami and the sultry ganglands beyond. But they had shared London connections, and Grauber suspected he had been drawn into the ploy that had preoccupied them in recent times, maybe making a few European runs. He could see smiley Joe in his mind's eye – gangly, blond, hopelessly attractive, wilful and vulnerable.

By the time they were over Delaware, the ocean haze stretching to the horizon and the plane scything into its descent, Grauber knew these were the only preparatory thoughts worth assembling, fragmentary though they were.

He was content that he had done all he could with what he knew. Maria would lead him on.

She was a star. Tall, with black hair, a swan's neck and marble-white skin, she carried herself and her secrets with gutsy élan that concealed everything. Grauber goaded her as an obvious Irishwoman – green Mafia, St Patrick's Day madness, the Celtics – and they had a store of jokes that they would mine when they met to cheer themselves. She had a laser brain that allowed her to concentrate in a way that Grauber had seldom encountered. She was always there before you, spotting the complications that were going to multiply. He looked forward to dinner, eased himself down to the next level with the plane, changing his mood easily, almost asleep.

His companion spoke for the first time since New York.

'Work?'

'Kind of. You?'

'Fun in the nation's capital.' He paused. 'Family wedding. I care about family. You?'

'Sure,' said Grauber. 'That's all that matters.'

He turned to the window, and the skyline. They had circled southwards and were following the Potomac upstream as they dropped towards National. He watched the sun strike the dome of the Capitol and send out an ivory-white gleam, and as they touched down he saw the shimmer of heat moving across the city. He wished his companion well with his wedding, following in his wake to the arrivals door.

Using coins instead of his credit card, he made a brief call from a phone in the arrivals lobby.

'We're nearly home. He's coming in at last.'

The response was just as brief. 'Thanks, Abel.'

FOUR

Will Flemyng spoke as if dealing with an arm's-length matter of fact that would not directly touch him. 'The real question here is whether or not I know this American person. He may know me, but so what?'

Lucy said Paul Jenner had offered no clue, only a summons to attend.

'I've not been expecting anyone. There's been no message. This dead man has come from nowhere,' Flemyng said, shifting papers around as if he had to maintain physical contact with his desk. 'That's the first thing to consider. A friend or someone unknown?'

Lucy was straightening her hair in the mirror near the door, finding calm in familiar rituals. She said, 'The old story. Strangers or brothers?'

At this, Flemyng fell quiet for a full minute, and Lucy filled it by leaving the room with an embarrassed bustle to check her desk. 'A straight question,' he said when she returned, tapping his desk with two fingers. 'D'you think I'm in trouble?' His head was down.

'I haven't the least idea,' she said, her voice almost as steady as his, 'and nor do you. But we're going to find out. Paul Jenner's expecting us.'

Flemyng stood up and put on a tie, checking the knot in the

mirror. Turning round, he asked if she felt any excitement, and she responded without hesitating. 'I'm afraid I do, a little. This is the kind of thing I think I may have been waiting for. A change in the pattern. Is that embarrassing?'

Flemyng shook his head.

'I understand, you know. I really do,' Lucy ploughed on. 'Thank God, for conferences and treaties. Ivan the Terrible.' The signing in Paris, five days away, would account for the topmost layer of government, and there were preliminary visits that had cleared the field of their masters, overseas trips planned on the assumption of summer calm and torpor. The great illusion.

Walking to the window, he turned his back on her again and drew the flimsy white curtains back, forcing a change in the atmosphere. He was pulling himself down. 'How would you describe it?'

'A nightmare, wherever it leads us.'

He was staring towards a blazing sun as she said it. Lucy was arranging the same papers on the desk that he had shifted around more than once, but her voice had recovered a businesslike tone. He turned his head as she spoke again. 'A mysterious man' – he noted the extra information – 'has been found dead, cause unknown, and the whole hen coop has gone mad. That's all.

'He's turned up in a strange place, apparently. Paul wants to tell you himself. Bells have been ringing from here to Kingdom Come.' Then she put both hands on the desk and leaned forward in the pose that he knew so well, her hair hanging forward so that her face was half masked. She tossed it back and made a characteristic modification of a statement that she considered too loose. 'Well, not quite. Nobody out there – even along this corridor of ours – has a clue that it is happening. No press, nobody. Believe me. Paul said only two things, apart from requesting us to get you to him soonest.

'One, your phone number has turned up on a death scene, and two' – here she paused for a moment, fixing Flemyng's eye – 'the Americans haven't been told. Don't ask me why, or why he should say that to me.'

Flemyng left the window and went to sit in a corner of the room, as if to postpone their departure. The reading chair was an introduction of his own, a gesture of independence against the government-issue stage set, and stuffing poked out from under the seat. His blue linen trousers were rumpled and his shirt well-worn. One hand massaged a cheek on which stubble still showed – it had been a dash from home that morning – and the other kept up a regular beat on the arm of the chair. 'Who is he?' he said, without expectation of an answer. Then, with the ease that Lucy loved, he said, 'It might be nothing. Nothing at all.' His head was still and he looked straight ahead.

She brushed herself down. 'Let's go.'

Flemyng said, 'Has anyone been in touch in the last hour or so?'

'Jonathan Ruskin's office wants you. Personal. That's it.' She pointed to his phone and went to the door. 'Two minutes. Then it's Paul. Are you going to ring Ruskin?'

Flemyng moved to his desk. 'Not now. One family thing. I'll be quick.'

Soon, they were walking together down the stairs and across the courtyard into Whitehall. Within four minutes they arrived at Paul Jenner's door, having passed from the street without being stopped, only giving a nod towards the glass box at the end of the corridor. A sleepy guard behind a whirring fan waved them through.

Inside the cabinet secretary's lair, high summer seemed to be at bay. The heavy curtains on the wide windows that opened towards the park were half closed, and someone had switched on a tall lamp that cast a pool of light in the corner under the Disraeli portrait. Paul's desk, set at an angle so that visitors coming through the door didn't meet him face-on, was an elegant defence against chaos. Flemyng could see three files of different colours lying closed, side by side, and not much more: a metronome that seemed marooned there, a few pens in a fish-shaped glass dish and a small bronze figurine keeping watch over the three phones, her arms meeting over the head. Paul was a balletomane. Otherwise, the desk was clear. Behind it was a bookcase that reached to the ceiling, each shelf neatly packed.

Paul himself was standing in the corner away from the window, and as he approached them he unfolded his arms as if he'd been practising a formal pose before they arrived. 'So.' He said nothing more as he helped to pull two chairs into position in front of his desk. 'Let's try to straighten this out.'

Paul was jacketless but still formal. He had more than ten years on Flemyng, but no one would have thought the gap so wide because Paul was in good shape, with a helmet of flecked grey-blond hair and a fresh complexion. He wore a pale blue shirt with faint stripes, his daily uniform, and a loosened cricket club tie. As he opened a file, Flemyng watched the tilt of his face, which was dominated by wide, light grey eyes. Long lashes gave them extra power. Everything else played second fiddle – the short nose, his full lips, the ears scrunched up as if someone had nibbled them. When he spoke it was in a classless voice devoid of any drawl, clipped and precise, like his grammar. He was hard to place, except as a man of decision.

'We have a delicate problem here,' he began.

'Where?' said Flemyng, familiar enough with the Jenner style to know that Paul would not think him frivolous.

'Well may you ask. In a bloody cupboard somewhere in the bowels of our beloved parliament.'

Flemyng shifted in his chair, head forward.

'As awkward a place as you could imagine for this kind of business,' Paul continued, as if he had been expecting just such an event to come his way some day. 'I needn't tell you what the House authorities are doing.'

'Crapping themselves,' said Flemyng quickly and quite softly, to make clear that he didn't want to interrupt.

'Indeed,' said Paul. 'The very few who know. I'm going to let you hear the story first hand.' His grey eyes fixed on Flemyng, as if he might ask him to swear an oath first. 'I tell you now that it has become more complicated than I would like. There have already been mistakes, and…' – he produced a rare unpolished phrase – '… we've hardly started.' Flemyng saw him glance at his watch, and felt a jolt: everything must have happened within the last hour or two. Paul was still standing, one hand resting on the edge of his desk.

'Will.' Flemyng could hear longing in Paul's voice: he needed reassurance. 'You're here because your phone number has turned up in strange circumstances. We'll come to that. But there's more. Your boss, like mine' – he looked back at his watch with a touch of theatricality – 'is leaving the country as we speak. Mine *en route* to watch a military exercise in the northern seas – and to be watched in turn by our Russian friends, naturally – and yours on a quieter African swing for lots of handshakes and not much else. That's his lot. Then both to Paris for the signing on Tuesday. Good news. When prime ministers and foreign secretaries are away, we're a little more free, as you well know. We can operate in our own way.'

'You might even say we were alone,' Flemyng said. In an enterprise that they both knew might involve deceit.

'You'll gather,' Paul was continuing, 'that I have already started to play this one in a rather unorthodox manner. I may regret that. History tells me I almost certainly will, but there we are. I've set a course. Some of it, I'm sorry to say, has been set for me. I'm going to produce for you the nearest thing we have to a witness. Gwilym is the best we can do.' He lifted the phone on his desk.

Gwilym. Red-striped shirt askew at both ends, with the collar splayed wide, leaving his black tie to hang down like an afterthought, he stumbled through the door. He was what he appeared: a blue blood who pulsed with confidence and bonhomie, a kenspeckle presence in parliament and government, drinking with backbenchers one minute and secretaries of state the next, for ever appearing around corners. He carried the misleading label of private secretary to the government chief whip, true as far as it went but catching none of his significance. Half manipulator and half honest broker, oiling the wheels, he was family solicitor to parliamentarians who had to be extricated from an affair or a plot that had backfired; did the deals that had to be done across the floor, behind the arras. Got the government's business done. Along the way, he saved marriages and broke them, gave a career his blessing or prepared it for the end. Knew every corner of the political landscape, and all the darker secrets that moved events.

A daily cry went up, 'Send for Gwilym!' – it was rare to use his second name, which was Crombie – and he was there, often before the message was sent, having a nose for trouble and a genius for never being far away. He was ready with a hand for any shoulder, a confidence to offer in exchange for a confession of weakness or terror. Treasured and feared, he lurked, and almost always smiled.

Flemyng had seen him the previous evening, doing his rounds. They'd exchanged a cheery word about parliamentary business for the last few days before the coming summer recess. 'Harry Sorley's education bill is a mess,' Gwilym had said. 'You saw it coming, which is more than he did. Well, I've got it in hand. He's going to have to swallow his medicine. Chaos otherwise. Do help, won't you? Speak to him as a friend. You have a way at these moments. We don't want the rising of the House postponed, and trouble.' Unthinkable, with the summer sun so high.

But the Gwilym in front of him now was a different man. His face was blotchy, his straw-blond hair matted in violent spikes, cheerfulness transformed into a visible nervousness that had him clutching the top of his trousers with one hand and waving the other like a flag of distress. Flemyng was stirred. There was a hint of terror in the room. Paul seized the moment.

'Will, I know how good you are at this kind of stuff.' Flemyng gave no acknowledgement. 'I need you on board.' That he wasn't yet in cabinet, hadn't yet taken the oath that made brethren of the highest ministers, was neither here nor there, it seemed. Paul pressed on, 'Who cares about seniority? An advantage, really. I know what you've done in the past, under the radar, before you got out.' He did a half-turn of his head to look directly at Lucy, who stayed stock still. After a few moments, when he had received a slight nod of understanding from her, he turned back to Flemyng. 'I do need you now. All the advice you can give. It's your political brain I want, your feel for things. I can't read them the same way.'

Flemyng's response was largely for Lucy's benefit. But he looked to Paul. 'Do you trust me?'

'Do you think you'd be here...?' He rubbed his head. 'Of

48

course I do. I think I may be in great difficulty and there are people in this building who mustn't know that. Not until I've got a grip of this. I don't even know what I want you to find out. I need your understanding, that's all.'

Flemyng interrupted. 'You know what I'm saying. Really trust? On board to solve a problem, or to be watched so that you can make your judgement of me – if my phone number's tied up in this somehow.'

He appeared not to have stiffened in the course of this awkward exchange. His legs spread out wider, he loosened his tie and across his face there was no sign of alarm. He seemed to draw in energy in preparation for springing to life and racing from the room. 'I'm with you, of course. I'll work with you, as best I can. But I know nothing.'

'Fine,' said Paul. 'I do want you, from which it follows that I have trust.'

Flemyng muttered, 'Are you sure? Which phone? Home…, office?'

'Let's hear from Gwilym,' was Paul's answer. He gave the signal to begin.

In the pause that preceded Gwilym's account, the scene took on the appearance of a staged photograph, which Flemyng saw in sepia, drained of colour and everyone held in a pose by the moment. Gwilym had steadied himself in the comfortable armchair Paul had placed in the bay window, the strong light from behind him keeping his face dark, by contrast with the circle of brightness round his head from the sun. He'd dropped his jacket on the floor in a heap. Lucy was sitting upright with her hands folded over a closed notebook, the perfect servant. At the centre of the tableau was Paul, in command behind his wide desk, quite still, eyes turned towards the window, their grey untouched by the sun.

'I'm afraid it was a bugger's muddle from the start,' said Gwilym.

'It begins with Denbigh. You'll know him, by sight anyway, one of the younger clerks in the House. Hair everywhere, beard and all the rest of it, child of the decade past, I suppose. Odd-looking chap, but conventional underneath, funnily enough. Sorry for rambling.

'He was going about his business this morning, trundling through the shortcut that they use down from the Speaker's office. I think myself that he was heading early to the strangers' bar for a swift one, but that's by the by.' His voice was rising to its natural confident tenor. 'Anyway, he noticed that the door to one of the store cupboards was open – a walk-in thing, full of boxes and spare bits and pieces. There's a bust of Gladstone for some reason, old door handles, ghastly candelabra, you name it. They put the Baldwin portrait in there, the one that was slashed. Rolls of wallpaper, lanterns and brass rails dangling all over the place. Anyway, tried to pull the door shut. Natural thing to do. Couldn't.'

He hadn't lost his sense of timing, and waited for a moment.

'It was jammed open by a dead man's foot.'

Though Gwilym's eyes were in shadow, Flemyng could see that he was looking up at his audience. Lucy's concentration had kicked in. She was holding her hair behind her head, so that her broad mouth, usually turned up, was her main feature. Her face was expressionless. 'Denbigh took a minute to realize what it was,' Gwilym said. 'Thought there might have been a statue or something that had fallen over. Silly, but fair enough when you think about it. You don't expect corpses in his line of work.' Paul showed no sign of impatience but allowed Gwilym time, to let him settle. 'As he put it to me, the body was twisted and contorted, pale – you'd hardly expect anything else, would you? – and the eyes were open. Horrible, of course.' He paused, an attempted mark of respect.

'The man was so obviously dead that Denbigh realized he wouldn't have to touch him, or speak to him. That was a relief, of course.' Gwilym added, 'I mean, he wasn't still alive and in need of something. Rescue, kiss of life, I don't know. He had another reason for relief – knowing them all, he knew that it wasn't the body of a member. Better or worse if it had been? I don't know.

'Then Denbigh did something a bit silly.'

'But understandable,' Paul put in, to help.

He took in expectant glances from Flemyng and Lucy and raised a palm. Wait.

'He did his best to conceal the body without disturbing things too much.' So he had tried to move the foot, using his own, to allow the door to close. 'It was bloody difficult,' said Gwilym. 'Not because it was stiff, but because it was floppy. Denbigh kept thinking it was going to come to life again. Ghastly, and he was a youngish man, too. Blondish curly hair, fit-looking if you know what I mean. Wearing jeans, believe it or not, in the House. Must have stuck out like a sore thumb. Anyway, no blood, not a drop. That was a relief. But an awful look on his face. Anyway, Denbigh got the foot, leg I suppose, back far enough and shut the door. There was a key. He locked it.' Flemyng noticed that Paul was shaking his head slowly, for the first time.

The police officer who should have been on duty down a few stairs, round the corner near the strangers' bar, had taken a walk on to the terrace, Gwilym said. It was a hot morning; no one around, wind-down time. 'This is where he bent the rules a bit. Didn't look for an officer, but came to me. We'd been together a few minutes before, so he knew I'd still be in the chief whip's room a minute away.'

Paul made his first intervention, knowing the answer, but wanting it laid out. 'And what did you do then?'

'I'm afraid I made a mistake. Me too.' Gwilym's head was down again. 'This was so odd that I didn't want to leave it to ordinary policemen.' Aware of the childish phrase, he hurried on. 'I know the number for the Special Branch folk so I rang it. Panic, I suppose. Friend of mine helps me out there from time to time – you remember when we found the IRA boys on the kitchen staff – and it seemed their sort of thing. Chap called Osterley picked up the phone; an officer not known to me. I gave him what information I could.' At this he stopped, and seemed to be about to offer an explanation, but Paul gestured to him to resume the core story. 'He told me to get to the scene, wait with Denbigh and say nothing.'

'You mean, not to tell the House authorities? Which you should have done first?' Paul as head prefect, getting Gwilym to repeat what he already knew.

'Exactly.' He nodded miserably. 'I pressed the alarm bell when I shouldn't have. Tourist keels over. So what? But a body in a cupboard… I suppose that's what did it; that and what we found at the scene.' There was a moment's silence, as if to give sympathy in his predicament.

'And so a sequence of events began,' said Paul, like a solicitor obliged to take a client through an unhappy story. 'Rapidly.'

Having stood on the other side of the door from the dead man for a few minutes, Denbigh, according to Gwilym, had gone into a kind of trance as a way of preserving his mental balance, but even in his torment he had recognized the origin of the dark blue passport that was making a little tent where it had fallen on the floor.

'When I made my call to Special Branch they asked for any information I had,' said Gwilym. 'Well, all I had – apart from a corpse at my feet – was an American passport. So I read out the details, naturally. Osterley asked me to stay on the line and I waited. Disappeared for a good five minutes, then he gave me the third degree. Name and passport number that was recognized, national security, blah, blah, blah. The works. Stand by your beds; stay dumb. Well, what else could I do? I was in it up to my neck if I did anything else.

'There was panic. Imagine us. Denbigh was as white as the corpse. He was guarding the door like Horatio on the bridge and I was shaking. Apart from his aunt, he said he had never seen one,' he said, with a theatrical hand gesture in gesticulation at the memory of the body. 'Great-aunt, actually.'

Denbigh had asked him a clerk's question, Gwilym said. 'He wondered if it helped– made a difference – that he was American.'

Happy to have a procedural problem to explain, Gwilym had recovered his fluency. 'I understood how his mind was working, trying to find a way out. We all know about deaths in the House. Denbigh was hoping it might be easier with a foreign corpse. 'Tisn't, of course. Makes no difference. Worse, if anything.'

His listeners understood, but allowed him to tell his story without interruption, explaining a difficulty that was well-known, but kept quiet. The parliamentary authorities had more than the usual dislike of dead bodies, because their building was still – technically and anachronistically – a royal palace, with one irritating consequence. The royal coroner was responsible for investigating sudden deaths on all such premises, medieval-style. Complicated, and a cause of public fascination. A legal horror show always best avoided.

Flemyng knew that, as a consequence, no deaths occurred in parliamentary precincts. They were not allowed: custom, and therefore fact. Whenever they did take place, they were officially denied. Gwilym had known the junior minister who had dropped dead in the middle of a speech, toppling to the floor like a stone obelisk, and was said to have expired in hospital some hours later. At least three members in his time, who had succumbed in different parts of the House to various kinds of sexual acrobatics, were said to have died safely outside the precincts, usually in the ambulance that took them away. A benign hypocrisy descended at life's end.

'I think that's why Denbigh got on to me first, not the serjeant-at-arms and the rest of them. He was hoping that it might be dealt with at once. Awfully quickly. He didn't think it through at all.'

Gwilym was wearing his hangdog look. 'Well, it was dealt with, but by the wrong people. My fault. Sorry.'

He told of his instruction from Osterley, speaking from Cannon Row police station only a couple of hundred yards away. 'You know Special Branch, how they work.' Flemyng dipped his head. 'I was instructed to wait for some workmen. Workmen!'

'They were in dark blue overalls and I realized on the spot where they must have come from. They walked like an undertaker's burial party, very downbeat, and there was one in a dark suit. That was Osterley. He'd summoned up a team from you-know-where.' He jerked his head.

Paul said, unnecessarily, 'Security Service.'

'Of course,' said Gwilym, 'I realized then I was losing control of all this. What would the House authorities say? I didn't dare to think. But I'm afraid it was all because of the big mistake I made at the beginning. Or was it a mistake, Paul? I don't know.' Paul nodded, a signal to continue.

He took them through his encounter with the emergency

squad, which he said he immediately recognized as the kind of team with which you would hope never to have any dealings. Gwilym said the most unpleasant moment for him was when he'd realized one of the men was a doctor, because he began some preliminary poking around with the body, got out a ther-mometer. Osterley, the besuited officer, took Gwilym aside. They stepped on to the terrace a few yards away. Osterley expressed his gratitude for his discretion and for the call. He asked if anyone else had appeared, and, by Gwilym's account, looked him in the eye in a deliberately unsettling manner.

'I'm afraid I began to burble about the royal coroner.'

'What did he say?' Flemyng asked.

'Stuff the royal coroner. Or something to that effect,' look-ing at Lucy. 'Then his exact words were, "He's the least of our worries. Don't fret, we're getting him off the premises anyway."' Gwilym said he recognized fret as a patronizing word.

'By this stage, I'm afraid I had an odd feeling of familiarity with the corpse, though we'd never met. Sorry. You know what I mean. I felt that I was sort of on its – his – side, if you follow me.' Flemyng nodded, to keep the flow going.

'I realized that they were about to cart off the body. What could I do? Osterley told me that I wouldn't have to worry about a fancy inquest. He then said that other people were on their way, and didn't leave me in much doubt where they were coming from. He waved across the river.' Flemyng managed not to smile. His old friends were in on it already. Paul was shaking his head again.

'I'm afraid it gets worse,' said Gwilym. Denbigh had taken the next bit badly, and had to be spoken to by Osterley in a manner that verged on the brutal. 'The policeman told us not to worry. He – the body, the cadaver, call it what you will – would be found again, somewhere else. That's when Denbigh protested, started to melt down really, and was told to shut up. I didn't like Osterley's ghoulish grin – it's the only way to describe it – but you can see how stuck we were. Frankly, we were scared. And I knew that we had rather messed it up.'

Flemyng asked if the policeman had given any indication where this second coming might occur.

'No,' said Gwilym, miserably. 'Of course,' he said, 'we're assuming natural causes. Surely?' His eyes moved from Flemyng to Paul and back again.

Having pulled himself round in the course of his story, he now slumped back in the chair. 'What could I do? They backed a bloody van, a black one, right up to the point where the passage gives on to Speaker's Court, locked the door at the top of the stairs beyond the store-room, and before I knew it they'd wrapped it up – the body – and it was gone. They took all its… his things with them.' He paused before the significant addendum: 'And the piece of paper that came out of his pocket.

'I'm sorry, Will. There was no name on it, but it's so distinctive, your number, I'd always know it – the last four digits stick in the mind. I use battle dates as an aide-mémoire, you'll remember. Just a trick. You're Agincourt. I'm Trafalgar, as a matter of fact. Nice. Anyway, when Osterley produced the paper I knew immediately what was written on it. Bells rang in my head, and I told him it was the private number in your office. Apologies.' His eyes were anxious, gleaming with the pathos of the moment.

'You did the right thing,' said Paul. 'They'd have identified it in a few minutes anyway. Quite right to help out. The question is – why?'

He signalled to Gwilym, allowing him to rest for a moment. 'I should tell you all that I have had a first account, on the phone, from Osterley. I want to go through some of it alone with you, Will, but there are a couple of things that we all need to know. This body will be rediscovered soon and normal procedures will kick in. The embassy will be informed by the police – not Osterley and Special Branch, but by whichever regular officers are called to the scene.' He looked down at his desk, and Flemyng understood the profound discomfort that was gripping him. He saw fear. 'From then on an investigation into the cause of death will continue.'

He added, 'as normal,' spoken in a near-whisper.

'There are naturally some complicating factors...' At this Gwilym snorted a laugh. He subsided. Paul went on, 'You and I will discuss them on our own, Will.'

Lucy rose and nodded to them both. Gwilym slung his jacket on and opened the door for her, following her from the room, to leave Paul and Flemyng alone.

'It's nearly two o'clock,' said Paul. 'I'm getting a full briefing by three, much of which I assume I'll be able to share with you. But I can tell you one or two things now, your ears only, ask you a couple of questions, and suggest what you and I might do next. There's also the opera tonight, and I hope that I can make that work to our advantage. You'll realize why when you get there.' Flemyng was surprised, assuming it would have been scratched from the diary.

'We don't need to rehearse your past connections, Will. I'm not only talking about the phone number when I say that you can't avoid this one.' Paul prepared to start the story proper.

'McKinley, Aidan. That's the name on the passport. I'm going to tell you now why it caused alarms to sound. Osterley was off the mark like a shot. An Irish name so he was thinking bombs, naturally.' Paul spread his arms. 'Rang the bell to see if there was any current interest, and indeed there was, but of a quite different kind. I think you can forget any Irish connection.' He poured two glasses of water from the jug on a side table and gave one to Flemyng. 'You'll get something stronger later.'

Paul began to pace the length of the room. 'The passport was clocked at Heathrow, early yesterday, Wednesday, because it popped up as one that caused us a little difficulty not long ago in Colombia, of all places, and was put on the watch list. Your old friends' – he waved a hand towards the door, as if they might be gathering just outside – 'were surprised it had turned up again. They didn't expect that, so a decision was made on the spot not to challenge him but to find out where he went. They got help to put a scratch team together and saw him check into his hotel. The Lorimer, at the back of Harrods.'

Flemyng, knowing of the pressures on such operations, was surprised that they had taken the trouble. 'Any more on him?'

'Nothing yet. I'll be better briefed later today. But you won't be surprised to learn they couldn't put a full surveillance team on him. Frustrating, but how could they justify a twenty-four-hour tail? An American posing no threat? We're friends, after all.'

He put out his arms. 'Same side.'

'Now to the guts of it. This man, we're all but certain, was operating for his government. Did he try to ring you? Your office will have a note, even if it was your private line.'

Flemyng met his eye. 'I've been told of no call of that kind. What exactly do you want? Time to tell me, Paul.'

Instead, the cabinet secretary returned to his story and began to add pieces to the jigsaw, laying them down one by one. 'There are things you need to know. First, that we are dealing here with an overdose of drugs. I'm told – it's preliminary so I must be careful – that it looks that way, and there's every chance that will be the finding at a post-mortem and an inquest. Not much doubt. I don't want to sound callous, but that's a relief. Second, I am positive that our two American guests at the opera tonight will know of it. It will certainly tell us something if they don't. No more now, but if we assume that the embassy's official channels learn in the next couple of hours that one of their citizens has expired in his hotel, which I am told is how it will happen, and then do a couple of basic checks, I can assure you that our visitors will come prepared. That's the sort of people they are. Think carefully how you want to proceed.'

Flemyng looked out of the window towards the park, where two hours earlier he had dodged Lucy and made for his rendezvous. Paul Jenner's story gave no clue to the operation that had caused that nervy summons and Sam Malachy's warning about surveillance. Instead there was a hint of supplication in it. Flemyng wore the lopsided smile that in him always signalled excitement. 'I think I know what you want. But we'll come unstuck. You realize that?'

'I'm betting we won't,' Paul said, 'because we can't afford to.'

He turned towards the books behind him, as if to search for something he had lost but gazed blindly at the shelves. 'I'll try to explain why. You need to be aware of something that I can't yet describe to you in detail. Only half a dozen people in this whole jungle have the picture, and most of them only fragments. In all my time, I've never known anything like this. Deep, with not a trace on the surface.

'I can tell you this much. There's a negotiation going on with Washington right now that's bloody sensitive beyond words.' His face was hidden from Flemyng. 'A big one.'

Turning back, he said, 'We can't afford trouble on that front. There is no evidence that this guy is connected to it, whoever he may be, but anything' – he was almost growling – 'anything that upsets this apple cart could be a disaster. Not just messy, I promise you. A nightmare. But no more of this now. I'll have a word with you after the opera.' He sat down, resting both his elbows on the desk, and finished, 'Believe me.'

The exchange had swung increasingly fast between the two, the questions flowing from Flemyng and the answers from Paul. Now was the moment to switch. Flemyng wanted clarity. No misunderstanding.

'I'm not going to ask, I'm going to tell. Forget the stuff about wanting my political brain. You know my past. And you know that Lucy knows, because of where she sits and the papers she sees from my old friends in the course of office business. You're taking me back there, without telling anybody, aren't you?'

Paul leaned back behind his desk, perfectly relaxed.

'You want me to be a spy again.'

Paul smiled, and it was over.

FIVE

Francesca searched for a card to send to Lucy. Another conversation so soon after the first might raise alarms; a note should do away with any awkwardness and be a natural progress for them both. In her office, she had a stack of cards showing operatic scenes, but didn't want an image that might be thought to carry its own message. She shuffled through and discarded the broken heroes and mad lovers, with all their tears, choosing instead a painting of an Italian garden with a still pool at its centre, the cypress trees casting long, solid shadows on the water. The scene calmed her. She turned it over, and wrote.

Lucy – let's make that lunch next week. Wednesday? It's a day when the diary says Will should be out of town. I was so touched by our conversation, and there's much more to say. Let me know. I hope the office is not too wild.
  Warmly,
  F

She considered what she had written, re-read it and placed the card in an envelope which she addressed to the office, confident that it wouldn't reach her husband's desk by accident. Everything passed Lucy first, and Francesca could be sure that it would stay with her. She took the back staircase and walked to the post box in Bow Street to catch the first afternoon collection. But she slowed down as she went, disturbed by a thought that swept over her without warning. She stopped, and after a few moments tore up the envelope and dropped the pieces in a litter bin on the corner. It took about ten minutes in the sun for her feelings to settle, then she went back to prepare alone for the evening, first to the private dining room behind the royal box near the stage.

With a seating plan before her, she wrote names on place cards for supper in a free-flowing hand. Three to each side of the oval table and one at each end. She looked round the small, high room, saw the flowers in place beside the ormolu clock and the drinks tray ready on the table. From the opening that led from the dining room to the royal box, muffled by a curtain drawn across the door, came the sound of a single horn. A player had slipped into the pit for some private practice, the gleam of his instrument just visible in the gloom under the overhang. Above him a crew was banging around on the stage, making the last checks on a revolving set that would turn for the first time in public that night. Their voices were louder than usual, and reflected the excitement that had crept through the building. A new production, an atmospheric Thursday, and Francesca shared the shiver of tension that everyone around her craved. 'Penny Jenner,' she wrote. Then one for Paul.

The American party had almost arranged itself, doors flying open. She knew that the visitors – one from the embassy in Grosvenor Square and the other from Washington – were aware that their host would be Paul Jenner, the mandarin of mandarins, and she'd learned from his office that they were turning up the heat with two cabinet ministers. Yet it would be a chance for Flemyng to relax, free for a while from the family troubles that were disturbing Francesca because he had told her nothing of their origin. She saw brother Mungo as one of her charges, needing a woman's helping hand without asking for it. He had said how well she understood him and his gratitude touched her, but she knew he would never call for help. That was beyond Mungo, who with every year that passed settled more firmly into the solitary routine at Altnabuie. She made a mental note to ring him, and turned back to her plans.

The guests would use the private staircase that ran up from the quiet side entrance in Floral Street and led straight to the dining room, from where they could enter the box in the auditorium after the lights went down, to take their places in the shadows, only noticed by those in the audience who were watching for them. They could slip in and out without fuss. She checked the cards, wrote 'Mr Wherry' and 'Mr Sassi' for the Americans, listened to the horn player doing his runs for a few moments and then walked round the horseshoe of the grand tier to start the obstacle race through the warren of corridors behind to her office high above the stage, looking out to the old market square.

She played with the seating plan in her mind. It should be easy, although there were only two women in the eight, and she turned over the permutations as she approached her tiny office, stopping to make way for a high trolley hung with wigs that creaked past her as it wobbled towards the chorus room.

The two ministers who were coming, neither bringing his wife, would add colour. She liked Jonathan Ruskin, known for being the tallest man in the cabinet, which was a useful identifier and had served him well, who was gently spoken and always an engaging companion. She enjoyed his bookish side, and he'd spent long evenings on their sofa in Putney chewing the fat of politics. She and Flemyng enjoyed his sense of adventure in all things – his account of a walk along the Rhine had been their holiday reading the year before, and he'd almost won a literary prize for it. Because he had to bend his elongated frame most of the time to avoid aloofness, he appeared in company to be a natural listener, always leaning towards the person who was speaking. He had no choice, but it made him seem willing. His eyes were as blue as gas jets. Francesca knew him rather better than Harry Sorley, his ministerial partner for the night, although there were tales of hidden depths.

Physically, Sorley had none of Ruskin's style, being porky. There was a reputation for womanizing and sexual adventure. Dark where Ruskin was fair, he exuded a mid-forties vanity, his curls well-tended and not to Francesca's taste, because they oozed with a seducer's oil. She knew, however, that the effect on some others was different. And he was sometimes fun, if you didn't mind the eyes, which reminded her of Malcolm McDowell in *A Clockwork Orange*. Not enticing. But the friends who clustered round her husband made a happy gang, and she enjoyed their naked relish for the game. She was a natural collector of the tales they told but protected her own sense of propriety with the promise that she would never keep a diary.

The favourite stories clinging to friends and rivals were shadows that never lifted. 'Everybody has a past and we all know it,' Flemyng had told her on one of their first weekends together. But she enjoyed them, stags of a common age including Ruskin and Sorley, who'd both slipped ahead of him by virtue of having started earlier, and the likes of Forbes and McIvor who were at his level, waiting for the next jump to a cabinet seat, and looking for a helping hand from anywhere. Sparger too, although he had once propositioned her when drunk, whispering all the while that music made him cry. But

Francesca knew that one day their band of brothers would break up and there would be pain. Their life of rivalry made that a certainty, the fervour of the moment coming from the knowledge that it would pass.

Because she loved the risks of the stage, the life of politics worked on Francesca. Flemyng's friends confided in her in ways that she found surprising, leaving their own wives in ignorance, and within months of Flemyng falling for her she'd been adopted by the gang. Forbes had shared the story of his failed marriage; Ruskin his desire for children and his wife's distance from politics. She kept their secrets.

With her husband she'd developed the honesty that he needed. Her love for him, which had grown, obliged her to be tough. He wanted nothing less, and she could often see in his eyes, behind the dancing smile, an appeal for an openness between them that might one day be uncomfortable. He'd told her that without it he feared that he would drift, and maybe fall.

There would be politics around the table later. Francesca opened her window in search of some air, checked her clothes, and responding to the chatter from the cobbled street below, set off in search of strong tea to ready herself.

*

Back in his office, Flemyng dived into a red box of paperwork and sat alone. He was told that Lucy would be delayed so he took relief in his work. He spoke to the Beirut embassy, composed a message for Damascus about his September visit, and re-read a hostile Treasury paper on the cost of embassy entertaining in North Africa. The note on tactics from the official representing him at the following day's budget wrangle seemed to do the job, so he scribbled a quick note of thanks and support, read the daily batch of embassy telegrams, which took an hour, and put away the last of his papers. Lucy hadn't returned. He asked her assistant to let Ruskin's office know they could talk the next morning, and made sure that the message would be passed on immediately. A letter of thanks to his party chairman in the constituency, and he was done. There was time for a quick shave and shower, in the poky bathroom he shared with the minister next down the pecking order, and he thought he had won himself some thinking time.

Instead he was summoned to a meeting, for the second time that afternoon. 'Thomas Brieve rang,' Lucy's assistant announced through the doorway. Because she was junior, she used his full name.

Brieve. Prime ministerial foreign affairs adviser and, in Flemyng's mind, the most obnoxious of the new breed. Fixers appearing in ministerial offices, confidants hired to do their masters' business round the clock, and known for their lapdog loyalty. Brieve was their model – a Cerberus at the gate who sent unwanted ministers on their way, the boy scout who followed the paper trail wherever it went, the man who never missed a meeting. His memos, Ruskin would say, were like toxic lava from a volcano: get in its way and you'd be swallowed up. Tom Brieve, although his skinny, angular frame was physically unsettling and he had a boyish manner that multiplied the effect, had power. Gatekeeper and enforcer, he had secrets stuffed in his pockets. But Francesca was always surprised by Flemyng's reaction to him, and puzzled. Brieve hardly seemed like Rasputin, she had said after first meeting him. Nor even Machiavelli. Flemyng said that she would be wise not to bet on it.

She remembered, however, how he had spoken of his own awkwardness and confessed that he felt it lifting in her presence. He understood the effect of his manner on his colleagues, he said, and Francesca remembered his relief when he realized that she found nothing embarrassing in his decision to speak to her intimately.

Flemyng made his call, and Brieve answered the phone himself in Downing Street. 'I'd like to see you if I can, Will. Away from the office, now. Do you have a few minutes?'

Briskly, Flemyng agreed without asking why he was making such an unusual request, and suggested that they went to a subterranean bar near Charing Cross, a dingy, dusty place where they both knew it was easy to hide. There were corners where the shadows were deep. Half-burned candles, almost always unlit, stuck out of green bottles on each table, and the air reeked of the sherry dispensed from four great barrels lying end-on behind the bar, their bulging wooden ribs shining as if they sweated alcohol. Flemyng knew of a few affairs that had started in these premises, and some that had ended there. It wasn't natural Brieve territory; so much the better. They'd meet in fifteen minutes.

Before leaving, he made one careful rearrangement in his office. Making sure that the door was closed, he took a plain envelope from his briefcase. It had no name on the outside and the flap was open. He checked the sheet of paper inside, read the words again, and placed it in the drawer of his desk, putting the key back in his pocket after he had unlocked it. He pushed the drawer carefully so that it was nearly closed, but not quite.

He walked across Whitehall, stopping to buy late-afternoon editions of the *Standard* and *Evening News* from the wooden shack at the Ministry of Defence corner – the water workers' strike was still hogging the front pages – and was soon on the precipitous stairway to the cellar bar. Brieve was already established in one of the brick alcoves, seated at a rickety wooden table with two schooners of pale sherry in front of him. Flemyng shook hands and sat down. 'Tom.'

Brieve was carrot-haired, freckled and pale. He was taller and thinner than Flemyng as well as a year or two younger, but the gawky façade was misleading. When he opened his mouth Brieve was smooth as silk, speaking in mellifluous tones. From the Foreign Office fast stream, he'd swum off to life at Harvard when he was barely out of his twenties, returning in triumph to the diplomatic whirl. With a speed that his contemporaries thought indecent as well as infuriating, he abandoned the department that once commanded all his loyalty in favour of his new ante-chamber adjacent to the seat of power. In Whitehall, his tracks were visible everywhere.

'Will, I wanted to pick your brains.' Flemyng drank some sherry and thanked him.

His curiosity rose as Brieve began a ramble that seemed to have no destination, without any of the discipline that was his hallmark. Flemyng had never heard him speak so aimlessly. 'I wonder what you think,' he said more than once in the course of his Middle East tour, but never paused to allow a reply. The coming Paris conference was thrown in, although it had little connection with Flemyng's territory, and he told a long anecdote which he described as the only funny thing to come out of the latest session of disarmament talks in Vienna, which had stalled again. This was the excuse for some further musing about the Russians, and the scelerotic Kremlin succession that must surely come. Finally Flemyng interrupted him.

'Tom, what's this all about?'

Brieve flinched. 'Why d'you ask?'

'Because you're all over the place, and that's not like you. What's up? You can tell me.'

Brieve's natural pallor was touched by a flush of pink at Flemyng's interruption. 'The first time I met Francesca, I realized she was somebody that I could talk to more frankly than is often the case with me – this job, and so forth. I've often hoped that the same might be true of you, although we tend not to speak to each other in that way, or often enough.' For the first time in Flemyng's experience, Brieve showed symptoms of rising embarrassment.

'Be my guest.'

Flemyng was sitting back in a wooden captain's chair, and could feel its struts on his back. Brieve was hunched forward over the table in an attitude of supplication, and he spoke hesitantly. 'This isn't about a crisis, it's more nebulous than that. An atmosphere…' His head was still down, but his eyes had come up to observe Flemyng's reaction. 'Do you know what I'm referring to?'

Flemyng's expression didn't change and he made no effort to ease Brieve's discomfort. 'Out with it, Tom. Who?'

The answer surprised him. 'It's not a question of who, more a nervousness, a fear really, and I can't work it out. I've got masses of stuff to put together before the Paris conference – the communiqué's only halfway there, and there are all-nighters to come – but that's manageable. Drafting's my business, and we'll fix it. That's not my worry. I wanted to ask you if you'd had the same feeling lately – that things are unravelling. People keeping secrets, working against each other, that kind of thing.'

Flemyng confided none of his own worries. 'Politics, Tom, politics.'

If this was a prompt for Brieve to elaborate, to name names, it was ignored. He appeared to regret that he had made the

69

overture, perhaps even that he had suggested a meeting. His expressions of alarm gave way to another rambling foray into the Paris preparations, this time his own skill in winning a concession from Washington. But it was obvious to them both that his enthusiasm for confiding in Flemyng was waning fast. Brieve's physical awkwardness, always highlighted by its contrast with his actor's voice, betrayed a desire to get away. He had taken fright.

Flemyng tried to rein him back. 'When I asked you "Who?", it was because there's always someone in the middle of these upheavals, isn't there? Somebody pulling the strings, or someone in trouble.'

But it was too late and so was Flemyng's rush of regret. His chance had gone. Brieve was slurping his sherry, and with some crude stage business involving his watch he excused himself – Washington calls to take, French egos to be massaged. So it went. ''Bye, Will. I really want to have this talk some other time.' As he left the table, he paused and looked back. 'Please.'

Flemyng sat alone for a few minutes when he had gone. Later, he would explain to Francesca his sadness at having allowed the conversation to be sabotaged by his instinctive irritation with his personality. But Flemyng had learned something: there was fear in Brieve's eyes.

He walked north towards Covent Garden, unaware of his surroundings, coming close to stepping in front of a number eleven bus. A minute later he was in the dog-legged lane leading to the opera house, aware of a sense of expectation that made him quiver. It was a short walk, fresh in the relative cool of the narrow passage, well-sheltered from the last of the sun, to the side of the theatre. Fifty yards away he stopped at a shop window to check his tie, then followed the cobbles towards the private entrance. As he passed the stage door he could see the flowers piled inside for the ritual first-night celebrations. A slow-moving black limousine with diplomatic plates passed him and pulled up about thirty feet ahead, its nearside wheels on the narrow pavement.

The Americans had arrived.

SIX

They met at the bottom of the steep private stair. Flemyng introduced himself. 'Guy,' said the taller of the Americans, his first word carrying the assumption that Flemyng would know the rest. A moment passed before he added, 'Sassi. And this is Jackson Wherry.' Hands shaken all round, they were borne upwards on a cloud of aimless and cheery chatter, Sassi leading the way. At Flemyng's first assessment he was a year or two younger than him, just on the good side of forty-five, and lithe. Having touched him already on the upper arm, by old habit, Flemyng realized he was in good shape, player of a hard game. His black hair gleamed, and flopped over his collar. Wherry was broad, white and crinkly on top, and older than his colleague. His face bore the traces of wild times past. He was dressed in striped seersucker, the olive-skinned Sassi in dark blue. Each wore a flag pin and Flemyng noted a chunky fraternity ring on the little finger of Sassi's right hand. Their shoes shone and they left a faint trail of scent as they climbed the stairs.

Waiting for them was Paul, displaying his gift of dressing neatly on the right side of formality when he was away from his desk. His civil service pin-stripes had made way for a summerweight grey suit with a bright green tie and a button-down shirt that was a subtle gesture to his guests. He had a quality of timelessness, which allowed him never to make a point with his appearance nor offer a challenge. His wife Penny was beside him, bubbly and wide-eyed, with the side-to-side gait of a country girl that was deceptive because she knew more about members of the cabinet than some of them knew about themselves. And then – Flemyng turned to his left – there was Francesca.

She was preparing to bring the two ministers forward. First, she pulled Flemyng towards her and they brushed cheeks. She wore the jasmine perfume he'd brought home from Cairo the previous month and her long dark hair was swinging free. In a cool blue-green dress she seemed immune from the heat. 'Great night,' she whispered in his ear. But then she felt the tension in his shoulders.

'OK?'

'Later. Don't worry.'

'What's going on?' She tried to keep him from turning away.

'Too much.'

The ministers, out of his line of sight, stepped forward together. Though Francesca was tall, Jonathan Ruskin seemed to tower over her. For a moment Flemyng seemed thrown, as if he had expected someone else, and his eyes veered from one to the other. Francesca saw Paul moving towards him from one side with hand outstretched. But Flemyng had bounced back. 'Jonathan!' Then, 'Harry!' as Sorley appeared from behind Ruskin. It seemed to Francesca that the scene froze for a moment.

The ministers went through the preliminaries with the Americans and champagne was poured, so the volume of conversation rose. The bright red programmes went round. *Eugene Onegin*. Paul checked that everyone knew something about the opera without making it a test. Sassi was beaming and, taking the floor with ease, revealed that he'd studied at the Julliard and still played in a friend's string quartet when he was in New York. He gestured to Wherry. 'And Jackson's a Broadway man, music in the veins. So we're grateful that this was possible. Truly.' He inclined his head towards Paul, who had his hands out ready to receive thanks.

Sorley, who always carried with him a sensitivity about his place, was getting the idea that his role might be to set himself up as Wherry's partner, and launched into a clumsy question-and-answer session with Paul to set the scene. Director, singers, the conductor's reputation. 'Bonkers, I hear,' said Sorley, missing the beat as usual. Flemyng listened without a word, and began to smile. Wherry was a type he recognized, and would have done his homework, with Pushkin at bedtime to avoid mistakes. He watched Sassi scanning the room.

They enthused about the atmosphere, although none of them had yet seen a single member of the audience. Francesca said there was pandemonium backstage with a coughing scare in the principals' corridor, but nerves always helped. Flemyng winked at her, and she realized he was trying to reassure her. 'English asparagus,' she announced, and they sat down. Sassi, next to Paul with Ruskin to his right, opened things up wide. 'So we're off to Russia tonight. Familiar?'

He grinned straight at Flemyng as he spoke, apparently looking for a sign of pleasure.

To the table at large, he added, 'Jackson's an old Moscow hand. He sings the songs.'

Flemyng glanced at Paul, who stepped in. 'The thing about *Onegin* for me – shaming, I think – is that Russian children know the story by the time they're seven.'

'Life,' said Wherry, 'a tragedy.' And he hummed a phrase from the climactic scene. Sorley clapped.

'You'll like the crowd here,' Ruskin said, gesturing towards the auditorium. 'Getting less stuffy. Mind you, the roof is start-ing to fall down.' The American said, 'I care, you know. Some of us do, even in Washington.'

Ruskin knew Sassi missed nothing that went on in that town. And London couldn't compete with its political obses-sion. 'Just as well when I think what sometimes goes on at Westminster, especially in the heat. It's good to have those walls around us.' With Sassi's encouragement he launched into one of his party-stoppers about a girl being dangled by her ankles over the terrace on the Thames on the hottest night of the previous summer, the happy climax to a night out with a posse of drunken backbenchers. A cross-party group, he added to get an extra laugh. Everyone at the table watched him use his long arms to show how she'd been held just above the waterline. 'Thank God there weren't any voters in sight,' he said. 'We chase them away when it gets dark.'

Even in the bubbling cauldron of the whips' office, he said, where a melodrama was cooked up every day before lunch, they'd talked about it for a couple of weeks. The girl visited Westminster occasionally, until she realized that no one had forgotten. They never do, she was told.

'We know each other's past. That's the thing,' said Ruskin.

Sassi laughed. 'It's why I'm glad I'm not in politics.'

And Ruskin leaned across, his eyes bright. 'Your game's even worse.'

Paul shot him a glance, and he flinched.

Francesca saw that he was screwing up a napkin in his hand, as if he might throw it, although his smile stayed in place. Ruskin stopped in mid-flow and the moment was strange enough to bring silence down on the room for the first time. Flemyng took it on himself to lift it as a matter of duty, but Francesca sensed anxiety when he spoke.

'Well,' he said, with emphasis, 'let's hope we don't have any of the troubles we're going to see in the next three hours.' He finished weakly. 'I've never fancied a duel.'

The company ordered itself, splitting into twos, everyone well-versed in the rules of the table. Flemyng watched Francesca at the far end being amused by Ruskin next to her, leaning forward with a wide grin and now relaxed. He was in the middle of a story. Wherry was on his other side, with Sorley beyond him, trundling on about the education bill, though its interest to the Americans was zero, as Ruskin leaned across to point out, interrupting his own anecdote to slap Sorley down. Being cursed with a face that gave everything away, he folded in embarrassment.

Flemyng knew the reason for Francesca's squeamishness about Sorley – the hair on the back of his hands. As he made a point to Wherry, he stretched both of them out on the table and revealed the thick black whorls that disappeared under his cuffs and up his arms. Francesca used to say that it must culminate in a thatch on his chest that needed work with a little lawnmower at weekends. She had once wondered if Sorley had a special wax to make it grow, and for a moment, Flemyng was transfixed. But Wherry was asking questions about parliamentary procedure, putting on a show of interest at Sorley's explanation of an arcane legislative wrinkle. 'It's hard to explain… It just happens. One of our funny ways.'

Wherry gave a sympathetic nod, and drank.

Both Ruskin and Sorley were able to contribute something from their American experiences long ago and Ruskin chipped in with an anecdote about his own time at Princeton, his dalliance with the anti-war movement in the high old days – 'I even marched on the Pentagon,' he said with a laugh – and rolled out a couple of tried and tested routines, one of them featuring Flemyng as hero when he'd become a Foreign Office minister two years before on the lowest rung. Europe was the new diplomatic game, and at his first Brussels summit as a stand-in Flemyng had run rings round the Germans in such a way that to the few who understood what was happening he became an instant celebrity. He'd been promoted six months later. 'Ministers don't come much smoother than our Will,' said Ruskin, finishing it off with a friendly salute.

'One of our gilded boys,' Sorley added, betraying a touch of sourness. 'Brings some class to proceedings.'

But Ruskin kept command, giving a health check on his own government that verged on the reckless, and had Paul smiling. Then, from the box alongside them, they heard the sound of the theatre filling up. Paul got to his feet and gave a soft clap. The orchestra had tuned up, the lights were down. They filed through the door at Francesca's gentle urging and took their places in the box, moving the chairs, high ones like bar stools at the back, so that they all had a good view of the stage below. Flemyng was in the shadows towards the rear when the curtain rose on a Russian cornfield.

The atmosphere was high, everyone on alert. It was hot, with a sea of red programmes waving as makeshift fans down below, but they had a stream of air from the half-open door behind them, and there was none of the soporific feeling that might have taken hold. Wherry and Sassi were at the front, intent. They barely moved. Ruskin and Sorley were behind them, and from his perch at the back Flemyng could watch them all.

For more than an hour there was almost no movement, the cheerful patter having been a preparation for an intense and wary period of stillness that couldn't be attributed to the music alone. Francesca wondered about Sassi, pondered the length of time he had devoted to Ruskin and not to Paul at the table, concluded that Wherry was an odd fish but a friendly one, and watched Paul maintain his familiar state of relaxation that she compared with an athlete's ability to be loose and alert at the same time. Then Sorley scratched a hairy wrist and the spell was broken. Gathering her thoughts when the curtain came down for the interval, she was convinced that the company was waiting for something, and knew not what.

They chattered their way to the table at the interval where a platter of lobster and crab was waiting. After fifteen minutes the party broke up for the first time. Paul stood and said, 'Would you please excuse us?' He and Sassi moved back into the box, clicking the door shut behind them. The auditorium was almost empty, only a few members of the audience lingering in their seats, and the long velvet curtains round the box gave them cover. They could talk unseen and unheard.

Wherry became more animated in Sassi's absence, doing the work of two. He was the heart and soul of the table as he revealed his foreign-service travels, in a pattern that Flemyng recognized. Vienna and Moscow before Delhi. As he spoke, Flemyng's two ministerial colleagues sitting directly across from each other were finding it difficult to keep their eyes off the door, though it was awkward for Sorley who had to glance over his shoulder, so that he looked even more inquisitive than Ruskin.

With two empty places at table, Ruskin was alone on his side and leaned across to try to engage Flemyng's attention and perhaps give him relief from Wherry. His angled smile, appropriate for the extra-long body, was hard to resist. He had a way of using his eyebrows as question marks, over the startling blue eyes, and Flemyng had long admired his ability – not shared by many fellow ministers – to listen, and to stay still while he did.

This was, in part, because of a hearing loss that he'd suffered as a young man, which had taught him to concentrate on every conversation. It was an advantage for Ruskin, which had been practised over many years and turned to good use.

Ruskin had good luck in his roving cabinet job that let him wander freely from his base in Downing Street, and he spent a good deal of time in the corridors of Flemyng's building and on the other side of Whitehall in Defence, advertising himself as the most discreet listener in the business. He had also, like Flemyng himself, a particular fondness for the parliamentary maze, where he had made himself popular. He would cock a friendly ear, hear a personal story of difficulty, pass the word through the right channel. 'Let's have it out,' he would say in his confiding way, perfectly mannered and easy at the same time. Francesca often remarked on the musicality of his voice. He was nearly two years younger than Flemyng and, unless fate intervened unkindly, would finish near the top. Wherry asked him to describe his role, and he gave a shrug and a smile. 'Continuity, I suppose. Calm. Will's speciality too.'

He looked at Flemyng. 'Agreed?'

Engaging him directly, Ruskin gossiped with Flemyng about the Paris signing, and the coming French state visit. They turned to the government's bout of summer nerves. 'Summer heat and inflation in double digits… can't beat it for panic. We know the pattern.'

'The madness of July,' Ruskin said. 'There's never a year when people don't say the government can't go on, we're falling apart.' Flemyng agreed. 'It passes,' he said, 'like a fever.'

The summer term was always wild, especially when the temperatures rose. People said silly things, the newspapers fantasized and parliament fretted. All to be expected. 'Tennis next week before we go our separate ways?' Ruskin suggested.

He was a member at Queen's, and Lucy would fix a time. Settled.

'Your office rang this morning,' Flemyng said. 'Anything up?'

'Forget it,' said Ruskin. 'It can wait.'

About ten minutes had passed and Francesca wanted to signal time to Paul and Sassi. She knocked gently on the door to the box and opened it a crack. Everyone turned round. The two men rose but seemed reluctant to part, still bound up in conversation, heads together, their shadows intertwined on the dark red curtains around them. Francesca leaned towards Paul, and they came forward. Neither of them had alluded to acquaintanceship, but there was closeness on display.

As he emerged, Sassi said, 'Good, Paul,' as if to put an end to their conversation, and turned to the table, lightening his face as he did so. 'We've sorted everything. The special relationship lives.' Wherry said, 'Bet it was baseball.' Sassi put a playful finger to the side of his nose, as if it was a joke and his private time with Paul had been a mirage. The bell rang for Act II. Two minutes later, as the conductor entered the pit to take his bow, they were settling themselves in the box again.

Although Francesca could identify her husband's unease, whose cause she had no means of identifying, he had the ability to conceal it from everyone else. Things might be shifting around him, but Flemyng looked untroubled. Alarms were hidden, except that she could sense that his easy balance had gone. To calm himself he would be thinking of a visit home to Altnabuie at the weekend. The lights were down, the applause died and she turned towards the stage.

An artificial silence descended on the box. Sassi was leaning forward, both hands on the velvet-covered rail. The stage lights were bright, and Francesca saw the guests' dark outlines on the brilliant backdrop. She saw their box as a second stage set, on which the action had paused. Everyone around her, the Americans at the front and Flemyng and Paul at the back, was refusing to move.

The gunshot that brought the duel and the second act to an end was a loud crack, coming from the prompt corner just below them, and they could smell the powder. Paul sprang to attention in his chair, and took a moment to calm himself. Flemyng unfolded his arms. Wherry, sitting in front, remained quite still at the sound of gunfire. A hunter, for sure.

Paul didn't waste a minute in the second interval, but took Flemyng aside. No one seemed surprised. The Americans were talking to Francesca, and she found Sassi exploring her Italian background, more distant than his own. 'We were Naples,' he said. 'You?'

'The north,' said Francesca. 'In the Veneto. But it was generations ago. I take it you're more recent.' Sassi offered little more. He continued, gently, to probe her. 'I don't often talk about my family,' he said. '*Omertà*, you might say.' Francesca laughed, enjoying his game.

Penny was dealing with the ministers and Flemyng and Paul were free to speak, standing in a corner, Paul with his back to the others. 'Let's talk about Washington and one of our bigger problems,' he said, keeping his voice low. 'An ambassador.'

Flemyng started and his eyes came up. 'Dennis is home and dry,' he said. 'On his way. Surely.' Old Inskip was getting his move from Paris, after years of manoeuvres, and the office was happy for him.

Paul said, 'No. We're changing horses, I'm sorry to say. Can't say more, but you'll be pleased. A grown-up appointment.' Francesca had broken from Sassi but saw Paul's serious expression and turned away.

'It's another damned complication that we don't need,' he was saying. But the calendar couldn't be denied and it was time for the greatest diplomatic prize of all to be passed on. Runners and riders headed for the line, straining at their bridles. Malton at the UN, Colquhoun in Pretoria, O'Hare in Brussels, his unorthodox love life notwithstanding, Glendinning in Bonn looking for escape from a one-horse town and a last chance of glory, and the permanent secretary himself, Finzi. No one else in the running save for Dennis, who had got Paris as a consolation prize when Moscow slipped through his fingers. They had all been at it for two months, making unscheduled visits to London to sit at the right lunch table ('happened to be in town… half term for the youngest… time to catch up') and at first Dennis seemed to have faltered.

But he had put in a wondrous late run, with the help of Flemyng's boss who admired his style with the French and had managed to fix it for him with a discreet conversation at a Downing Street dinner. 'Steady and classy,' he'd said. 'Washington will like him. A good vintage and at his peak. Drinking well, you might say.' He regretted the phrase afterwards, but never mind.

All of a sudden Dennis was the man: throwing a wild party in Paris to celebrate in advance, the excuse being the visit of an artist whose name would bring French ministers flocking to the embassy, where he could quietly pass the word that, sad though he was, he would soon be taking his leave of the Faubourg St Honoré for the big Lutyens house on Massachusetts Avenue, Washington NW, which he told his guests was almost as lovely a residence.

Everyone knew of Dennis's problem with the third Courvoisier, but his comfort with the American scene, his grace in public and his happy ability to write a political précis laced with the tartness of a natural diarist meant that his colleagues put it to one side. Everyone was happy; Downing Street signed it off. His appointment would produce small headlines and minimal comment in the public prints. Relief all round.

'What happened?' said Flemyng, in a tone that suggested he already knew the answer.

'Well,' said Paul, 'Tom Brieve did for him.' Flemyng's face darkened. 'He was in Paris the other day, a pre-conference thing. Dennis *en fête*. Completely pissed at dinner, pardon my French. Prattled on about tennis on the White House courts, how the secretary of state was junior to him when they were both in Moscow. I got this from Marilyn in the embassy, who was there, poor girl. I'm afraid he did his Jacques Brel impression. Twice.'

'Oh, God,' said Flemyng.

'Catastrophic. You know Brieve can't stand him. Wanted another. So he scampered back to Number Ten and pressed the panic button. Dennis was a hopeless soak and insecure. Roped in Yves from the French embassy to put in a bad word. He's a mate – they're cooking up some deal with the state visit. All rubbish. Dennis is just prone to the odd good night. Sharper than our Tom any day and trustworthy, as we both have cause to know. But I lost that one, I'm afraid, and so did your boss.'

He went on, 'I don't know if you've picked this up...' He was looking closely at Flemyng, who neither nodded his head nor gave it a shake. Paul hesitated.

'... but it's felt...' He was adjusting his grammar to cover the source of the idea '... that maybe we shouldn't just be looking at career people for a replacement. Maybe we should cast our net a bit more widely.'

'You know what we think about outsiders,' Flemyng said. 'There's a great fuss, fireworks on the Thames, then a bloody explosion. Ugly, and it never works.'

Paul said, 'I know. I bear the scars. But this is different. Keep it to yourself – entirely – would you?' Flemyng raised his hands in a gesture of assent.

'There's a thought,' once again authorship was concealed, 'that we might think of a minister.'

Flemyng flinched. Paul said, 'I know – by-elections are dangerous, reshuffling cabinet a pain. All that. But there's a reason.' And then, as if it had struck him for the first time, he looked Flemyng straight in the eye and put a firm hand on his shoulder. 'Don't worry – if that's the appropriate word in this context – the fickle finger of fate isn't pointing at you. Probably.'

And added, 'Would that be disappointing?'

Flemyng was serious. 'No. But why change course? There's no good reason I can see.'

Paul turned his eyes towards the Americans. 'It's not done yet. But we think it will work. And I think you'll be pleased.' He looked Flemyng in the eye again. 'It's necessary, believe me.'

As he spoke, Flemyng saw Francesca and Ruskin in a close exchange. He could hear nothing, but saw that she was startled, maybe annoyed. Her eyes had widened a little in the way they did when she was thrown; she was touching her forehead as if she felt a headache coming on. Ruskin was smiling as he spoke and laughed when he leaned back. Flemyng moved towards them, and took his wife's arm.

She was surprised at his quiet whisper as they went into the box together, because it seemed too melodramatic for him. 'Another complication. I don't know when it's all going to stop. And what was going on with him?'

'Afterwards,' she said. 'Please.'

84

It was half-past ten when the curtain came down. Flowers sprouted from the singers' arms as they came forward for their second curtain calls, the director got some boos from high up in the amphitheatre, and the throng began to pour out into Bow Street. The party in the box gathered for post-match coffee and drinks in the dining room and Flemyng found himself with Ruskin. Summer troubles again.

'What's up in your patch?' Flemyng asked.

'Bloody Treasury mostly. And timetable nerves in the House. Talk of postponing the rising.' Ruskin raised his eyes to the ceiling.

The party broke up in the course of a few minutes, Flemyng and Wherry promising to lunch after the summer sojourns, Sorley giving Francesca a hug that she would have been happier not to receive, Ruskin seeming a touch distracted but giving everyone a benediction with one long arm before he slipped down the stairs and disappeared. Francesca and Flemyng would soon be alone. First, Paul. He asked Francesca to give them a few minutes, and she headed along the grand tier to pay her backstage calls.

Paul checked that the door had clicked shut.

'I told Sassi some of what we know. They're aware and it's taking its course.'

Flemyng asked a blunt question. 'Whereabouts?'

'The dead man, Aidan McKinley as we know him – was found at the Lorimer, where he'd checked in. Natural choice, I'm told, and used by our boys quite a bit. Anyway, police called from Kensington, embassy notified, preliminary view – no post-mortem yet, obviously – that he took a drugs overdose. And remember this, Will, the Americans have every interest in confirming a natural death. Tourist expires; sad business. Why would they want anything else? And it's true, so I'm told – he was a heavy

user, our medics confirm it. You'll help with the story underneath? There are many complications. Tomorrow, please, at ten.'

The evening was over. He opened the door, saw Paul down
the stairs, and in a few minutes Francesca was back. After a
hug, he said, 'Did you hear anything in the box when you
opened the door to call Paul and Sassi?' She didn't smile.

'Why? What's up? You're so tense. Not yourself. I didn't
enjoy this evening.'

'I need to know,' he said.

She said that when she'd opened the door to invite them
back, they were close together in conversation – so much so
that she pulled back and was about to close the door when they
caught her presence and broke quickly. A few words had
floated towards her, that was all.

'Sassi was talking. He said they were seeing Berlin at its best
and its worst.'

'That was it? "The best and worst of Berlin?"'

'Nothing else. They weren't smiling, though.'

'Thanks, Bat-ears,' said Flemyng with a smile. 'No names?'
She shook her head.

'Another thing,' he said. 'Jonathan. What was he saying to
you?'

'Something quite odd,' said Francesca. 'We hadn't even been
talking about you, but he threw something in. Said he'd heard
you were knocking around with some old friends. Made a joke
of it – said people like you could never let go.'

'Names?'

Only one, Francesca said. 'Sam Malachy.'

She saw his surprise.

They were alone in the dining room, sitting on either side
of the marble fireplace, with the extravagant clock above them,
the table alongside empty except for some unfinished wine

glasses and bundled napkins. Flemyng, without raising his voice, asked how she had interpreted Ruskin's mention of Sam. Francesca said he hadn't seemed interested in getting an answer. 'A message, then?' Maybe, she said.

'Have you been seeing Sam?' she said. Flemyng avoided a direct answer. 'Jonathan's probably had dealings with him, one way or another. He's all over the place in his job. That's the point of him, after all.'

Standing up, she faced him and there was fire in her gaze. 'What the hell is going on? Because I don't want it to get between us. You're down and you're worried, and I don't believe it's family and nothing else. I just don't.' She reached out for his hand, but with no apology for her words.

'Can we leave it until the morning?' He put an arm round her. They took the stair down and found Lawrence waiting, to drive them across the river and home, an unhappy silence between them.

*

Near Hyde Park Corner, Sassi and Wherry were having a slow journey through the post-theatre traffic, Wherry to his Kensington house and his colleague to a favoured townhouse hotel near Sloane Square. In London the day was almost done. As they wheeled round and looked down Constitution Hill they could see Big Ben. The light above the clock face at the top of the tower that stayed burning when the Commons was sitting had now gone out. They turned towards Knightsbridge. A curtain of black velvet had come down over the park; the city was going to sleep. Will and Francesca were on their way back to Putney. Paul was nearly at his office, where he wanted to spend the last few minutes of the day.

Wherry said, 'What a mess. A real beaut.'

Sassi sighed. 'We need that eight o'clock meeting. I'll have a plan by then.'

He looked at his watch, and the dial glowed green, the only light in the car. 'It's quarter of seven in DC. Not even dark yet.'

SEVEN

As the embassy car dropped Wherry at his home, Grauber was checking into a hotel a short step from Union Station on Capitol Hill. The sun was setting. He used the nondescript place quite often, because it was run-down enough not to be inhabited by any colleagues and only a six-minute walk from Maria's house. He liked the shabby lobby and the sleepy clerks, who changed with a helpful frequency. Like the guests, they were birds who never nested. He showered in a sprinkle of water, went through a quick exercise routine in his tiny room, diverted by insect life in the carpet, and changed into jeans and a loose shirt.

He savoured the walk in the fading light across the east front of the Capitol and veered left into Independence Avenue towards Maria's house, past a gang of staffers and interns churning the gossip mill in the Hawk 'n' Dove. A congressman crossed the road, a boy skipping at his heels and reading loudly from a legal pad, his pace set by the rattling commentary of his master, who chopped the air as he walked. Grauber gave a couple of quarters to a guy propped up at Maria's corner, rattling a tin cup in the old style, stopped at the liquor store for a bottle, and turned towards her house.

The door was painted a warm yellow, but everything else was scruffy. The trash can had almost tipped over and the shrubs round the steps were scrawny and dried out. There was a bike chained to the short fence, which he thought too tempting, even with a heavy lock. The upper floors were dark, but by contrast the big lower room to the left of the door sent out a welcoming glow through its window. When he rang the buzzer she was there in a flash. 'Hey!' They hugged, and he handed over the bottle of wine in its brown paper bag. She gave no clue as to her mood, looked along the street and closed the door behind them.

He had his arm around her shoulders as they walked in, rediscovering the comfort of a room that he loved. There were South American rugs on the walls, half a dozen candles burning, warm wood everywhere, a welcoming round table set simply for two, and wide, inviting New England chairs arranged at angles to face a sofa with richly patterned red, green and orange cushions piled up. He sank straight into them. Maria was comfortable in this home, which she sometimes shared with an on-off lover who worked at State and whose existence was known only to a handful of friends. They guarded the fact. Grauber understood how difficult it was for both women, even with Maria's experience of the shadows. Tonight, as so often, she was alone.

He was pouring wine, expecting a few minutes of catch-up before business. There had been the lunch, after all. But Maria was quiet as she went to stir a pot that was filling the room with promise, checked the bread in the oven, letting loose a heady garlic cloud, brought in a platter of glistening peppers, and finally sat down in the low light with her hands resting on her knees. 'Thanks for the Bendo news,' she said. 'I need a drink.'

He said nothing, waiting for the explanation.

'You're going to London. Tonight.'

Grauber moved to one of the wide chairs facing the window at the back of the house. Before he sat down he leaned over and reached out a hand. Maria came first. He breathed in. 'Your message said I wasn't. Tell me everything.'

She said, 'I wish. It's not here yet, but there's a storm coming our way, a big one, and it's moving fast. Could blow itself out; my guess is not. A hurricane gathering speed.' She circled a hand above her head.

They both knew they did not have long. Grauber assumed he would be on the last red-eye from Dulles and there was time for her to tell him what he needed, and not much more. Not one of their happier evenings, but he felt a pulse of excitement. The atmosphere in the room was begging him to slow down; his mind sharpened.

'Here's a name you don't know,' she said. 'Aidan McKinley.'

He nodded, spread his arms. Maybe it was on a passport she would have ready for him, one he hadn't used before.

'Here's a name you do know. Joseph O'Connell Manson.' Spoken as if she were giving him a citation.

Joe, dear Joe. Grauber thought of the first time they had played the street together. They'd concocted a New York operation of their own, targeting a Mexican at the UN who fell into their laps like a game bird brought down with a clean shot. He was a joy, and Joe had taken him with such delicacy that for the brief few weeks while they shared the intensity of the sting, Grauber had been rejuvenated by the bubble-haired, womanizing, danger-seeking bundle of fun that was Joe. A moth always drawn to the flame, he had a dash and an energy that Grauber associated with his happiest times. Such was Joe's flair; but he recognized in him, too, a capacity for melancholy and self-destruction. Maybe that was why when they first met they had smiled instinctively like brothers, or lovers electrified by a single moment in the wildness of the dance floor.

When the operation was over, Grauber had helped him out with a couple of contacts in London, together with his invariable warning: only if in trouble. He wondered if this was a summons to work with Joe again. 'I adore him,' he said.

Maria reached for the bottle, and didn't speak until she had topped up both their glasses, turning them ruby red.

'He's dead.'

In silence, she raised a glass. Grauber, shaken but as quiet as Maria for a moment, did the same. Then together: 'Joe'. They drank.

Grauber shook his head to clear it, and put both hands to his brow. 'When did you know?' There had been no hint earlier in the day. 'How?' The tears for Joe had to wait.

She got up and moved to the fireplace to fiddle with a candle on the mantelpiece that was reaching the end of its life. She found another one, lit it with care from the first, waited until the flame sent up a confident flicker up the wall and turned to Grauber in shadow before sitting down again. In memoriam, she repeated 'Joseph O'Connell Manson,' saying it with a nice flourish, her hand raised at the end.

'I asked you to come here because I learned today that he'd left the reservation, gone on a private expedition,' she said. 'That's all. A tricky one, about which I'm afraid I knew little. I was livid when I found out – you can imagine. Then I had a message this afternoon – did I know it was coming? – telling me this. He's gone. You'll remember Wherry. Well, Jackson has fetched up in the London embassy. Remembers old times. Gave me a call. Kind. He didn't have to do it so quickly, but he wants to help.

'My dear boy, Abel...' his first name a sign that they were changing gear '... we're in a hole. Joe, poor Joe, may have screwed everything up with his last fling.' She sighed and almost thumped her arms on the cushions piled up around her. 'Why? Trouble is, I know. We liked him 'cos of his weaknesses, that indifference of his, the mad passions. We loved it all, and now he's gonna haunt us. Abel, I'm weeping for him. And for us.'

The scene was familiar to him – the talk racing away, a story getting ahead of itself, the need for calm, which would come in time because he had never known Maria succumb to panic. He sighed to insert some heavy punctuation, watched her flop out, waited for a long minute or so, and said, 'Explain. Take me there. Berlin. Bendo. Everything.'

Maria gazed directly at him. 'I have to start somewhere else, in this town, and tell you a straightforward story that most days wouldn't lose us any sleep. Familiar... amusing, I suppose. But this has turned dangerous, unpredictable. A serpent worming its way into our business, yours and mine.

'There was a time when your path and Joe's never crossed. Different territories. Then the Mexican business, right? You remember how he was when he had his own patch. Miami, sunk in Little Cuba – that madhouse. You know Joe played both sides of the street, stirring up the exiles with their dreams and their fury and their guns? Well, he was even comfortable when he was away from them, with what we might call regular Miami. There's a joke. But he did so well – that Spanish of his. They'd have thought him Colombian if it wasn't for his hair. Then the Mexico swing – the drug gangs, rough stuff. Good times; you know what I mean. We all understood that he had a problem from time to time. I thought he'd got on top of it. Maybe not.'

Abel realized that he was still in the foothills on this expedition, felt the steepness ahead.

'So what happened? Why scramble to London tonight? Tonight!' She took a chair and stretched out, long legs straight ahead of her, head back, face to the ceiling. Ready.

'Patience. This goes back and involves coincidences, of course. Our business. They've happened, and that's why you're here. It's why we exist, I suppose – to wait for a collision, which is what we've got.' She turned her face towards him and gave him the old smile that they'd shared so often. He sensed behind it an anxiety that he hadn't seen for a long time. 'More oncoming trains,' she said, 'heading down the line at us.'

Abel knew better than to try to steer the story, although he was already letting his mind think through their operation, which had preoccupied him for so much of the day, that she now thought at risk. In the stillness, he felt the room become gloomier.

'You need to know more about Joe's life before your time with him.'

Maria took him back years, to a time when Joe was a callow conscript cutting his teeth in Washington, before her own era in the city had started to bloom. She was in Europe, laying down her tracks in Paris and in the thick of it at the Sorbonne. Threw the occasional paving stone, as she used to say. Joe was straight down from the north of Maine, sharp and lively, big on the street. The story was that he had befriended – Maria's careful choice of word – a Spanish woman, then single and a mover and a shaker around town. In her late twenties and well-connected, she was a cut above Joe's normal level, maybe two, but because he was getting a taste of the diplomatic life for the times that lay ahead, and was charming and sexy in his way, they made contact. Hit it off, said Maria, which summed it up without need for extra detail. She was at her embassy, apparently in a humdrum role;

he was doing whatever he was doing and pretending to be something else. Never mind. Joe's job, in part, was to log everything he picked up – everything! – and lay down stores for the future, which he did with the aptitude that he later showed off in the fleshpots of Mexico and Miami, via some strange places in between, God remember him. He was an accumulator. But so, it turned out, was she.

Before Maria got too distracted, she forced herself back to Joe's time in DC, and what he'd left behind. The lady – still no name – told him a tale that was spicy enough when she first passed it on, startling and piquant, and had matured with the years. 'It's ripe now,' Maria said, bulging with promise or menace, depending how you saw it.

As Joe's friend had put it to him, it concerned the ruination of her life. Not the word he would have chosen, but never mind. It was no less than that. She had lost her innocence and dignity and her position all at once, so she said. 'We're talking here about a high-born woman, and a Spanish Catholic. Worst of the lot. They can see off the Irish any day.' Maria smiled.

The woman had been raped – legalities aside, that was her word for it – by a man who had done the deed and walked away, leaving her in despair to guard her secret shame. Not American, but someone who subsequently gained prominence in public life. She'd kept his name to herself; still did.

'I only know one thing about him,' said Maria. 'He's a Brit.'

The secret festered throughout the years. Maria said that Joe's story was that the memory had been controlled, laid to rest because she had to survive the day-to-day, but it was never lost. It could erupt at any time.

And the moment had arrived. 'For you and me, my friend, at the very worst time. This little tale starts to become the plot of something far bigger. It's not Joe's fault, but mine. He knew' – Abel noticed how the tense had changed for good – 'too much about Berlin, did some runs for me there, and made connections. Connections I wish he'd never understood.' Maria closed her eyes, and Abel understood the pain that came from loss of control. Joe had got a step ahead of her, and one way or another it was the end of him.

Maria began to trace the links, to try to see a pattern. 'Joe told me this story not long ago. He was back in touch with her. Bad news. And here's your second curve ball of the evening. You know who she is.' She lifted her glass towards the Capitol dome around the corner. 'Our friends on the Senate intelligence committee? You know what they think of us. One in particular. Got it?'

They didn't need to use a name. The senator whose wife had been Joe's lover flashed into Abel's mind at Maria's simple gesture. He felt the force that had almost flattened her.

'We don't need to ask if they resumed their relationship in every respect – I couldn't be surer of it, incidentally – but Joe was agitated when I talked about it. I had to turn the screws on him to get him to say why. It worried me; he was obsessing, and she's a lady we should handle like an unexploded bomb. Unstable, corroding from the inside, dangerous to everyone. Eventually Joe let it out to me. Here, on Monday.'

Abel knew, from the way Maria now stretched out her arms with a sigh, and raised her legs as if she were going to do her exercises, that she had come to the turning point.

'She'd had a child after the rape. Not known to us, and well-protected. Kept carefully out of sight, until now.

'That boy has just enrolled in a masters program at Georgetown U.'

'Ah.'

'Exactly. That's why she decided never to shout her story from the highest hill – she wanted to see him quietly through the years. A mother's duty. He's only just arrived in town.'

Abel sipped his wine and asked, 'What changed?'

Maria smiled. 'It would be beautiful if it was a piece of math, some kind of perfect equation. Joe's history and our game in balance. Except it's ugly. The Brits have nearly – nearly! – decided to help you and me. Right? And for us the prize is big. With Bendo fixed, it could be ours.' Abel inclined his head.

'They don't know it yet, but they may have decided to do something stupid at the same time. This woman, whose influence we know, believes that her humiliation is going to be paraded before her eyes, and she can't bear it. For the first time she's faced with something that's greater than the price of her own private shame, the one thing that could break her. If it comes about, she's prepared to tell her story and bottle it up no more. No matter what.'

Abel waited, saying nothing.

'From friends of the guy, her assailant as she would have it, who've kept in touch with her she has learned that the demon in her life, the father of her son and the source of all her pain, may be about to become Her Britannic Majesty's Ambassador to the United States of America.'

Abel stayed quiet for a few moments, frowning. There had to be more. Ambassadors could be stopped, friendly governments warned. Happened all the time. For some reason these channels weren't open, which was why he was here.

Maria smiled at him. She began to walk around the room. 'You're right. It should be the simplest thing to fix. Overnight job.' Not this time. His eyes were on hers and he saw in them, for the first time since he'd walked in, a wariness that he associated with their most difficult moments. There were the times when her natural lightness was a disguise, and he knew the symptoms.

'Two things. One – we don't know who the guy is. Two – we don't know who the Brits want to send to Massachusetts Avenue. Are they one and the same, or not?'

Abel leaned back and put his hands behind his head. 'And Joe is dead.'

'Precisely.'

They were two players in a long, smooth rally. Abel picked it up. 'Joe knew too much, but we don't know exactly what.'

'Or who he told.'

'About Berlin?'

'And Bill Bendo.'

'Or how he died?'

'That too,' she sighed. 'That too.'

'And if there was a reason behind it…'

Maria mimed a scream, then laughed. 'It's our fault. Like always. We're supposed to know these things before they happen, and we never do. We're stuck with our reputation. Right now we have one piece of information… a precious advantage and a curse. We use it or do nothing. Our choice, and either way there's trouble.'

He saw the fork in the road as clearly as she did, but she wanted to spell it out, as if to help herself decide.

'If we find out that her guy is going to be sent here, and we have to warn people that she'll call him a criminal – suggesting, obviously, that we believe her – then you can take it that two things would happen. The Brits would take fright, and our deal, yours and mine – the biggest of them all – would be over. After all we've done to pull it round, out of the fire. Dealing with Bendo. The works.' She looked straight at him and he was completely still. 'Second, we'd be over too. The fall guys. Swept away to save embarrassment.'

Maria drank some wine. 'The killer is that we don't know if she's even telling the truth. You know her reputation, and she might have been spinning Joe a line for purposes that we can't begin to guess. So think of this. We say he's a rapist – privately, to the folks that matter, which would be like sticking it on a billboard in Lafayette Square, signed by the fucking State Department – and it turns out that he can prove he isn't.

'White House and everyone else in total meltdown. Shit everywhere. *Everywhere.* The works. Me and you and the rest of the boys cast into outer darkness. For good.'

She asked the last question herself to get it over. 'And the other option – doing nothing and letting it happen?'

The painful answer. 'We don't say he's a rapist, and it turns out that he is… and we knew all the time.'

She painted the scene. 'He comes here. She goes nuts in the papers, spews it all out, he hasn't a defence, the kid shouts "Dad" on the news, ambassador resigns, horror story. Our deal's off – things are blown that would finish you and me for good – relationships screwed on all fronts. For all I know the government falls in London. I'm told, incidentally, that that's exactly what would happen, 'cos if this door opens there's gonna be a pile of horeshit that flows out, and she'll be spreading it all around this town. Joe isn't there to stop her. And, as we know, her loyal husband would throw himself into the task, with his committee piling in behind with their shovels.'

Maria was on her feet now. 'I say again' – the formal touch seemed right for the moment – 'who did Joe tell about Berlin? And what? The guy himself, whoever the hell he is? God save us.'

Abel got up and they paced the room together, had to move. 'It's unfair, old friend – it's always unfair – but we're piggy in the middle here. No win. Go one way we're screwed, other way we're fucked. Crude, but that's how it is. Joe got us into it; he can't get us out.'

Abel said, 'Sassi. Still in London town?'

'I've sent him a message,' said Maria. 'Knows there's trouble. Got most of the loose ends tied up, too. He'll try to keep them sweet. Guy's a charmer's charmer. If anybody can see us home, it's him.'

Abel was conscious that there was another chapter to come. He asked the question that he knew would open it up. 'What might Joe have done?'

Maria sat down across from him, and put a hand out to take his. 'The thing we've been managing all this time… I used Joe, more than you knew, to help with messenger jobs. He spent enough time over there to learn… too much. He could blow the whole thing wide open. And, sad to say, he was in a frame of mind where he might have done just that.'

And Abel knew why he was there.

'You know what we need from London. If Joe's tongue has been too loose, just because he went mad about this woman – for the second time, God save us – the game could be over. There are things London must never know.'

Abel got up and walked to the table, as if looking for a place to think. His head was down. 'All that work, digging our gold seam. And it's dust.'

Maria sighed. 'Yeah. The Brits will retreat, which is what some of them are inclined to do anyway, as we know. And then we're screwed. And let's be clear about what we both know. I don't mean the American national interest, I mean us.

'You and me. Our people. Nobody out there' – she flung a

hand towards the window – 'has an idea that any of this is happening, or not happening. We don't exist. But Joe and a stupid ambassador threatens everything. Ambassadors! Who needs them?' Abel, if our deal goes down, we'll be absorbed, reorganized, reconfigured. Fucked.

'The bureaucracy's human sacrifice. Roasted alive.'

His thoughts were turning, as Maria would know they must, to his own story, and the decision that had taken him to America. His calling, his family, and the secret that he'd kept down the years. Maria shared it and no one else around him knew it, not even Hannah. Not his brothers. He had long since decided that it was no deceit, but a necessity. All the years on the road, times of darkness and days of fun with Joe and Bendo and all the others, sprang to his mind. His life. 'Unthinkable,' he said.

'You know what everything here – us – means to me, and why. It's family. My inheritance. Well, one of them…'

'Believe me.' Maria spoke quietly, aware of the pain. 'We're all at risk.'

'I've been away from home for ever, but I still worry about Will. Brother Mungo's on the trail of the family story. He's got on his historian's hat, and he's fascinated. We're going to have to talk about it. Now this, just when we don't need it.' He shook his head.

'Is Will OK?' she asked.

'When you knew him in Paris he was happy-go-lucky. Loved it all. Same in politics for a while, but he's got a dark side. I sometimes speak to Francesca – his wife, you won't have met – and she's worried. He doesn't know we're in touch. He's troubled by the game he's in now – more than he ever seemed to be in the old one, which is strange in its way. He won't get killed in this one, but he might be destroyed. So I guess he feels as vulnerable as he's ever done.

'Meanwhile, Joe's dead in London. Meanwhile! How can I even say that?'

Maria stayed with Will. 'He was the life and soul in Paris. Style. Everybody loved him. I'm sorry things have changed for him, but it's what he always wanted. The political life.'

She left Abel alone then, going through the archway into the kitchen, whose aromas had now infected the whole house. He lay back on the cushions, watched the candles burn. The last of the light was fading from the windows, and the evening breeze filtering through the bug screen in front of him was a relief at the close of a long hot day. He was looking west and caught the livid stripes of the sunset through thin broken clouds. He thought for a little, while Maria sang softly in the kitchen as a counterpoint to the alarms of the last few minutes. He heard the pasta bubble and she clattered plates and salad servers, shouting to him to get water on the table, and more wine.

'It's gonna be a long weekend, one of the longest. I don't think we have more time than that.'

He felt the night drawing in quickly, darkness only a few minutes away. The high spirits of his arrival had slipped away; there were no smiles as they sat down at the table. Maria, whom he knew to have the ability to stay cheerful at the height of a crisis, was serious, eyes cast down. They both thought of Joe.

'First of all, I need to know where and how,' said Abel.

'He was found in his hotel room. Place called the Lorimer. Maybe known to you. Curled up, lots of stuff around. A mixture of substances, they say. A syringe, used – remember that. Passport in the name of McKinley – only one – stupid when he was told to ditch it after that shit hit the Colombian fan. This from our people. Wherry says the red light went crazy at Heathrow when he came in. Don't know what they did about it.'

'Followed him?' said Abel.

Maria tilted her head to one side. 'Would you? They're strapped, like us. They'd need a good reason.' Suddenly she smiled. 'And we're friends, aren't we?'

There would be an autopsy, but the local police who were called to the hotel – Wherry knew they weren't aware who Joe was, and only had the McKinley passport – took the straight-forward view. He'd overdosed. Died in the morning sometime, maybe topped up from the night before. That's how it looked. Maria said there would be another examination of Joe by embassy people, but they wouldn't get the body for days and days, at best. Coroner's call.

'That's it. All yours, Abel.' Their old intimacy had kicked in easily. A team of two. She went to her desk, and took out the passport which was ready inside. 'You've never had this one, Zak Annan tells me. Plane ticket's there. Credit card in the same name. We're getting faster at this. Lehman.' Abel laughed for the first time since he'd arrived. 'One *n* or two?' He scanned the documents. The photo was fine.

Maria said, 'I'll call a cab.' He'd pick up his bag on the way to Dulles.

He called information on the other line from the phone on the kitchen wall, and after a wait for the number rang the Lorimer, Hans Crescent, London. 'A room from tomorrow, please... Four days, probably. Is that possible? I'd like to check in around noon, if that suits you... Mr Lehman. One *n*.' They didn't ask for an address, only his first name. 'Peter.' A pause.

'Thanks for your help... Hot? Glad to hear it. Until tomor-row then.'

They said little for the next four or five minutes, exchanging murmurs of reassurance that didn't take them far. Abel was anxious for movement. The air was stifling, and for the first time since he'd got off the plane there was, just under the surface, a fearful pulse. The thrill of the chase was overtaken by the feeling that he and Maria were gripping each other tight, rolling headlong into a dark tunnel.

'All these complications,' she said, a finger raised like a teacher's signal. 'But so simple. What did Joe know, and who did he tell?'

Maria was smiling now. 'It was like this with him,' gesturing to the table, 'on Monday night.' Joe was heading home to Miami, and no talk of London. 'But he left me with the story I've told you. He stepped out there to the Diamond cab. Last I saw was his head catching the street light at the corner. A wave, and he was gone. But he'd decided to take himself over there. Didn't give me a hint. I think he went a little mad, and that's why I'm scared. I'll miss him.'

Abel shook himself and stood up. 'Come on. This is what we're for. It's us. We'll do it.' The truth was that Maria's mood had shaken him. She was the leader, the playmaker, source of all fun. Now she stood by the fireplace – tall, white, but half lost in shadow and darkened by a distant thought or a memory. He managed to grin. 'Let's go.'

As if he'd given an order, they heard the cab draw up. At the door, Maria put a hand on Abel's back. A police car, siren blaring, rolled past quite fast; from a neighbouring street came the sound of another, an echo of the first. The noise hung in the thickness of the night and died away. The cicadas chirruped in chorus, and a little gang of kids shouted their way past on the far sidewalk. Maria leaned towards him to say goodbye, and they embraced.

He whispered, 'Like I said from the airport, Bendo's ready.'

She pushed him away slightly to hold him at arm's-length, as if she wanted to examine him from top to toe. 'And you?'

He felt her arms go around him again before he could reply, and she wouldn't wait for him. 'Listen.' She spoke more softly than at any time that evening. 'I saw Joe through all his troubles. I knew what he'd fallen into, how he got out and slipped back, time and again. But he had a fear that never left him. And it tells us everything.'

Her grip on Abel was still tight, and he fancied he felt the beat of her heart.

'Joe was scared of needles. He never used a syringe in his life.'

FRIDAY

EIGHT

'When are you going to tell me what you're keeping from me?'

Francesca's question came after a weary night. Flemyng had pleaded fatigue when they went to bed after the opera and spoken of complications that needed the clear light of day to explain. Each woke once or twice in the dark, said nothing. And when the morning sun was brightening their bedroom, nothing much had changed.

'I don't even understand the family stuff you've been talking about, because you won't let me in,' she said. 'You mentioned Mungo in your sleep. I heard his name. I care about him, but you won't talk. And what's been going on in the office? I've never known you so dark.'

He asked for time. 'I'm going to sit outside for a few minutes,' he said. 'Please.'

Francesca sat up abruptly. 'Is there someone else? I deserve to know.'

He was stricken, and with Francesca beginning to weep, found it impossible to give her an answer. Instead, he said, 'I love you. Never forget that.' And closed the door.

He stepped softly downstairs, stopping twice to calm himself. He opened the door from the kitchen and went outside, disturbing a squirrel and some blackbirds breakfasting on the lawn. There was a swinging chair under a canopy of white climbing roses near the chestnut tree that marked the far limit of their garden and he sat down, the swing squeaking softly with his weight. He realized his cheeks were damp with tears.

But deliberately he turned his mind away from home, and concentrated. Methodically, placing each conversation and each event in sequence, recalling words and gestures from Paul and Lucy and Gwilym, he built up a picture of the previous day, piece by piece. To make sense of it, he then turned back to Wednesday, the night before his long walk to meet Sam and then Paul's bolt from the blue, the arrival of Sassi and the opera night. There had been a strange encounter in the dark.

He'd not expected to see Paul late on a Wednesday, because the cabinet secretary had seldom any need to cross the road for a long parliamentary sitting. But he was around, and they'd fallen into conversation on the terrace alongside the river, surrounded by members enjoying a late night (Sorley's bloody bill, again) because they could escape between votes for blissful drinking and banter in the dark, a balmy orgy of politics at the end of the day. Flemyng had responded to the unexpected quality of the encounter and now, sitting in his garden at dawn, could remember how their conversation had developed and, as he recalled, got out of hand.

At first, a routine canter round the course. The temper of government, how summer crises were ephemeral storms, strikes and inflation and the Europeans, and Paul's vague concern about the Americans, which had intrigued Flemyng. They'd leaned on the stone balustrade with their drinks and watched the river, letting themselves relax, and Flemyng had spoken of the forest fires of politics, the flames that sprang from nowhere and left the landscape bare. 'I can feel the heat,' he'd said. Paul was listening, refusing to interrupt.

Like a penitent getting close to the point with a confessor but stopping short, Flemyng had edged on to risky territory with thoughts about the nature of friendship in politics and his own troubles.

'You think comradeship is the greatest gift in this game, and for a while it is.' But the higher you got, the more certain it was that the closest friendships would break, and probably break you in turn.

Paul had asked how he could enjoy his world.

'The intensity,' said Flemyng. Then, as if that wasn't enough to be truthful, added, 'And the danger.'

Before they had parted, Paul had said enough to encourage him to go a little further, turn over a few more cards. So Flemyng had added: 'The more you concentrate on behaving sensibly in politics – rationally – doing the right thing, moving up, the more the rules of the game are bound to make you behave irrationally. It's so obvious. I'm the one they say has all the advantages – the silver spoon, the confidence. If they only knew.'

Paul had said nothing, letting him continue. Two party boats passed them on the river, weaving away towards the south bank, their music carried off into the night. The cover of darkness had encouraged Flemyng to continue.

A point was reached where you invited destruction, he'd said, as if it were inevitable. 'Maybe madness isn't an aberration, but the natural end to our game.' Everyone aspired to it in politics, even if they didn't recognize it for what it was.

Before they parted, half an hour later, he had been drawn into a conversation that courted yet more danger. 'I've found out something that troubles me, Paul. I don't want to say more now. I'll choose the right time. But I've seen the fragility underneath. I've always known it was there, and I suppose that's my trouble. I want it all. Need the promise, enjoy the fear.'

Paul hadn't pressed him. 'Tell me when you feel it's right, or necessary.' That was all.

Now, in his garden at the start of the day, he recalled how he had been disturbed enough by his own frankness to tell Lawrence to take the car away, and had walked home along the river in the warm and soft darkness. Near Chelsea Bridge, on a whim, he had taken the slimy stone steps down to the water's edge for no purpose but solitude, with the tide rising and streaks of light from the street lamps breaking on the water. He spent a few minutes in isolation there, standing on the lowest step, hidden from any passer-by at the railing above, one hand touching the damp weeds clinging to the stone embankment wall. The world retreated, granting privacy. Above him, the traffic was thinning out. One o'clock struck. Then he heard the faint swish of an oar on water and saw out of the blackness a single rower, sliding rapidly westwards and almost noiselessly along the surface, alone on the waterway in the dark. His blades left silver traces picked out in the patches of light, but soon he was gone. His wake disappeared, and the river looked as if nothing had broken its surface. A city of the unexpected, always. When Flemyng climbed up the steps to the street and began to walk again, it was at a faster pace.

Half an hour later he had reached home. Francesca was already asleep.

On the inside doormat lay the message with its handwritten summons from Sam, using an old workname. He noted the time of delivery on the postcard inside the envelope on which Sam had written 'Will'. It had been dropped off only a few minutes earlier. Flemyng had read it twice, then torn it into four pieces which he'd pushed to the bottom of the kitchen bin. He'd immediately planned his route for the next day.

He could still remember every step of the walk on Thursday

morning, Sam's alarm, and the atmosphere in Mansfield Mews where the government car had been parked outside number six. The movement at the window. Paul's revelation of the American's death had come only an hour later and now, in the stillness of the morning, Flemyng began to think through their next meeting, four hours away.

Francesca's arrival in the garden with coffee jerked him back to the present and the misery that he'd felt when she began questioning him. She interrupted his apology with her own. 'I don't mean to be hard on you. But can't you see, I'm worried sick?' They hugged, swinging back and forth on the seat. 'Can you reassure me?'

He squeezed her to him. 'Of course I can. Of course. How could you think anything else?'

'What am I supposed to think?'

'I can't tell you much,' he said. 'You know how it is. But I've learned something about what's going on around me – hidden deep down and dangerous, I think. Forget policy, all that. This is about people, and what it's like when they break.'

He asked her, as he had asked Paul, to give him time. Holding her hand, he turned to his plans for the weekend. 'I'm still planning to go north tonight. . . I'll fill you in properly on the family thing when I've talked to Mungo. That's his territory, not mine. I owe it to him to wait.'

He got up and walked across the lawn, turning back to her after a few moments. 'As for the office, I've been thinking about something you've often said to me.'

'Which is?'

'That I enjoy the thick of it, the camaraderie. Thrive on the fun. But that's not the whole story, nor even the true one.'

For the first time that morning, Francesca smiled. 'I know,' she said. 'You'll always be the cat who walks alone.'

Then they heard the doorbell. Lawrence was waiting with the car to take Will to the office.

He picked up his red box, and the morning folder was waiting for him on the back seat of the car. He checked the diary, revealing a lightish Friday, although there were ominous signs in Lucy's typed note of a queue of visitors forming in the building, all wanting decisions before the office powered down for the summer. And, Flemyng knew, so that they could wipe clean their consciences before they cleared their own desks. An ambassador from the Gulf was in town and had been promised lunch – that could go – and there were awkward phone calls to make to disgruntled backbenchers. His constituency chairman still wanted him, and Gwilym had to have a word about parliamentary business next week. Two big red boxes were threatened for the weekend in Scotland, fishing or no fishing. About the events that were consuming his thoughts, there was only one simple line: 'Paul, 10 a.m.'

He flicked over the newspaper front pages as they drove alongside the river. Serene. He'd clear the afternoon.

He leaned forward. 'Lawrence, could you drop the box at the office? It's a fine day. I'll walk the last lap. Work off last night's indulgence.' He got out of the car a hundred yards before Lambeth Bridge, and crossed the river. As he turned towards Whitehall, he rehearsed what he was going to say to Lucy, on the assumption that she had done what he had planned.

The pavement was busy, and he felt the holiday spirit abroad in the crowd moving around him in the direction of Parliament Square. To the world beyond his own, politics was entering its summer hibernation. He stopped to talk to a backbencher with whom he was friendly, giving his visiting constituents their ministerial moment, then negotiated the traffic in the square to get back to base.

As he did so, Lucy was ringing Francesca. 'If Lawrence is on time, which I'm sure he is, Will is in the car and on his way. May we talk?'

Francesca was cool. 'We have to. What's going on, Lucy?'

'You mean, with Will?'

'Of course. I just can't get through to him,' Francesca said. And without any further acknowledgement from either of them, the conversation took on a different tone. They were still feeling each other out, but understood that they were going to take the risk and trade information.

'You know he's been a bit distracted in the last week or two. I don't know how much he's told you,' Francesca began. No response.

'May I be frank?' Francesca continued. 'Will had a bad night last night after the opera. He was secretive, unhappy. And he asked me a strange question out of the blue when he was half asleep – about how I'd define madness. I don't know whether he even realized he'd spoken. No context, just that. I didn't know what to think. Has he said anything like that to you?' Then she added, 'Please.'

Lucy didn't hesitate. 'Yes, end of last week. Don't know why. He passed it off with a laugh. I think he was surprised it had slipped out.'

Francesca asked, 'Did you have an answer for him?'

''Course not. Made a joke of it.'

Francesca, not ready to resurrect her lunch invitation, said they both had to try in their different ways to help him through.

'I'll try as best I can, and it'll be fine,' Lucy said. 'We've been here before.' Francesca thanked her, and prepared for her day. Lucy straightened her papers and asked the rest of the office staff, bustling around, to leave her alone. She took an envelope from her locked cabinet, stood still for a moment, and placed it on Flemyng's desk.

*

As she did so, the two other ministers from the opera party were across the street, together in a small conference room in number twelve Downing Street, where the chief whip had his headquarters, with a disagreeable problem on the table. Harry Sorley's bill was caught in a parliamentary struggle that seemed to draw added heat from the rising temperature outside, and had the whole of Westminster complaining about long nights and the prospect of postponed holidays. The bill was being eviscerated and the entrails, as the chief put it, were beginning to stink.

'Sorry to call you together at this God-awful hour,' he said. 'But we need to get this fixed, and quick.'

Extricating themselves from Sorley's muddle would be messy, but that was politics. The whips were ready. There would be a concession to the unhappy mob and the threat that if they didn't buy it, maybe had the gall to ask for more, the House would stay sitting into the school holidays. Deal done, as the chief knew, but there would be pain. Jonathan Ruskin had fetched up, Sorley's friend at court, to dispense wisdom and warmth.

The chief whip was large and sometimes cheery, but kept his job because he had a relish for black politics, coloured with a scatological turn of phrase and a love of verbal violence. Sorley was dressed more smartly than usual, as if to make the point that he was going to keep his self-respect to the last. The chief whip sniffed his shaving balm when he entered, and blew his nose loudly. He noticed that Gwilym wasn't smiling, which was unusual, and said to him, 'You look terrible. You should piss off for a while. Let's get on with it.'

Sorley had put up a terrible performance at the party meeting on Tuesday, and there was a panicky interview in the *Telegraph* the following day, in which he had unwittingly revealed his fear, giving the scent of blood to a parliamentary pack on the prowl and stirring their ravenous urge. He'd be dead meat before the weekend was over. A firm hand was needed. As far as Ruskin was concerned, the detail of the bill was of no moment. 'It's piss and wind, I'm afraid,' he'd told the chief whip the previous afternoon, though he'd flexed his muscles in arguing for it in cabinet a few months before, when the wind was coming from a different direction. An age ago.

Gwilym pulled himself together to begin. 'Harry, it's obvious that this could drag on for a longish stretch, to no one's benefit. Clause three, which I know is what you're most concerned to save, isn't going to make it through this side of the recess, I'm afraid.' He paused to chew his pen. 'Maybe not at all.'

Sorley felt on his cheeks the first brush of the kiss of death. Gwilym said, 'The boys won't wear it – backbenchers are in a funny summer mood. Jumpy.' His pen was passing to and fro above the offending paragraphs in his copy of the bill, circling for the kill.

He lightened things, aware of the tension. 'The party's in a state. I think we should do something dramatic. Cut loose and get the advantage.' With this, he threw a thin smile in Sorley's direction.

'Chief?' In response, there was a sharp nod from his right.

Sorley drooped miserably. It was Ruskin's moment. He spoke softly. 'Harry, drop clause three altogether. Out it goes. Get up there and make the concession. Be forthright – make a virtue of it. We don't do it often enough. Just say – "I've changed my mind." We can do an all-night sitting on Tuesday, get the whole damned thing through and sail off on holiday, with Sorley the hero who's saved the day.'

He lifted his arms from the table with a flourish. The chief whip grunted again. 'Done,' he said.

'Not quite,' said Sorley, 'because it involves me getting up in the House, standing on my head and then sticking it up my arse.'

Gwilym, now in the groove, was ready with a reassuring word. 'Come on, Harry. There's not a minister in any government you can remember who hasn't had to do this. Forbes had the frigate procurement balls-up and put his hand up. Mr Humility. The papers were fawning at his feet, and he hasn't been out of the news since. You can do it and prosper, you know.'

'Damned right he did,' said Sorley. 'We both know he's a complete shit, but you're not allowed to say it. Out there, they think he's fun. He screws up something, they say "Good Old Jay"; with me it's "Sorley Sinks Again".' His listeners realized there was a real danger of tears.

Gwilym ploughed on. 'Jonathan's right. We can make this work. The foreign debate on Tuesday we can ditch easily; it was always a filler in case we needed a slot in the last week. I'll fix it with Will Flemyng. An evening on Iran he could do without anyway. It means we can have a last all-nighter before the summer – they all enjoy it at this time of year in the heat and the dark, as we know – and by the time we're back in the autumn, your bill will be safe and ready for the statute book.'

Being a broadly honest soul, he added, 'Well, most of it.'

'You're right about our Will, anyway,' Sorley said. 'He'll carry it off, Flemyng the Glamour Boy. Some of us don't have the bloody ancestral estate. Only have one spare suit. He'll always power on, when the rest of us fall away.'

There was silence. The chief whip broke it, but offered Sorley nothing. 'Stop it. Flemyng's one of your friends. Don't you forget it, or you'll have none left. It happens damned quick, in my experience.' Peering across the desk at Sorley, and refusing to offer him a hand, he repeated, 'Damned quick.'

With Sorley looking sick, and turning pale at the inevitability of it all, Ruskin rode to the rescue, which was his special skill in gloomier moments, dropping his voice even further to a consoling level. His perfect grooming, and his taste in shirts, made him the picture of confidence. He put a hand on Sorley's and inclined his head to talk in confessional mode, keeping his voice steady. Ignoring Sorley's outburst against Flemyng, he said, 'Listen, friend' – the formula perfect at that juncture – 'you're understandably browned off by our folks over the road, and their silly games. Our own lads who make it difficult. We'll get some of them, you can be sure of that. But there's life for you beyond this bill. You're in favour.'

To be clear, he repeated it, 'You're *in favour*,' making it sound like a priestly indulgence, offered without need of grubby payment. 'Act big now and you'll reap your reward. 'He touched Sorley's arm, feeling the thick black hair and nearly being jerked into what would have been an unhelpful recoil.

'We'll brief on your steadiness under fire.'

Sorley's head was down and his fingers were drumming on the table, making a quiet tumbril sound. He understood that whatever chutzpah he might manage to summon up for his speech on Tuesday, he had surrendered his dignity around this table. Everyone knew it. 'Fine,' he said, looking down at his hands. Then, realizing that he had to make a show of it, he added, 'Let's do it!' and gave the table a feeble slap, which was more embarrassing than doing nothing, because it revealed that all conviction had left him.

They turned quickly to their own affairs, with Ruskin leading Sorley from the room under the protection of an arm long enough to clutch the far shoulder as they walked. 'It's a rough old trade,' he said as he saw him out into Downing Street. 'We've always known it. We just have to rely on friends, and you have them in spades. Including Will – don't forget it. Now we'll all stick together. Nil desperandum,' which Sorley found irritating but knew was kindly meant.

'Thanks, Jonathan,' he said. 'Bloody awful, but there we are.'

Gwilym went to his room to phone Flemyng's office and tell Lucy to forget the Iran debate, tying up the job. The business of government went on.

A normal, hot Friday.

*

Flemyng had arrived in his own office just before the chief's meeting broke up and Sorley was led away. After settling at his desk, with his first coffee drained, he asked Lucy to come in and close the door. She was in one of her maroon shirts, which he'd told her he liked, and her long reddish hair was managed as well as ever, tumbling free across her shoulders. She was not in a mood for compliments, and Flemyng saw weariness in her pallor and downturned mouth.

'OK?' he said.

Lucy had difficulties at home. Her teacher husband was not looking forward to the next foreign posting, due to come her way soon. She was turning thirty at the end of the year and wanted a move. There were no children yet, and Flemyng knew enough to be aware that they argued about whose career should prevail. It was unresolved. 'I hope everything's better back at base.'

She ignored the overture and said sharply, 'Why are you avoiding the point?'

Flemyng's eyebrows rose. He picked up the envelope on the desk in front of him. 'This?'

'I've read it,' she said. 'I assume that's why you left the drawer open overnight. So that I would find it.'

He smiled.

'It was sneaky – I'm being blunt here – trying to make me feel bad, or putting one over on me in some way? Why not just show it to me? I can only think of one explanation.'

'Come on then,' he said, smiling.

'That you wrote it yourself.'

The cruelty, born of anger, was deliberate and Lucy saw him stricken with shock, eyes narrowing and creases appearing on his brow. The hollows in his cheeks seemed to deepen. But she said, 'I think I deserve an answer, don't you?' without giving way.

Flemyng got to his feet. 'Of all the things you might have said, I didn't expect that, I promise you. Surely you can't believe it, if you've read that letter carefully?'

'All I know,' said Lucy, slapping the table with her hand, 'is that you've been sunk in some kind of gloom for the last week. Everyone's seen it. Then you put on a pantomime to lead me to discover this. If it's a game, it's a weird one. So you can see how I reached my conclusion.'

Taking his time, he walked round his desk to the chair and sat down again. He took the single sheet of paper from the envelope, unfolded it and put it squarely in front of him, smoothing the folds. 'Well, let's read it again, together. And I'm very sorry, Lucy. You didn't deserve this.'

Then, with his gift for surprise, he leaned across the desk towards her and said without warning, 'I'm scared. Can't you see it?'

She stared at him.

He splayed his right fingers on the paper and turned it round in one movement, pushing it slightly towards her. It gave the letter an untouchable quality, as if it were liable to explode if interfered with. She placed both elbows on the desk, pulled her chair in, and looked down without setting her own hand on it. For a moment Flemyng imagined her sitting an exam paper, or having a first look at some teasing cipher that resisted explanation, and was excited by the intensity of her gaze. She settled gently to the task like an archivist in a quiet cloud of dust.

He watched, knowing that she was clearing her mind and reading the letter as if for the first time.

Before her lay a sheet of House of Commons notepaper without a member's name printed across the top, only the portcullis crest and no other indication of its origin. It was a photocopy of a note, dated eight days ago with the month rendered in roman numerals, *vii*, typed like the rest of the letter. Her discipline and fingertip concentration allowed her to begin at the beginning and not to try to jump to the last line, although from her study of it the previous evening she could have recited some passages from memory.

There was no salutation at the top and no signature at the bottom.

Flemyng leaned back and watched her work her way through the letter, her only movement being a slight shifting of the elbows. She didn't touch the paper, and her head stayed perfectly still. She didn't look up as her eyes moved down the page. He heard her catch her breath a couple of times, very quietly, as if capturing some meaning that had previously escaped her. She read deliberately slowly, as if she was starting on a paper that was much longer than the thirty lines of this letter. Twice she stopped and went back to give a passage a second chance. On each occasion a twitch at the corners of her mouth suggested that she had confirmed an opinion, not changed it.

Lucy could devour a complicated government paper and get to the point in a flash, but she was controlling herself here and forcing her eyes to take their time.

Finally she read it aloud, and he leaned back to listen. He knew almost every sentence by heart.

'I cannot express the pain your disdain caused me yesterday... why have you repaid me like this? You must know how deeply this hurts, after everything we've done. How are we going to continue?

'I may be losing my mind.'

Flemyng assumed that she shared the surge of embarrassment and guilt that he had felt on first reading these words, but that she was also engrossed in analyzing the personality laid bare on the page in front of her. There was now no outward sign of the stab of alarm he had felt when she accused him of having written it. He appeared content.

Lucy decided, without any appeal to him, to continue to read aloud.

'I have come to the conclusion that you are bent on a cruel destruction of our relationship. This can't be happening by chance. I would beg you to stop, but it may be too late. Is this inevitable in our lives? Did you always know?'

For the first time, she looked up, drew breath and turned back to the letter.

'Where do we go from here? I'm desperate.'

Lucy glanced over the page at him. 'Desperate? The trouble is, I believe it.'

'How can you pretend that this is not happening? For you it's business as usual; but agony for me. When I need your help

you're not there. All the others are driving me insane. We need this game, both of us, but we have to play it together. The only way.'

She had almost done. She saw that the last paragraph had words that were heavily underscored in ink, some of them several times, and that the typed text took on a rattled character, with wayward punctuation, as if it had been composed in fits and starts. She read on, without losing her rhythm. One line near the end held her attention, so she repeated it. Flemyng watched her closely.

'This could kill me, or both of us. Don't you see that?'

She lifted up the sheet of paper to try to catch the light better, and let her eyes examine it from an angle. 'From the same typewriters as we use, so familiar.'

She returned to reading aloud the last line. *'We may not have long. Help me.'*

Sitting back, she looked across the desk at him. 'Well?' said Flemyng.

'I've never seen anything like it.'

'I take it,' he said, 'that you now understand what I meant when I said I was scared.'

Quietly, she said she did. Then, considering the seriousness with which Flemyng had approached the letter, his horror at the suggestion that he might have written it himself in a storm of despair, and his concentration on her reaction, she decided to take a chance and leap over the first fence. 'I'm assuming that your interest in this means that it's either addressed to a minister, or written by one, or a senior official using this notepaper. There's nothing low-grade about this. Otherwise it wouldn't matter. It's from our level or above.' She moved one hand back and forth, palm parallel to the desk. 'Although I find that a difficult thought. Unbelievable, in fact.'

'Yet you thought it could be written by me.'

Lucy said she was paid to think the unthinkable, take nothing on trust. 'I'm sorry if that hurts. But you always say you want honesty.'

'It does sometimes hurt. Forget it.' He turned away as he spoke. 'I think you're right that it was written by a minister. That's my own conclusion.'

She revealed that her first impression matched his. 'Can you tell me where this came from? It's odd as well as scary. At first you might think it was – well, about sex. Naturally.' Lucy gave no sign of embarrassment. 'But somehow, and I'm not sure why I say this, I don't think it is.' He put out his hand towards her, to show that he'd reached the same conclusion, with the same level of incomprehension.

'I'll describe the origin precisely,' said Flemyng, 'or as best I can, because in some ways it's the most important part of the story. I still don't know how to account for it – who wrote it, or for whom it was meant.' He said that the way he had come across it might help to lift some of her anxiety about him. 'And Francesca's,' he added, producing a flicker of guilt on Lucy's face as well as his own.

'Do you see why I had to let you see this? I can't keep it to myself.'

He said that after Thursday cabinet the previous week, to which he'd been summoned as an auxiliary because there was a paper on the Americans and the Middle East that lay squarely in his territory, he'd lingered for a few minutes outside the cabinet room to speak to Paul about a parliamentary statement he might have to handle for the office in the coming days. He'd perched on a private secretary's desk in the anteroom beside the double doors that led into the cabinet room, and talked it through with Paul. Tom Brieve was there too, lounging in a chair and occupying himself with a thick file. Ears red-hot as usual, said Flemyng. By the time he'd left, all the members of the cabinet had passed through the corridor that led towards the front lobby. One of Paul's secretaries was making sure that no papers had been left on the long coffin-shaped table at which the cabinet sat. Everyone else had gone. Flemyng needed to make a copy of a constituency letter he'd found in his box, so took it from the back of his bright red folder and walked to a photocopier newly installed in an alcove off the corridor on the little passageway that led through to the Number Ten political office. He lifted the lid and saw a document lying face down.

'I turned it over. It was this letter.' He tapped the desk with his thumb. 'The most extraordinary document I think I've seen in my time in government. And you know some of the stuff that comes across my desk.'

'So what did you do?' said Lucy. 'Give it to Paul? Somebody in private office at Number Ten?'

Flemyng smiled and gave a shrug that combined embarrassment and self-satisfaction. 'I did the only sensible thing.' He looked up and grinned at her, opening up for the first time that morning. 'Just what you would have done.'

Lucy pursed her lips, knowing what was coming.

'I pressed the button, copied it, left the original where I'd found it, face down on the glass, and took the copy. This one. Put it in my briefcase and walked away. There was no one around. I checked.'

He had then made an excuse to go and see Paul about something he said he'd forgotten, passing through the connecting passage to the cabinet office where Paul had returned to his lair. He'd managed to spend ten minutes there without any trouble, came back through Number Ten on the pretext of passing on a word to Brieve about a conversation he'd had with the Israeli ambassador the night before, and made a detour to the photocopier on the way out. The letter had gone.

'That makes the whole thing even stranger,' said Lucy.

Flemyng was smiling now, his eyes alight. 'This was typed, and given what it says, the writer wouldn't want it left lying around. I'm sure the usual carbon copy wasn't made for the file, nor that it was photocopied in the office where it was typed.'

Lucy's eyes were scrolling down the letter. 'Maybe he – or she – panicked afterwards. Wanted something to keep.'

'Yeah,' said Flemyng. 'I'm certain you're right. Whoever wrote this wanted nothing on file. So why take the risk in copying it afterwards? In the cabinet corridor, for God's sake? And does anything else puzzle you about the wording? Take a step back and think about it.' He straightened the sheet of paper once more, leaning over towards her side of the desk.

As he had expected, Lucy didn't waste time with the obvious point that it was surprising that anyone who had written such a letter – assuming it was the writer who had left it there – would be careless enough to forget to remove it from the copying machine. Instead she got straight to the heart of the question that had most interested him.

'If it was left there by the person who wrote it – and it's dated on the day of cabinet, which started at ten-thirty, so that's a sensible starting assumption – I find it very strange. Inexplicable by the usual rules.'

'So do I.'

'It probably means,' said Lucy, 'that someone wrote this intimate letter, which is about as personal and private as you can get, and poured out these feelings. And then, instead of sending it or handing it over, or tearing it up, which is what anyone else would have done, decided afterwards, quite deliberately, to make a copy – before, during or after a cabinet meeting. A change of heart, in panic, or for another reason. It seems that he wanted some kind of proof that it had been written.

'A copy! Of this?'

She paused, and shook her head slowly, spreading her arms out for the first time since entering the room. 'It's… mad.'

'Exactly,' said Flemyng, looking happy for the first time that morning.

NINE

Sam Malachy was planning a morning of exploration. He had devised a winding route of meetings and pit-stops that would take him to three separate floors in his dingy tower block and bring him, he knew with certainty, a rich haul of gossip, all in the name of an ambitious operation that he was putting together for Finland – if only in his head. It had a name, Sam had found an alluring objective for it, and even an old agent whom he could say was willing to be revived for the game. Fiction from top to bottom, but it wouldn't be the first time. In a week it would be forgotten, one of Sam's flights of fancy and gone with the wind. A risk to be taken, for Will Flemyng's sake. Loyalty demanded it, Sam having remembered in recent days his friend's calming cheerfulness in moments of darkness, most of all his arrival in a clinic one Sunday night when Sam thought the world had left him behind. A smile out of the darkness and a hand on his shoulder.

He had cleared files from his desk and spun the combination on his safe when a secretary knocked and pushed open his door. He seemed to have known her for half his life, Jean being a pillar of the service, born and bred in its embrace, and a mothering presence to all the boys, ready with a bucket of healing balm when they came home from scrapes and adventures, bruised and sometimes broken. Sam often thought of the shock he'd experienced on learning she was two years younger than he was. She smiled. 'An old friend rang for you yesterday, after you'd gone. He said his name was Mr Massie.'

A Flemyng work name from Vienna long ago. She knows, Sam thought.

'Rang from a call box. He said he's in town briefly, and would like to see you. Same place as last time, at five this afternoon, if you can manage. He didn't leave a number. That's all.'

'Thanks, Jean. You are kind. Forget it, won't you?'

'Always glad to help old friends.' She smiled.

It was with a cheery expression that Sam set off to start his morning calls on the floor above, certain that Flemyng was operating once again. He turned his mind to Helsinki and his own Operation Endymion, which he was sure would bring him rewards for ingenuity. 'Hey, Maurice,' he said to a young colleague on the stairs. 'Bend your ears. Have I got a story for you,' and steered him into the empty back conference room.

Across the river, Flemyng was preparing for Paul's council of war with Lucy at his side. The letter they had read together was back in his briefcase, and by silent agreement had been set aside for now. Lucy was busying herself with embassy telegrams for his box, and a draft of his speech for his Sunday seminar in St Andrews. 'It'll be in good shape by lunchtime, never fear,' she said. 'I'll leave you to apply the polish.'

Flemyng said he wanted to spend a few minutes alone before meeting Paul, and asked Lucy if she could find him a London telephone directory. 'Switchboard can find anyone for you,' she said. 'Don't waste your time.' He shook his head. 'A to D, if you can find one. I want to check something.' She rummaged under her desk and found a battered directory, with clumps of pages missing. He took it and shut himself in his inner room. Ten minutes later he was ready for the meeting.

His first impression on entering Paul's office a few minutes later was that morning had turned into autumnal afternoon. No one had pulled the curtains back properly to let in the light, and there were shadows on the desk. Heaps of paper had appeared, and Paul appeared to have sunk under their weight. He didn't rise as Flemyng came in, and compared with his performance as presiding officer at the opera house, when he had pulsed with good humour, this was a thinner and darker character altogether, his sparkle gone.

'We're expecting Gwilym in a minute,' he said. 'This is Chief Inspector Osterley,' gesturing to his left.

The short, neat policeman, pleasantly open-faced, sprang to his feet. 'I'm Jarrod,' he said, with a smile that suggested he knew that Flemyng would be wondering when officers, even in Special Branch, began to acquire such names. 'I'm not sure whether or not I should be here,' he said with a grin, and Paul flinched. He was shaking his head, the stuffing seemingly knocked out of him.

Gwilym's arrival compounded Flemyng's feeling of shock at seeing Paul's unsteadiness. Their confederate was grey and dishevelled as if it was the end of a long day and not the beginning. Paul's office seemed to have developed its own micro-climate and become a place of fear and alarm, where anything might happen without warning. Osterley, however, whom Gwilym greeted with notable wariness, appeared immune to the atmosphere. He was alone among them in having no gleam of sweat on his face, which was deeply tanned and looked as if it had been shaved moments before. He cheerfully laid a couple of sheets of paper on Paul's desk, side by side.

'Shall I tell you where we are?'

Paul waved a hand, and said, 'That's why we're here. Please carry on.' Flemyng had never before seen him surrender command in such a way. Paul sank lower in his chair.

'Right. I'll bring you all up to speed,' said Osterley. 'I'll be quick, starting with what you already know.

'First, let me explain that Aidan McKinley doesn't exist. Well, obviously he does in Dublin and points west – bound to, of course – but not here. Not in our midst. The passport that the boys picked up at Heathrow was a dud, one that we knew, although it's a classy one, if you follow me. We'd known it for a couple of years, and it was safely there on our watchlist. Odd that it should be used again, when there'd been trouble before, but there you are. There's no rhyme nor reason for some of the mistakes people make. May have been in a rush, who knows?

'The man who was carrying it was Joseph Manson, thirty-seven, resident of Miami, Florida, and known by us to be a representative of a small, bespoke outfit of American intelligence that – if I may put it like this – we know a little about, though far from everything. And rather admire, so I'm told by those who paddle in that canoe.'

Flemyng's attention quickened. Where Paul's wide grey eyes were dull with weariness, his had the quality of jet, black and alive with light. But he was motionless.

Osterley described the loud ringing of bells when the passport was logged, then the observation through the one-way glass of McKinley at the baggage carousel – 'they were nice and slow with the bags as ever, I'm glad to say' – his progress to the taxi queue, and the tail that they managed to scramble to find out where he was bound.

'Quite a fuss,' said Flemyng, one hand massaging his neck. 'Unusual these days. Why?' He looked at Paul, not Osterley.

'You may think it was over the top.' Paul's expression was

sombre when he spoke. 'There was good reason, believe me. Sadly, as it turns out, we should have done more. Forgive me for leaving it there for the moment. Press on, will you?' A long look at Flemyng.

Now Osterley made his great leap, leaving aside events at Westminster and dealing with the second coming.

'My uniformed colleagues from Kensington were called to the Lorimer Hotel at just after three o'clock yesterday afternoon, Thursday. The chambermaid dealing with room four two five noticed that the Do Not Disturb notice had been hanging on the doorknob for more than twenty-four hours, so she followed the instructions they're given for that eventuality, and knocked very loudly several times. Called out. She hadn't been in the room since the guest arrived the day before. She then opened the door – very carefully, she says in her statement, in case the guest was sound asleep... or busy in some other way.' He gave a grin that got nothing back from Paul. 'What she found was the very unpleasant sight of which you're already aware. She called the housekeeper, who rang the police, and here we are.'

'We certainly are,' Gwilym murmured, raising bloodshot eyes.

Osterley was watching Flemyng, not Gwilym. 'My uniformed colleagues called a doctor, surveyed the scene, and after the person was officially pronounced dead, rang the American embassy to inform them that one of their citizens had been found, apparently having succumbed to an overdose of drugs. The doctor had no doubt at all. Naturally, the name given was McKinley. We had the other passport that was with his things in the room, the Manson one. Much better like that. Safer,' he said, as if dealing with the aftermath of a street disturbance. 'It will be returned to the appropriate people in due season.'

He described how the police had contacted the consular officials for help with family, if there was one, getting the settled procedures under way. 'The presumption was of an accidental death, which means a formal inquest at some stage, so the body remains in our care *pro tem*.'

Paul intervened. 'I have made certain enquiries in the quarters that you would expect. I can help with a little bit of the background to the day that McKinley... let's hold to that name for the moment, I find it easier... McKinley spent in London, before all this happened. Before he died, I mean.

'As the Chief Inspector – Jarrod – has explained, he was picked up from Heathrow on Wednesday morning and it was established that he was staying at the Lorimer. We couldn't keep a full-time watch on him. It would never have been agreed for an American and I didn't really want to ring all the alarm bells at that stage. But our man who followed him to the hotel did keep on his trail to lunch – young and enthusiastic, so it appears, and he stuck to his man. McKinley met a junior guy from the American embassy – he's called Halloran – who seems to operate in the same line of business, broadly speaking. They ate at an Italian place called Le Ville off the Fulham Road.'

Gwilym said, 'I know it,' surprising them by taking on the role of aimless commentator. 'Nets on the ceiling, dangling Chianti bottles. Charming in its way.' Flemyng wondered if Gwilym would be able to stay the course.

He asked, 'And what did the target do next?'

Paul clasped his hands together on the table, preparing himself. 'We don't know. I wish we did.'

Gwilym said, 'So do we all, so do we all,' resuming his gravedigger's commentary.

'From then on,' said Paul, 'he rather slipped under the radar.'

Flemyng said, 'You mean there's no information at all.'

'Yes.'

And Gwilym said, 'God Almighty,' as if he had known nothing of it.

Despite Osterley's care, and perhaps generosity, in editing out of the script the first discovery of the body, they had no choice but to return to the subject. Flemyng watched for Osterley's response.

Paul said, 'Manson wasn't seen again after that lunch on Wednesday until he was found, for the first time, in the parliamentary precincts on Thursday morning.' A glance at Osterley, no more. 'I hope you are following me. There were drugs on the scene. A syringe.

'The medic who had a look at him before he was… taken… I'm referring to the first discovery,' Paul found it hard to leave anything unsaid, 'is apparently convinced that he died of an overdose. Probably a long-time user. Anyway – not much doubt.

'But the first people couldn't do a great deal – couldn't intrude, so to speak – bearing in mind that he had to be found again. Properly.' He gave an unnatural, nervous cough. 'Our man couldn't leave any traces. He did say rigor mortis was only just beginning to set in, so the victim died on Thursday morning. Not before.'

No one in the room asked for more detail.

Paul added, 'I wish I didn't know this, but I can't pretend that I don't.' His first concern was to avoid breaking the rules, let alone the law, but the speed of events had left him on the back foot, for the only time that Flemyng could remember. 'Here's our problem. We don't know the circumstances in which he died. That's the truth of it.' He gave a sudden, loud sigh. 'Had he spoken to anyone? Why had he gone there in the first place? What was his game?

'The syringe was nearby and had his fingerprints on it, I'm told. Just what you would expect. It was on a bookshelf. But where we go from here, I'm not sure.' He looked towards Flemyng.

'God save us,' said Gwilym, still flailing around, despite having heard everything for a second time.

'Let me spool back,' Paul said. 'In McKinley's room, we found his real passport in a pile of clothes. It confirmed that he was the person who had used the McKinley one before. A Mr Manson. As the Chief Inspector said' – a glance at Osterley – 'we'll hang on to that for a little. The Americans will be up to speed by now, and dealing with it in their own way, I've no doubt. The police officers who found his body – the second discovery – never saw the other passport so he remains McKinley to them. There were drugs of various kinds, I'm told. I haven't heard of any of them. The syringe, of course. Wallet and keys. A small leather notebook. And that's about it.'

He looked at Flemyng, to pass the silent message that Osterley had agreed that there was to be no mention of his own phone number. Another gesture. No matter that everyone in the room was aware of the piece of paper that had been fished out of the dead man's pocket at the first discovery, the deal was that it would not, as Gwilym had put it to Paul, be placed on the table for all and sundry to peruse at their leisure.

Flemyng asked the question that Paul was expecting. 'What does the notebook tell us?'

'Quite a bit,' said the policeman, and smiled.

There was a pause. Gwilym looked to be imagining the scene in the back of the van with no windows, transporting a stiffening corpse wrapped in blankets despite the heat, through the streets of London to a hotel where a second team of dark servants in overalls would be holding open a service lift, perhaps forming another bearer party and clearing the way to whisk it upstairs to its new resting place. He was sitting quite still, with his head at an artificial angle looking straight ahead, and Flemyng caught the shake in both hands.

'I made arrangements, I should say right now, for the notebook to be given to me. In other words, it was not taken to Kensington police station with the other personal effects. That seemed the obvious course in the circumstances. It will not appear on the list of items found at the scene. Just like his real passport.'

For a fair man, Paul's face had taken on a strangely dark look. His forehead was lined, his short hair ruffled as if he had been wakened from a deep sleep. 'Tell us, Jarrod. I should perhaps warn you both' – a gesture to Flemyng and Gwilym – 'that there are some disturbing entries in that notebook.'

Flemyng waited.

'For example, in relation to one senior civil servant in particular. His name and private office number. All underlined. He has a page of the notebook to himself.'

Looking miserable, he said, 'Tom Brieve.'

Another heaving sigh from Gwilym, who was producing a chorus of groans while lighting another cigarette. Flemyng had never seen him smoke, and such was the surprise of it that it seemed as if Gwilym was now operating in another dimension.

'Brieve.' Flemyng's voice was flat and gave no hint as to whether he was surprised or not.

Paul said, 'I've spoken to Tom. He'll soon be on his way to Paris for the conference, with pretty well everyone in this whole place. But not until the morning. He has a dinner tonight, apparently.' He then swept his hand high. 'He has explained to me,' this with a careful glance around the room, taking in everyone, 'that a call did come into his office from a man who called himself Manson. His real name, as we know. One of Tom's secretaries took the message. Manson wanted to have a conversation, and mentioned the name of a congress-man in Washington whom Tom knows, saying he was the conduit who had suggested the call. Didn't say what he wanted to talk about.

'I should say here and now that with some effort we con-tacted the congressman in question last evening and he knows nothing of Manson, nor of the supposed introduction to Tom Brieve, and is as mystified as we are. It was a tale Manson told for his own purposes. I need hardly say that the congressman is neither aware that Manson is dead, nor of the nature of our interest. He will doubtless have forgotten it all by now. Let's hope so. The boys in the Washington embassy handled it well.' As always with Paul, praise where it was deserved.

'The long and the short of it is this. He wanted to speak to Tom Brieve himself, but the conversation didn't take place. Tom's secretary told Manson to ring back the next day, put a brief note on Tom's daily list and says he thought no more of it. Put it out of his mind. And, of course, Manson didn't get in touch again.'

'For reasons we know,' said Gwilym, with another sigh.

Paul was on his feet, a straight-backed figure beside the high white marble fireplace, his hand resting on the mantel. 'So there we have it. We know who he was.'

Gwilym said with relish, 'A spy.'

Paul ignored him, and resumed.

'He was proposing to speak to an official in the most impor-tant office in this government, had got himself into parliament for reasons we don't understand, and ended up dead in a cupboard, apparently having taken too many drugs. And as to the question why, we don't have a sliver of an answer. Except that we can assume he wasn't here on holiday.'

'Or for the good of his health, you might say,' said Gwilym. Paul breathed hard.

'Jarrod, thank you. Let us know when you learn more.'

As Osterley departed, Paul turned to face the others. Flemyng was in front of him, Gwilym still in his chair by the window.

Paul went back to the desk and perched on one of its corners, one foot just touching the floor. 'Will, this is the oddest business I have ever known. Grisly, dangerous, you name it. Politically – explosive, though it's not a word I like. As I indicated yesterday, I need you to help in any way you can. And since then, as we have heard, it has taken another nasty turn, towards Brieve's office. You have to pitch in, full tilt.'

'We're in it up to our necks,' put in Gwilym.

Paul ignored this, and carried on. 'Your boss won't know, Will. He's away anyway. No one, not your colleagues, not your old friends elsewhere – Gwilym here, that's all. As I told you before, not another soul in this building, from the highest to the lowest. I'll tell you what I can.

'The body's the least of it.'

Flemyng moved quickly to pin him down. 'What do you mean by help, exactly?' he said. 'And pitching in?' He pulled himself up and, Gwilym also having risen, joined them at the desk, straightening his jacket as he did so.

'As I said last night, I want you to delve into your past a bit, wherever it might take you. I don't need to know all the details. But I'll protect you if you need that,' Paul told him.

He did also offer a smile. Gwilym didn't. He was still trembling, and had left several cigarette ends in a heavy ashtray beside his chair. He was watching Flemyng closely, head cocked to one side in a manner that looked affectionate.

Paul said, 'We don't exactly look like the Three Musketeers, do we?' That did bring a flicker of a grin from Gwilym. 'But we're going into battle, I suppose, together.'

At this, Gwilym produced a moment of unintended and touching comedy. He stood to attention, as if in response to a command, his shirt ballooning out of his trousers and his tie at half-mast. He pushed a hand through his hair, stirring up the blond thatch. 'Come on, Will,' he said, raising both arms like a nervous conductor.

For Flemyng, the minute or so that followed this display of innocence and supplication had the intensity of some vision come upon him in the night, vivid enough so that the shapes and colours of the faces and places that he saw were imprinted on his mind, where they would remain, clear and seductive, through the days that lay ahead. Paul understood that he felt the pull of the old game with Sam and the others; understood all the confidences they would share and the secrets they would have to keep. Flemyng was thinking, too, of Lucy hunched over a letter that was taking her into the dark heart of his trade, and a picture of a brother in happier days flashed on his mind, unprompted. Then home, where he was bound that night.

'Paul,' he said. 'You know that I'm due to go north later. Last flight to Edinburgh. I've got a little fishing planned at home, then the speech in St Andrews on Sunday. Should I go? I've got today, can make some progress first.'

Paul said, 'Go. That's where you think best. It's your brain I need, Will, not your swordstick. Prowl around today, talk, then take yourself home. We'll speak tomorrow and meet here again late on Sunday, if that suits, take it from there. Things will have moved on by then. No doubt you will have had some conversations of your own.'

Flemyng was with him and they locked eyes.

'Get into this, as best you can. I'll talk to Tom Brieve again. You'll bump into all the others who're involved in bits of the business, but they're not to know. The police will have to go through the usual stuff, although it will be as discreet as they can make it. Let them do their own thing. We're going to have to make the connections that may be beyond them.

'That I hope are beyond them, I should say.'

Flemyng, who'd been managing his own fear for days, recognized in Paul the same determination to keep panic at bay, the effort to hold the temperature down, despite everything.

'Better than being a minister, any day,' said Gwilym, managing a laugh at last.

'Mind you, you'll have to carry on as normal,' Paul said, having got up and moved back to the fireplace. 'What you're doing for me mustn't show.' Flemyng saw that the big clock on the mantel was signalling that it was nearly noon, its long filigreed hands almost on top of one another. In a moment there would be a chime to mark the height of the mad day, and from over the road they'd hear the deep boom of Big Ben counting them into the afternoon.

'I have plans for this afternoon that may help,' he offered.

Paul returned his smile with a nod of relief.

'Will. Thank you. And it's just like the old days. As I say, no one will know.'

Flemyng smiled at that. They shook hands, not without a little awkwardness, because Gwilym was getting into the swing of the adventure and seemed transformed. He did up his tie, stood straight, and for one brief moment seemed on a high. They broke up.

Flemyng knew what Paul wanted him to do. He walked to the courtyard outside his office, paused for a few minutes' thought, then went upstairs to his desk and asked to be left alone, even by Lucy. On his private line, he dialled the number of Abel's home in New York.

TEN

In Washington, Maria had spent the night on the edge of sleep, mostly awake. The figure of Joe seemed to be in the room and she felt she could have touched him, the playboy who conjured up moments of intensity that brought tears to the surface. He teased her, then drifted away. When the light did come and the phantom was gone, there was no chance of rest, and she set to work. She sent a short, careful message to Jackson Wherry about Abel, and learned that he would be welcome at dinner that evening in London. 'Peter Lehman' would have a place at a good table.

'Time's short, but we'll play this for as long as we can,' said Wherry when he called. 'Old ways are best.'

Maria's dark night had lifted. Abel would touch down soon, and set to work. She would be at her desk, and therefore by his side. Until then she had nearly two hours. She cooked a little breakfast, and heard Leila stirring in the bedroom. She had come to Maria very late, after Abel had gone. 'Let's go out, before the day begins.'

They took their bikes and headed west. After about fifteen minutes they chained them up at the canal and set off, occasionally hand in hand, their faces raised to a freshening wind.

They lived a life together that couldn't be admitted, and few people in the city were trusted to share the knowledge.

Even with some close friends, she deceived. In all her store of secrets, one of the richest hoards in a city where they were hidden all around, there was nothing that she wished more to release and let go. But the consequence of that hard discipline and the careful years they had shared was that their trust in each other, when they spoke of their work, was absolute. Neither had to enter into negotiation about the boundaries.

As they walked along the rough bike trail on the line of the old Chesapeake and Ohio canal below Georgetown, the Potomac sliding past them very slowly going the other way, Maria spoke of Joe. He'd seemed indestructible, a survivor who proved as much by spending most of his time living on the edge. Maria had pulled him back from the chasm a few times, and although she had always harboured the knowledge that it was bound to happen again, she had held on to the illusion that his old habits – in truth, the one habit – had been discarded.

He'd spent long months in clinics in Arizona and Montana, the empty places where you can disappear. 'The word from Miami was that he was clean. I believed it,' she said.

She thought of him as a tree-dwelling creature springing from branch to branch, scampering from the forest floor to the highest tops in easy bounds, lying quiet for a while in the shade and then making a spectacular jump into the sunlight. He was never still for long, always watching and ready for the next move. He'd lived high in Miami, getting his energy from Maria's messages which assured him that his networks matched her highest hopes and that he would always be one of her best boys.

Leila understood some of Maria's connections to the apparatus of which her own office at State was a distant part, although there were almost no names that she would recognize. Abel's was one; Joe's was not. Fat Zak Annan and Barney Eustace, the short and the tall, appeared at the house from time to time as sentries come in the night to protect the citadel, and were familiar shadows. Annan always chose a corner chair from which he seemed to fill the room; Eustace was ever on the move, a thin figure who could slip through a doorway almost unseen. They were protectors of Maria's secrets, and now she was talking about Joe. She said he represented the wildness that they all had within them, and never wanted to lose.

'I cared for him so much. He tried it on with me more than once. An experiment. Wanted to see if I might melt, knowing all along that I wouldn't. We laughed about it a lot in the end.' Her voice was quiet, though she was enjoying the memory.

Leila asked, 'How did he die?' Straight out.

'Drugs, for sure. Cops have no doubt.' Maria held her hands like scales of justice and weighed them back and forth. 'The embassy's waiting for the autopsy report from the Brits. We'll do our own in good time, when Joe's handed over. Cold, so cold.'

She paused. 'But I need to know if he talked to anyone about things that should never have been spoken of, and I'll never be able to ask him.'

Maria stopped by a bench hewn out of a wide tree trunk and sat down. 'The thing is, they found a syringe beside him.'

Leila sensed her lover's mystification. 'You said he had an old habit.'

Maria was watching the water. 'No. There was someone with him, must have been.'

Leila was used to waiting in such conversations. When they happened, which was not often, they brought a new intimacy with them, and demanded special trust. She placed a hand on Maria's shoulder.

'I knew something about Joe that, through all the bad times, never changed. And I know it can't have been any different yesterday, on his last day on this earth. 'Course, I told Abel, too.'

Leila waited.

'Last thing I told him before he flew last night, before you came home. Joe couldn't take needles. So he was with some-one, near the end. In his hotel, where they found him. Why?'

Leila said, 'Unless it was planted afterwards.'

Maria nodded. 'Sure. Don't I know it.'

Once more she felt the distance to London yawning in front of her, and her inability to feel the atmosphere from far away: Abel's eyes, the tilt of Wherry's quizzical expression, the gossip among friends in their own shadows. With Joe dead, and the heavy mechanism of formal investigation engaged, the careful bits of cover being put into place, she knew the story was slip-ping from her grasp. It was going to be a long morning before Abel got back to her.

But he would be calling, that was sure. She stood up to put her hand in Leila's. 'Let's take a quick walk. I need to be home.'

They turned their faces to the sun and decided without a word to enjoy a few minutes of silence.

*

'My brother called New York,' Abel said, first of all, when he spoke to Maria from London. It was lunchtime for him; Washington was getting to the office. 'Will, I mean. Hannah hasn't spoken to him for nearly a year. She told him I was in DC; didn't know about London when he rang.' He could offer no more, and told her that he would choose the best moment to make contact. It would be later in the day; didn't want to call Flemyng in his office.

'How are things between you?' Maria asked.

'Much the same. Distant. No special reason, as you know. Just a drifting apart that neither of us wanted, but it happened all the same. Maybe we could never play the same game too close together. There was never a crisis, but neither of us has made the move. It's sad. For him, too.'

'Sure,' Maria said, aware of Abel's hesitation, and didn't push him. She had no wish to compound his awkwardness and weigh him down.

To business. Maria said he was expected at the Wherry home for dinner at eight – 'Jackson's a trouper, always was' – and rang off to settle down for the wait. In that moment of calm, when everything seemed to stop, she felt as if an engine were about to kick into life and set events on the move, remembering that it was always like this when the first surprise came along. Will Flemyng, drawn in already.

For her part, she called Annan and Eustace to tell them to be on hand for the evening, at home with her, and to clear the weekend. One of them, at least, might have to travel. 'It will break in the next three days. I know it.'

She hailed a cruising cab on the corner of South Capitol Street, rolled down the window to let the breeze blow through, and reached 16th Street in a few minutes. She walked two blocks to her office, in a building that gave no hint of its government status, and there extracted a buff folder from her personal safe. She took out four thick files and laid them on her desk. Opening the first, she looked at the title page: William Benedict Flemyng, born 5 November, 1930.

*

Flemyng had four hours before his rendezvous with Sam, and told Lucy that the office wouldn't see him in that time. She could make any excuse she chose: he didn't mind the paper piling up. He'd be going to Scotland as planned, so Lawrence could pick him up at seven to go home for a quick goodbye, then on to the airport. He assumed Lucy was surprised, but gave no sign. When he left, she set about preparing the red box that she intended to send after him to Scotland. It would be looked at by Sunday night, or else.

Two other projects were going to occupy her afternoon. She had a plan to crack the story of the Washington embassy, which Flemyng had reported from his conversation at the opera house, and she knew where to start. If Dennis had blown a gasket at the news that he was being dumped again, she had a friend on the bridge of that ship in Paris who would have the story. Second, she had a date of her own with the personnel department, which could be brought forward to coincide with Flemyng's absence if they had a gap that afternoon. Neat.

Flemyng walked to Parliament Square, lingered with a police officer at the gates of New Palace Yard for a minute or two, knowing that if there was a hint of spice in the daily round of gossip, he'd pick up the scent. Nothing. 'Quiet as the grave,' said the copper. A Friday heavy with tasteless phrases.

He strolled through the arches and turned into the service passageway running under the building towards the terrace and the river, the natural route for a habitué looking for air, or a drink. Within two minutes he was on the stairs that led to the room where Joe had been found one floor up. Flemyng kept climbing, to the main floor.

Lunchtime on a summer Friday, and silent. A party of workmen was attacking the ceiling in the library corridor, long starved of attention, and plaster mouldings were leaning against the walls. The men's newspapers looked incongruous on the green leather benches to each side, the Page 3 girls in *The Sun* still a novelty, and turned upwards. Further along, a pair of picture restorers was starting work on a wide battlefield canvas, brushing away the first layer of dust. He heard a gaggle of tourists being led from central lobby up the stone staircase to the committee corridor, and exchanged words with another policeman who was on his way down to the terrace, for a smoke or an early pint in strangers'. All quiet, and nothing to break the surface calm.

Doubling down a short stairway he was at the store-room door. There was no key. From inside he jammed a heavy oak chair under the doorknob. It held tight.

The room in which he stood was square and high. It was part attic, part church vestry, with a jumbled collection of furniture and ceremonial implements, cast-offs and broken remnants. There were two formal pictures hanging above head height, one of a prime minister, the other of a sea battle with the smoke of cannon wreathing the ships and tongues of fire on their sails. He examined what lay around him.

There was a set of damaged wall-hangings to one side, and a collection of broken pediments, window sashes and oak panels on the other. Beside them on the floor, a pitted stone gargoyle lay tilted back so that his eyes met Flemyng's. He had a sharp mental picture of the sight that had shaken Denbigh, the clerk who had found Joe. Gwilym had said that his open eyes, whose lids he could not bear to close, were the most poignant touch.

Flemyng lifted aside an old curtain and revealed two dark oak cupboards, with a collection of glass inkwells stacked on top and some metal boxes filled with doorplates, hooks and window latches. Covering them over, he turned to the bust of

Gladstone lying on the floor. The Grand Old Man had taken a grievous blow to the head. He was cracked from top to bottom through the left eye and, Flemyng fancied, would soon split in two. Apart from a glass-fronted bookcase, on the top of which the syringe had been found, and which was dust-free, there was a collection of institutional bric-a-brac, and a rolled-up carpet which would never grace the Palace of Westminster again, its threads rubbed bare.

On the floor where Joe's body had lain there was no mark. Flemyng poked around for a few minutes. Nothing. Then, as he took away the chair that had secured the door, his eye caught a flicker of white on the carpet. He was able to pick up a thin sliver of stone when he swung the door inwards. He turned it and held it up to the light. Then he placed it in his dark blue handkerchief and folded it carefully into an inside pocket.

Passing through central lobby and down the steps towards the public exit, he imagined Joe's progress. Had he met someone there, where visitors congregated for arranged appointments, and been spirited out of public view? A gamble. He need only have hung around for more than a minute or two if he'd got his timing right. On the other hand, getting into one of the inner corridors alone without being challenged would have been difficult, and for a man wearing jeans almost impossible. A police officer would have asked an awkward question. A meeting must have been fixed; it was the only way.

Flemyng considered the risk Manson had taken, then burst into laughter that startled the tourists waiting in line. So simple. Joe hadn't known he was on anyone's radar. The prospect of danger hadn't occurred to him.

Didn't know there might be watchers; didn't know he was going to die.

Flemyng left the building and strolled through the gardens along the river.

He'd ring from the call box in Smith Square to see if there was a message from Abel in Washington to Francesca or – even more unlikely – to the office, get some energy back, and then there was Sam. He'd take a cab to Mansfield Mews, confident that his friend would have understood the summons from 'Mr Massie'.

The temperature was refusing to dip, and everywhere he saw the comatose signs of a lazy weekend ahead. Building sites abandoned, grass patches turned into communal sun lounges, the pace on the pavements slackening in the sun. When he reached Mansfield Mews, deliberately early, he walked slowly past number six and was able to read the names on the brass plates. He got confirmation of what he'd expected, and understood why Sam had been bound for that black door. He rounded the corner, and a minute afterwards his friend had arrived behind him. He was smiling.

'I've pounded the corridors on your behalf this morning. Ministerial instruction after all.' He leaned in. 'I left no tracks.' Flemyng acknowledged the compliment, and the reassurance.

'I may be able to help, even if it's not as much as you'd like. To start with anyway. We're talking about the Americans, right?'

Flemyng dipped his head. 'Naturally.' They were off.

They had cut into a square where there was one empty bench. Sam threw his jacket across it, a signal that no one else was welcome, and they sat down. 'There's a game on,' he said, 'but I haven't got a handle on it. We live in compartments, now more than ever. Battery hens. For you and me, it's The Service and always will be, but believe me, they're starting to call it The

Office. Not I, mind you. Three-year plans and crap of that kind flying around. But people still talk, thank God. And I know there's something up, have no fear.'

Sam leaned in. 'Janus Forbes' – the proper name for once – 'is in on it. He was in the conference room this morning. Four of them altogether. Saw me passing the door and shot me a nasty look.'

Flemyng digested this simple fact. A ministerial visit to Sam's office was rare, business between their political masters and the spies more often done on home ground. But Forbes would love it, his grip on the delicious knot of status and secrecy. Flemyng dealt with a shiver of jealousy, and bowled a googly at Sam.

'I assume Guy Sassi was with them.' He got a wide grin in return. Sam said that was one of his little surprises, although he had others tucked up his sleeve.

'Bingo. Got it in one.'

'He's been in and out these last two weeks. Not in my little patch. I've been shoved up a bit of a siding, as you may be aware.' Flemyng shook his head, and said nothing, out of respect. 'I hear he's connected with an old Paris friend of ours.' Looking up, waiting for a response, which after a moment they gave in unison, Flemyng's eyes sparkling with enjoyment.

'Maria Cooney.'

The first piece on the board had moved. Sam picked up. 'And naturally he's a friend of all the brainboxes in their puzzle palace, dreaming up computer programmes for the new age that's coming. Very friendly, I hear.'

'So, my old fellow traveller' – Flemyng enjoyed Sam's relish for the story – 'I poked around and blew air on to the embers, to see what would glow in the dark.' His language, as always when he became the raconteur of the moment, was taking off in all directions. It was a signal that he was in charge, telling his tale at his own speed in his own time.

'I got one spark going, and it shed a little light. A mutual friend of ours,' said Sam, 'no name, not necessary, is just as intrigued as me. And he knows more than I do. Bloody should, I may say, it's his job. Came up with a name – not of a person, I should say, but an old operation. A clue. To be straight, I don't know if you'll remember this one, having been many miles away at the time. Your need to know was probably nil.'

Flemyng said, 'I remember how it was.' He drank in the warmth of Sam's presence, the generosity that lurked behind the lugubrious mask.

'Operation Empress?'

Flemyng's mystification was unfeigned. 'Means nothing.' He tapped his head. 'Not a sausage.'

Sam was pleased. 'Pin back your ears, then. The operation is buried these days, only used a bit for training – different name, mind you, and presented as a fiction. Old Tyson's work, I expect, God rest his soul. Gone to the big archive in the sky. Anyway, back to my tale. I'm not surprised you never heard the name, it was buried full fathom five. But it happened more recently than you might like to think… much more recently.

'And here's the thing, Will. I'm told the current little imbroglio has an echo of Empress. That's the link.'

He put out a hand in warning. 'Mind you – here's the bad news – I'm not sure in what precise respect that's true, why it's spoken of in the same breath, only that it is. I should take you back, shouldn't I?'

Flemyng said, 'I wouldn't want to stop you, even if I was meant to.'

Sam adopted an emphatic tone, and said Empress was unique. 'I don't use that word very often,' he said, which was a whopper, but never mind. He had known nothing like it. Perplexing, spraying embarrassment all over the shop, and the ones who were in the middle of it carried the secret with extra-special care, as if it might infect them, even when they gathered at the service's private ceremonies when gossip from behind the veil was allowed to flow free.

'And when it was over, the shutters came down with an almighty bang. Everyone's hands tied. Mind you, some of the boys could be heard speaking about a famous victory, and others – elsewhere on our battlefield – about the nadir. The end. I'll explain.'

Flemyng found it easy to be patient, liking to take his time at such moments.

'I would say,' said Sam, 'that our text for today is Pride, with a capital P.'

Flemyng remembered the unlikely fact that Sam was the holder of the office of churchwarden in a parish under the Sussex Downs, where those who enjoyed his reading of psalms at evensong in their Norman church were under the impression that he had spent his whole career in government public relations. Which, as Sam often said, was not too far off the mark.

'Pride,' he said. 'The cancer and the blessing of our trade. Cherished, but eating away at our innards all the time.'

He wasn't going to miss the opportunity to give the story his full treatment, language cavorting wildly now. In this mood of excitement, he had left his desk far behind and returned to the street, where he was most at home. Flemyng watched him turn once more into the wide boy he had loved.

'A long time ago, deep in the forest, there were questions being asked about someone in a position where he could do great damage.

'A minister, no less, and higher up the ladder than you. Well settled in cabinet, and the subject of nasty rumours. Very nasty indeed. No one knew where they'd come from, but they wouldn't go away. This person was accused of loose talk, perhaps indiscretions in bedrooms here and there, and worse. Maybe playing footsie with bad people, people on the other side.

'Blackmail, even. Who could tell? All we knew was that there were leaks, a bloody torrent it seems, and anxious talk, on both sides of this river. At the top – the very top – it was decided that he'd have to be watched, and listened to. The works, day and night.

'And who, my dear Will, was asked to do it?'

He gestured with his hands held up and outward, fingers curling in towards the palms. 'Come on! Remember we're talking about a minister here, not a poxy functionary like me. Maybe even a leader some day, who could say?'

Flemyng said nothing, wasn't expected to. Sam wanted to ring the bell himself.

He whispered, 'A friendly power did the deed.'

Knowing that he wanted to spin it out, Sam became a one-man chorus. 'I repeat – a friendly power,' his voice rising.

Flemyng was eager now.

'The God of Gods sitting at the top of the mountain over there, agreed that one of our own people – a minister of the crown, God save us – should be put under surveillance by the operatives of another country, working from their own government's buildings in London. Not ours. Theirs.

'Think about it. The boys with the bugs and microphones in their knapsacks, cut out on their home turf. Not wanted on voyage, while others padded the streets in their name, patrons of another master doing the Queen's business that we're sworn to pursue. All dressed up as a way of not breaking the promise that elected parliamentarians are never spied on. Balls on stilts, as we know. Humiliating, or what?

'Jesuitical hardly begins to describe it.'

Flemyng was enjoying Sam's free-flowing language again, which he thought of as some kind of jazz improvisation on the usual order of his thoughts, an expedition to who-knows-where. In another life he imagined Sam as a blues balladeer, with a soulful tune always ready.

He was up to speed now, keeping his voice down as they looked across the square. The evening passers-by saw nothing of the excitement they were sharing, but Flemyng's antennae were tuned to every nuance. Sam's curls lifted in the breeze, and his arms were starting to move like the sails of a stumpy windmill.

'Empress is lined up there with the best of them in the secret attic. The old boys are spinning in their graves just thinking about it, and trying not to.'

Flemyng was avoiding the obvious question, which he often did, and asked another instead. 'Did it work?'

Sam held up a hand. 'I've no idea what precisely came out of the washing machine when it was all done, old friend. But I know that it did work, and how.

'They got what they were after. He was nailed to the floor, although no one was allowed to hear the screams, and dealt with in the dark. No more politics for him. And, hear this, I'm told that when the stuff started to come in, everyone stood around and joined in a sing-a-long.'

Flemyng cocked an eyebrow.

'*The Maple Leaf Forever*,' said Sam, answering the unasked question. 'Didn't know the words, but gave it a good go.

'After all, what are allies for, if you can't ask them to spy on one of your own?'

He liked that one, and hooted with mirth. Flemyng smiled back.

'But sadly, old mate, that's where my story ends.' Sam had his arms out, a gloomy salesman with an empty bag.

Flemyng expressed no disappointment, but said, 'You spoke about pride.'

'It's what Empress was about. The game made sense – 'course it did. Got the stuff, relations closer than ever with the ally in question, great gratitude. But, oh dear, the pride that was hurt: we couldn't do the business without help, needed rescuing. Symptom of decline, they said. Same as the economy, unions, phones that don't work. The bloody gas board.' He stood up and took a few steps across the grass to loosen himself up.

Resuming, he said, 'Whatever is going on right now – and I'll crack it – there's pride at the bottom of it. Wounded, precious, self-deceiving, I don't know. But pride.'

One more word, said Sam, or four to be precise. 'A mutual friend of ours gave me a phrase. Make of it what you will.

'A surfeit of allies.'

Flemyng said he would remember that.

He asked no further questions about Sam's story, but said instead, 'Something else. I need your help.'

'Any time.'

He took an envelope from his inside pocket. 'When you told me yesterday that you had an appointment over there' – he nodded in the direction of number six – 'I am assuming this was who you were going to see. I've done a little research.' He showed him the name he had written on the envelope, and Sam smiled. 'You haven't lost your touch.'

Flemyng said, 'I want you to deliver this letter to number six right now. I shouldn't be seen going in there. You've been more than once, I'm guessing, so it's easy for you. Just drop it off, and there's no need for explanation. OK?'

Sam took the envelope without a word, and they shook hands. 'Thank you,' said Flemyng.

He was turning away when Sam spoke again. He was kind in the way he said it, because he understood the power of the moment and Flemyng's vulnerabilities. Sam's motto was that on such journeys there was always one more door to open.

'I don't know if you've heard,' he said, looking away from Flemyng for a moment, and pausing for a couple of beats, 'but we have an interesting visitor in town.' He spoke gently.

'Your brother.'

The parting was silent. Sam rested his hand on Flemyng's back, then hurried away without waiting for an answer.

Flemyng went the other way. As he faced the western sun there were tears in his eyes.

ELEVEN

A Wherry dinner party was generally a cheery affair. Their home, plucked from the second-top rung of embassy houses to match his status and the guest list he was required to attract, made its own determined and overdone pitch against informality with too much deep-polished mahogany, boardroom décor and a piano that was two sizes too big. But Betsy Wherry was better than that, and had swung into London with the small-town traveller's spirit that she'd protected like a candle flame in her years touring the world with Jackson, braving every hostile wind.

She had surprised American friends with her sprightly arrival, the town where they would talk about trains that didn't run and movie theatres where you couldn't get popcorn, where there wasn't a pizza outside London they said, a land of past glories and seeping alarms. But Betsy loved the old country, and had made it known that if anyone came from the embassy to her table and began a conversation about the British disease, she'd tell Jackson that they'd have to work a hard passage back to her house.

Her furniture was wide and comfortable, built of oak and cherry, the rugs and drapes the colours of the foliage of the New Hampshire fall that she loved, and she'd managed to infuse the high-corniced reception rooms with the personality of a jumbled den that was always a little out of control but had style. After its latest re-modelling her home boasted Indian silks and carvings from their last posting, giving it another layer of colour and what she called, in her rich cackle, 'a dash of spiritual chic'. The result was that first-time guests found themselves having the welcoming stiff drink in a mood of intense relief that often had them loosening their ties with one hand and reaching with the other for one of Jean-Luc's specials from the tray. And that was just how Jackson liked it. Surprise 'em, he'd been saying to Betsy for years, and you got 'em.

Tonight would be invigorating, because Wherry was a crisis man. Abel, alias Lehman, would play his part as foreign-service soldier and their footwork would let them follow their script like jobbing actors on tour, confident story-tellers both. Beforehand there might be time for a short briefing on Joe's demise, his whereabouts before and after, and the panic that Wherry had identified in the London authorities, for reasons he had only partly been able to pin down. Abel would have thoughts to share.

Before dinner Wherry planned to check in with Maria, think through his briefing for Abel. And his legendary luck had kicked in. Thanks to a date that had been in the diary for weeks, fixed soon after his own arrival in London as a generous hello, Thomas Brieve was coming round, and Wherry knew he would bring a loose tongue with him. The martinis would be fiercely dry to lend it encouragement. Wherry would make it his business to give his guest's natural boastfulness full rein.

Fortunately, it was one of Wherry's drinking nights – he had a rule that there were only three in a week, and never faltered – but he'd been long enough in the game to keep the lid on. He'd avoid the cocktails, then oil the gossip machine.

He patrolled the reception room, checking the stage set. The guests were a super-keen embassy colleague from the political office with his foreign-service wife, who both knew of Wherry's role, and a British banker and his wife who didn't. A visiting American writer had been recruited to give a splash of colour and unpredictability. That would encourage Brieve. It was unbalanced, but that never bothered Betsy, who gave every table the semblance of a chance gathering that had pulled itself together on a whim. It was approaching seven-thirty when they checked the place settings with Jean-Luc, who was usually in black jacket and striped trousers in his role as itinerant embassy major-domo, but had been told by Betsy that when on duty in the Wherry house he should put away his butler's gear and wear the brightest tie he could find. He gave them a tour of the table, perfectly laid without too much formality, and they prepared for the first of their guests.

*

As they did so Flemyng was leaving home for the airport, Francesca's concern enveloping him like a cloud. With her last embrace she had urged him to sleep on the journey. 'Get rest. You must.' She knew almost nothing, he was sure, and it nagged at him. When he'd arrived to say goodbye, she was playing the piano. He listened to Schumann for a minute or two at the door before interrupting. She was serious, but hadn't allowed herself the luxury of anger.

He could remember little of his walk to the office after leaving Sam, except for images of Abel's face flashing before him, as if on the last reel of a movie, playing the scene on an endless loop. He wanted to know when his younger brother had come, why he hadn't rung. Climbing the stairs to the office, he felt an ache in his limbs that hadn't been there before.

Trying to find peace in thoughts of home, he knew how right Paul had been to encourage him to go. By the morning he'd be thinking clearly. He would breathe the clean air, walk the old paths. The story would start to settle in his mind.

He'd managed to escape from the office with the promise that only one red box would be delivered to him over the weekend. Leaving Putney, Lawrence handled the Friday night traffic heading out of town with patience and they were able to stop at a call box to let Flemyng have a word with Mungo on the way, knowing that he'd make his flight and be home by midnight. It was quick, but tender. 'I'm on my way,' he said. 'Can't wait to see you. But don't stay up.'

After he rang off he concluded, with certainty, that Mungo didn't know of Abel's presence in London. He would have been unable to keep the secret.

But Mungo had sounded happy, on the up because of Flemyng's journey north. He'd said it was raining gently at Altnabuie, the wind bringing in heavy clouds from the west, but it promised to clear overnight. Everything was ready for him. He closed his eyes in the car, and tried to disentangle the events of the day.

Lucy, he knew, would have produced some alternative explanations for the letter, although she had said nothing about it as he left. Sam's nerve ends were twitching, and Flemyng assumed that he would find a way of seeing any reports on Manson's progress around London; he could concoct a reason, although since his day the old place had become a collection of self-contained cocoons and bubbles, all separate and territorial. Flemyng would give Sam twenty-four hours, then ring.

He thought of Francesca, about how he wished she could have dodged the next night's opera and come home with him, and then one word from the box at Covent Garden came back. Berlin. He let it sit there, a crossword answer without a clue, and left it to work away at his mind. He dozed for the last ten minutes before they got to Heathrow.

He had a few minutes in the lounge, and made a call to the office in case there was a message. Sorley's office wanted to find time for a meeting on Monday. Personal. Otherwise, nothing. As he walked down the gangway, the tiredness flowed back. He prepared for sleep.

*

Everything was happening in a rush chez Wherry, a fact to which the host later attributed the success of the evening when he recollected it in less happy circumstances. Chatter at the door revealed all at once the presence of the Biddles from the embassy, the banking couple announced as the Portarlingtons, and then Brieve and his girl, whom Wherry put at a full ten years younger than her man. The novelist tagged on, carrying a Barnes & Noble bag with some copies of his book, and he had affected a dark green Nehru suit in honour of the Wherrys' Indian sojourn. Betsy hugged him close, because she thought a table without an oddball was a bore. Everyone – save Abel – came in together, and a to-and-fro conversation began without prompting.

Betsy met Brieve for the first time. Her impression was of a pinch-cheeked and scrawny bird, and certain predator. His grey-green eyes were already at work on the room, and she noticed unusually pale lips, and bony hands always on the move. If he had nothing to pick up and play with, he would tug on an ear or rub his brow as if he were trying to erase the spidery lines that refused to disappear.

His red hair was well-shorn, with a few high tufts on top, and his straight, sharp nose acted like a beak. Betsy expected him to bob his head over his food as if he were feeding at a low trough, but discovered that was unfair. Brieve had perfect table manners, with only one public weakness. Having started on a subject he found it hard to stop, and had long ago perfected the feat of managing to keep up a steady flow of talk while he disposed of his food, clearing his plate before everyone else, which gave him time to bring his conversation to an end with a flourish while others were still finishing. He was therefore a wearing guest, despite his star quality as an unbuttoned dispenser of gossip.

'Let me tell you about the French,' he was saying even as he reached for the first of Jean-Luc's martinis. 'You might think you wouldn't believe it. You will.'

Wherry, who recognized a raconteur with wind in his sails, knew he'd be presiding at a lively table. He kept a weather eye for the guests' state of mind over drinks in the saddling enclosure, and Brieve was raring to go. This would be fun. He also noticed that the writer was flying high, and picked up the odour of his pre-dinner joint. Betsy cast her Jackson a knowing eye; she'd manage him.

Then Abel arrived, shown in by Jean-Luc. Abel had dressed casually, avoiding formal polish, and a sober black tie was knotted loosely, so that it could easily be discarded. Wherry realized his mini-briefing would have to wait, and greeted his latest guest with a familiarity that avoided the necessity for too detailed an introduction. 'At State with me, for ever,' he said to the room, 'passing through town,' and left it at that. Under the relaxed façade he could detect a tired and edgy man, because the eyes, as ever, were a giveaway. He'd seen them before in Flemyng, dark and quick. Though Abel smiled, his dimpled cheek sending out a friendly message, and made his hellos with a natural poise, his eyes were darting and refusing to stay still. Wherry found himself worrying without a reason that he could pin down; he smelled trouble.

At the table Wherry had Brieve next to him, and because they were one woman down was able to place Abel on Brieve's other side. He owed Maria that. During the warm-up, Betsy directed the conversation from the other end of the table and they spoke of India, cricket and its mysteries, food. A little banking talk broke everyone up, and by the time Jean-Luc laid a perfect pale pink salmon in front of Betsy, who insisted on serving her guests herself, Brieve and Abel were sizing each other up, with Wherry as host-eavesdropper.

Abel wanted the conversation to flow away from him so he began with Paris, and Brieve happily flew solo. He said nothing that his hosts did not already know, save for a few phrases from the speech he had to finish in the morning to carry to the conference. He showed no interest in the detail of Mr Lehman's life at State, which Abel had managed to turn into a bore. He was determined not to whet Brieve's interest, and when the subject of Paris began to flag, turned to a nicely neutral subject to engage the table. 'Any good theatre I should see in town?'

Marcia Portarlington was happy to seize her moment, and led them on a merry waltz for a few moments. The writer, who had been happy to snuggle at the end of the table with Betsy and seemed to be conducting their conversation with one hand, made a brief foray on the subject of his muse and gave his quotient of entertainment, happy to subside for the rest of the evening. Wherry wondered how Abel would make his move.

Brieve said, 'Somebody from Washington was trying to get to me this week and I was embarrassed I missed him. Probably State, I assume. Not higher up, or he'd have tried harder.' A prick, Wherry thought, despite the polish. 'That's the trouble with where I sit. Everyone's trying to get through the door next to my desk, but I enjoy sorting out sheep from goats. Half my job.'

Abel was cool. 'Difficult to know. Could have been anyone.' Then, a name. 'Maybe Joe Manson?'

Beautifully brave, Wherry thought to himself.

'Could have been. I felt a bit guilty because he said he'd been pointed my way by an old congressman friend. We coincided at Harvard. My secretary told him to ring the office again, but nothing. Paul Jenner asked me about it today, as a matter of fact, although there was no name. Must have banged on his door, too. Didn't come through you then?' This while looking at Wherry and then young Biddle, who each played dumb with a smile.

'I'm sorry... Peter, isn't it?' said Brieve, leaning towards Abel. 'Can I help? Is he still around?' Wherry shook his head.

'Could be, but not with us. If he's in touch, we'll let you know.'

Jean-Luc was refilling Brieve's glass. 'I'm back from Paris on Wednesday night. Rest of the week will be quietish. Summertime at last. So...'

Abel, still trying to assess whether Brieve's demonstration of innocence was unfeigned, allowed Betsy to pick up the conversation and it swung away from them. More wine, no politics, a happy chatter with everyone given the chance to tell a story, Brieve's girl surprising everyone with a brilliant piece of mimicry at the expense of Jay Forbes. 'We call him King William at home,' she said. 'He's shaped like one of the pears, the squat ones.' Brieve looked straight ahead. Then Wherry made one of his favourite plays, the simple and unexpected question. To Brieve. 'You got your Washington embassy fixed?'

Brieve was ready, though he hadn't expected it until after dinner.

'Pretty well. You'll know next week. It's going to be good – a story.' So there were still arguments, or Brieve would have blurted out something more. Wherry knew from the opera night how the ground lay, and was interested to learn if Brieve was aware of his encounter with Paul, and Paul's conversation with Sassi in the box. So he lied.

'We hear it's safe; one of the boys. Your diplomatic Four Horsemen.'

Brieve smirked, and shook his head. 'Can't say. Hasn't been cleared all round.' He rubbed his hands across the tablecloth, as if sweeping it clean. 'But you may be surprised. Pleasantly, I may say.'

Wherry concluded that the self-satisfaction was real: Brieve didn't know what Paul had told them, maybe not that they had met. And the job was not yet done.

Abel laid down another lure for Brieve, in case. 'I'm passing through, as Jackson said. Only here over the weekend, then in and out of Berlin. The strangest place. Your kind of town?'

Brieve was thrown, and Wherry could see it, but his recovery was quick. 'Get there now and again, no more. We've got a strong German team. Glendinning's one of the best in Bonn, as you know. And not – NOT – bound for Washington, Jackson.' He invited a change of subject.

Fred Biddle from across the table got a cue from Wherry's raised eyebrows and attracted Brieve's attention with a question about the coming arms talks in Vienna, which caused him to leap into action like a racehorse out of the gate. He gestured to Abel – 'A word later' – and settled down to a monologue.

Biddle would hear from Wherry the next day that it had been nicely timed. He was learning.

Wherry began the round-up at the table with some of his road-tested Washington stories, and let them run just long enough.

They talked American politics for a while, with Abel taking no part and letting Wherry manage the talk, which he did like a croupier with a sharp eye and soft hands. Abel admired the ease with which he cast another line towards Brieve, which no one else noticed for what it was. He heard Wherry allude with gentleness, as if it was a thought that had only floated into his head, to difficulties between Washington and London, using a particular word to describe the atmosphere: tenderness. He and Abel were watching Brieve closely.

'There are certain delicacies around the place right now, as you know', said Wherry, using a flattering tone.

Brieve said, 'You'll find – the ambassador knows this – that we're tying up the last loose ends.' He looked uncomfortable, and, sensing that himself, made a heavy-footed addendum, which they recognized as a sign of weakness. 'We both know what we mean.'

Wherry's expression didn't change, but he was surprised at this clumsiness. Brieve tried to lighten the moment immediately. 'I'm sure we'll all have a happy summer.' He picked up his water glass and gulped from it, and Wherry said, 'I'm sure', reaching for the water himself.

It was meant to be Brieve's last word, and Wherry got the drift that even he sometimes swam out of his depth.

Knowing it was the right time to probe, Wherry said that his colleagues were fascinated by Ruskin's new role, roaming across government. 'The wild rover, I hear.' To be sure, he said, London was getting more like Washington every day.

But Brieve was spent and didn't rise to the bait. All he said was, 'Lots of us get to spread our wings. Nothing really new.'

They soon broke up for drinks in the garden. Betsy had lit some flaming candles on bamboo canes and they dispensed jasmine and citronella into the night. They were the only lights in the garden and caught the lazy breeze of high summer, flickering on the faces around two teak tables set under one wide apple tree. She summoned the party to come and admire their Red Setter's new puppies in the basement, whose whimpers could be heard from below and who were said to be desperate for a mass visit. All of them went, save for Abel and Wherry. Good old Betsy.

They pulled two wooden chairs into a dark corner, and spoke quietly. 'I've been talking to friends,' said Wherry. 'They have Manson's passport in his own name, but haven't told us officially. They know that we know. They're counting on us wanting this to be handled as quiet as can be. And' – pouring them both a whisky – 'that sure suits us.'

They were aware that they had little time alone, so after a brief exchange about Maria and her boys, they transacted their business speedily. Abel wanted to run some communications to Maria through Wherry's office. Done. He would share what he could as he went along, assuming Maria's say-so. Agreed. He hoped that Wherry would keep him up to speed on any investigations the Brits might be carrying out that reached his ears. No problem.

Then Wherry asked, 'Why did he come?' Joe's friend Halloran, who had given Wherry a full account of their lunch on Wednesday, said he had picked up nothing of substance, only that Joe's journey was personal. 'Halloran said he seemed a bit... high.'

'He was right,' said Abel.

'Halloran and Manson went back a few years,' Wherry said. 'I'm assuming he told me everything. Who knows?'

Abel picked up. 'That's our problem. I can only give you a picture that's pretty hazy. Where Joe fits into it, and who else is part of it, I don't know; Maria doesn't either. Joe was on his own. Driven. He left us in the dark. The trouble is that he may have come here for one purpose, and screwed up something else in the process. A bigger game.'

Wherry sighed, 'Our lives, Abel, our lives.'

With Maria's agreement, Abel was going to give Wherry a whiff of the story, just to get him on the trail. Before the dog-admiring party returned, he revealed Joe's obsession: an embarrassing accusation against someone in or connected to government in London. Perpetrator unknown. And that it might touch on the coming appointment of an ambassador. 'That's all we know,' he said, turning away.

Wherry was straight. 'We don't know who they're going to send to DC, although I could give you a list of four or five obvious names. Jenner told Sassi and me on Thursday that they're working on a big appointment. A gesture, to fit in with… other things that I guess you're more familiar with than I am.'

For a moment they were both quiet, each knowing that their intimacy was constrained. Some veils stayed in place, on both sides, and behind them lay darkness. That was business.

'I took a chance when Brieve mentioned an unexpected contact,' said Abel.

'Good shot,' said Wherry, 'but where does it get us? Was Brieve his target, or just the way in?'

Abel said, 'We've no idea, and that's the truth. But it gives us a start. Listen, Jackson, I want to let you know something that's quite private. But you need to understand about my brother.'

'I know it's been a long time,' said Wherry.

They spoke quietly for ten minutes before the party from the basement was spilling back into the garden. The novelist was carrying a puppy, which Betsy rescued and returned, and there was chatter, with Brieve the life and soul of the party.

Everyone left in a bunch, including Abel, taking the chance to assure Brieve that he'd be happy to try to track down Joe Manson for him. Could he give Abel his phone number? Brieve passed over a card, scribbled a home number on the back and smiled as he handed it over.

*

Flemyng's flight had been a Friday night drag, and it was at just about the time that Abel and Wherry were sitting alone with whiskies after dinner that it dropped down towards Edinburgh. They banked over the firth, and he saw clusters of city lights and the black folds of the hills beyond. Five minutes later he was heading across the arrivals hall, and a familiar smile from Babble greeted him at the door.

'Will! Good to see you home. You're tired. We'll soon put that right.'

'How are you, old friend? I'm looking forward to this.'

'Capital,' said Babble. It was his favourite word. He took Flemyng's bag from him. 'Just capital. And the loch is fine. We had a wee shower in the afternoon and everything has freshened up. The trout will be grand in the morning, rods all sorted out.' He shepherded him to the car.

Flemyng put a hand to his shoulder. Babble was part of home that would never crumble. Although he was a loyal Londoner, born and raised near the Old Kent Road, Altnabuie had been his territory for nigh on forty-five years. He'd found himself looking for work as a young man, on the loose in the hills in the course of a long, wandering summer, and got an offer from Flemyng's father to do some odd jobs around his house, under the hawk's eye of a family cook and housekeeper whose regime had terrified him but won him round. He decided he could survive anything there, and stayed. Now it was his domain. Marriage had come and gone; he continued.

'How's Mungo?' Flemyng asked.

'A little bit distracted,' said Babble. 'Nothing obvious, but it's there. He'll be happy to see you, that's for sure. He worries.'

'And I about him.'

Babble had dark copper hair, still lush in his seventieth year, and overhanging eyebrows he had never tamed. His face was mobile, expressive, and it had taken on a redhead's vermilion hue from the sun. He was wiry and well-exercised, walking the dogs without fail every morning down the burn or up the hill. He was embedded in the countryside around Altnabuie and although, when he was in position at the Pole Inn, his watering hole on the high road through the hills, they sometimes called him Arthur – he'd been born Arthur Babb – the boys' nickname had stuck. Neither too intimate nor too formal, it was a happy compromise. To all of them, his smile and his rough hand were a welcome and his voice, which had lost all but the faintest sounds of London, spoke of home.

In the back seat, Flemyng folded his jacket, his locked briefcase stowed safely away. 'I'm switching off, I'm afraid. I'll dream about the fishing.' And in a couple of minutes, long before they reached the A9 and turned to the north, he was asleep.

Understanding Flemyng's need for rest, and knowing that his own news could wait, Babble let him be. They'd talk at breakfast. He'd enjoy telling him that he had spoken to Abel that very evening. But not yet. When they got home, he saw

Flemyng upstairs with a few words, and left everything to lie for the night.

Taking the air with the dogs after midnight, Babble enjoyed the softness that follows the rain and the fresh scent from the trees. He heard the water on the rocks in the burn, and the distant drone of a car on the high road that soon died away. It was black, quiet, almost everything still. He spoke softly to the old Springer Spaniel at his feet. 'You can feel it, Rousseau. Everything's on the turn.'

TWELVE

At Altnabuie, they woke to a trembling day. Flemyng had raised his bedroom window before turning in, and when he opened his eyes, very early, he could smell the highlands. There was an edge to the warmth and the damp, and the tang of tree and field lured him on. He looked towards the loch and saw swirls of mist rising up in thin pillars, like the guilty secrets of a multitude of hidden smokers, leaving a thin topping of cotton white on the water that crept over the surface and was beginning to disperse here and there with the coming of a soft breeze. It would be gone within the hour. The herons were on their favourite stone, prim and still like a pair of disapproving clerks. The crows cawed in the woods beyond, and behind him, on the eastern side of the house where the sun was already giving life to the place, he could hear the cockerel at work. Everything was crisp and clean, the stifling urban fug a world away.

In that early light, with no disturbance on the landscape and the silence holding, Flemyng was able to put his two lives in balance for a moment, their complementary spheres quite separate, letting him set the frenzy of a political life against a sense of spacious peace. A home where he felt no guilt or fear and sensed the intertwining of two worlds. But he knew that secrets were everywhere; certainty had gone, except for the knowledge that he and Abel would be changed by these days. So would they all. Lucy had seen the letter and she'd follow him on his journey.

The second chapter of the crisis was beginning. From the first, he had learned that none of the elements stood alone – the death itself, his earlier dark discovery and the decision to share it with Lucy, Paul's hint about a secret prize, Sam's first foray into the undergrowth, Sassi and Wherry, Berlin. Cross-currents flowed beyond his reach. But having learned of Abel's approach to the centre of events, Flemyng felt a mood of contentment in which relief was accompanied by even greater surprise.

He stood at the window for a while, then found his old jeans and boots, and dressed. He took the stairs carefully, walking from side to side to avoid creaks, and crossed the hall, with its stuffed wildcat in a cabinet on the wall, and pictures that took him back to childhood, to tiptoe into the dining room. The orrery was catching the first light, and he lifted the glass case before he sat down.

It was nearly as precious to him as the house itself. His great-grandfather had bought the machine because he was excited and bewildered by the cluster of brass planets, with the sun motionless at the heart of it all, controlling an elegant world of its own. People once believed, Flemyng thought to himself, that this was all there was.

With the mechanism well-oiled, the speed of the orrery never varied, and it made no sound. Teacher and companion. One of his first rituals each time he came home was to put a hand to the brass lever and watch for a while.

Mars, Mercury and Venus, Jupiter and Saturn, moved round the sun, and the earth turned slowly on its own axis while it went with them, all of them spilling tiny beams as they met the light. Around the rim, an etched ivory and silver ring showed the signs of the zodiac rotating steadily as the planets rose and fell, moved through their elliptical orbits, everything built to perform the same ethereal dance for the rest of time. When he watched the light glow on Mars, followed the progress of a lunar eclipse or measured the course of a year in a few minutes, he tuned in once more to the perfect music of his youth, which was the passing of the seasons at Altnabuie and the regularity and light that they bestowed on the place.

When he felt the sting of harsh words in politics – maybe a bitter reference to a life that was assumed by others to have been easy with too many benefits, or a sneer when his ambition broke through – he took refuge in the memory of evenings spent alone with the orrery, when he could feel the rhythm of a different sphere.

The cyclical comings and goings always had a soothing effect. He was excited at the same time, and often said to Babble, 'What more could you want?' An ordered world, which at times of distraction Flemyng said had the thrill of orthodoxy. When Francesca had first asked Will why he loved the machine, he'd explained that he couldn't conceive of a better encounter between mystery and precision.

This morning his limbs were loose, the tiredness vanished from his face. Time to go walking.

In the calm of these moments he was able to think of the two days just past, without the sense of alarm that had closed in. There was hope still. Sam was at work, and Lucy had the first glimpse of his own purpose. She was entering the locked room where he was keeping one of his secrets: by now she would have settled on a theory about the letter. He wondered whether she would make one of her intuitive leaps and turn the story on its head, which would lead her towards the truth.

With Sam's help as messenger, he had taken the next step. In three days, at most, the dam would break.

Flemyng believed – stubbornly, with the mild streak of arrogance that ran through him like his scar – that he could control the pace of events. He couldn't understand yet where the fire had started, but believed that it was burning deep inside his own government. The letter was wild enough to threaten anyone with knowledge of its contents – he had understood that from the moment he saw it more than a week before – but he'd convinced himself that his motives were unselfish. The flames might consume them all. So he needed time to think, alone in this place, and when he glanced through the windows to the loch, watching the brightness coming to the glen, he knew that the spell was working on him again.

Babble was bustling in the kitchen. When Flemyng came through the front door about half an hour later, dew shining on his boots and a smile across his face, there was bacon and fresh eggs, hot coffee on the range and Babble's own bread toasted and ready. They settled down. Babble asked about Francesca, the office, the parliamentary grind, which he followed day by day. 'You're rising on Thursday? Back up here?' he asked. He hoped so, Flemyng said, but there was still the summer traffic jam, with a pile of votes to get through before they could get away. A bore.

Then he said, 'I'm in the middle of something I don't really understand. I've had a glimpse, but that's all.'

'Nothing new there,' said his old friend, thinking of Mungo, and taking it as a family allusion. 'I've never had you here when you haven't been chewing away at something, like Rousseau with his bone at the back door.' The dog heard his name, and whimpered from his basket. 'Never mind. You'll sort it out here. Always happens.' He attended to the table.

THE MADNESS OF JULY

Flemyng said, 'You're right.' He stretched out, and Babble chose his moment.

'Abel rang me last night.'

If Flemyng was pricked, he showed nothing. 'Ah-ha. At last.' Babble wasn't fooled.

'Is that what's been eating at you? You're not yourself.'

Flemyng waved a hand, said nothing. There was no fight in him. 'Tell me,' he said. He ran a finger down each of the clefts on his cheeks.

'I've been hoping to see him.'

Babble stood at his shoulder. 'About time, if you ask me. The thing is, he's in London, and he knew you were coming home. Don't ask me how, but he did. I don't think Mungo's been in touch. He would have said. Anyway, Abel says he's looking forward to seeing you. Sudden trip. The usual.'

Babble said he looked forward to the day when Abel would come home again. 'You too?'

'Of course,' said Flemyng. 'It's been far too long.'

He'd wanted to know the weather, how the loch was, whether the river was high, what they were saying about the birds, the house, Babble himself. 'A catch-up. The whole caboodle. About you especially.'

'What did you say?'

'What d'you think?' Babble said. 'Everything's grand. Mungo's a wee bit low, but he's always like that in the middle of a book. I told Abel you were too busy. I know fine that there's more to it than that.'

'How did he sound? Abel.'

'As if he wanted to come back,' Babble said. 'Home.'

With that, Mungo arrived down for breakfast. He'd been asleep when Flemyng got home, so now he rose and the brothers locked arms. 'You look well,' said Flemyng, and there was relief on Mungo's face. Babble went to the pantry to leave them alone.

Mungo Flemyng looked the part of the eldest brother, his silver locks trained back in sleek wings, his dress always distinctive whether he was wearing an open shirt with sleeves rolled back or one of his rich greenish tweeds. He had brown leather on his feet, his face shone with a ruddy countryman's glow, and his movements were neat, although he carried weight, as if they had been considered in advance. His achievement lay in being commanding without hauteur, and his movements always seemed easy.

'We'll have some time, you and I, to talk about everything. OK?'

Flemyng said, 'I can start with a bit of good news. Abel's over.'

A shadow of anxiety passed over Mungo's face. There had been no warning. 'Really? Everything seems to be happening at once.'

'You too,' Flemyng said, and smiled.

'Where? I didn't know.' A sign of disturbance underneath.

Babble had kept the news to himself. Flemyng considered his brother's surprise, although Mungo followed up his questions with a slap of his hand on one thigh, to pull himself round. 'Good. We must get him up here.'

Flemyng said he had been thinking the same, and would try to make contact.

Babble came in and announced a plan for the morning: two hours on the loch and a drive up to the Pole for a lunchtime drink. The afternoon would look after itself.

The weather was going to be fine, but he hoped for cloud to persuade the fish to rise. Too much sun and they'd stay in the depths. 'Whatever you're worried about, forget it. You'll have sorted it out in your head by the time we come out of the Pole.

Alasdair and company will be there. Old friends. The whole catastrophe, as you might say.'

Flemyng laughed with him, remembering past times. Mungo was beaming now. He gave his brother a playful punch and ruffled the dogs' coats as they gathered round, sensing an outing. Sitting across from one another at the pitted wooden table, speaking softly, they talked of the trees planted on the hill, the burn, the state of Altnabuie in its fine old age.

Flemyng asked what Mungo was up to in his library, in the contented hours he spent at the desk above the iron spiral staircase in the gallery where he could absorb the silence and the view down the glen.

'You know it all started as a book that would explain our territory here – the topography, Gaelic turning to English in a few miles, the highland line the Romans couldn't cross, or didn't want to. All that. But a later family story's taking over, and I think of it now as private research. The eighteenth-century stuff is my bag, Jacobites and all their gang, but it's Mother now. We can't avoid her. What a story.' Flemyng watched Babble, who seemed untroubled by the course of their conversation.

'I want to show you the papers before you go to St Andrews, the ones I've mentioned to you. I've got plenty more, and the story is filling out. Quite a saga.' Awkwardness tinged the silence that followed, and Mungo's smile was forced, for the first time. They were quiet for a minute or two, enjoying the warmth and the smells of the kitchen, the light playing on the trees outside the window, the snuffling of the dogs at their feet, and the prospect of a morning on the loch. 'I'm so very grateful to you, Will. I wanted you here.'

His eyes were full as he looked at his brother across the table. 'Of course,' Flemyng said. Then, 'I miss Abel so much.' The words came from nowhere and surprised them both.

'Me, too,' said Mungo. 'We need him here for this. He can't stay away. It's family.'

For the first time he could remember, Flemyng felt panic in these surroundings, his attempt to conceal the turmoil wearing thin after only one night. He tried to keep it down. 'We haven't been alone together for a long while.'

Babble, standing by the sink, heard Flemyng's language change. He phrased things differently at home, dropped in old words. They both enjoyed that, and after a week at Altnabuie it was as if he had never left.

Mungo said, 'I suppose it's difficult for you to talk easily. And for Abel. Both of you. We've all had to be so careful over the years. The three of us' – a gesture towards the listening Babble – 'know how awkward it has been. I suppose, probably, how dangerous for you, and for Abel? D'you think we've been too protective?'

'Maybe,' Flemyng said. 'There's a reason why I must see Abel,' he added, and caught Mungo's eye. 'More than one.'

His brother sighed. 'I worry about you.'

Flemyng started to speak. 'You're the one who...'

'No,' said his brother with emphasis. 'You forget, I'm used to being here on my own. I can handle things. This place, and so forth.'

'I know.'

'Will, it may be that things are disturbing you more than you realize,' Mungo said. 'I know I've opened up this secret chamber in the family, or whatever we're going to call it, and it's disconcerting. Maybe frightening. Don't pretend. You may be the one who finds it hardest to deal with.'

'I can take whatever you have to tell us. I care, of course. But I'm not... unbalanced by it.'

His brother said, 'Neither am I. But maybe there's more going on underneath than you think. Inside.'

And Flemyng gave a laugh. 'There always is. That's what I've learned to live with.'

Then Babble at the door, with a clatter of plates and a shout to the dogs, said it was time for the gunroom and the rods.

The ghillie at Altnabuie was called Tiny, on account of his considerable height. He wouldn't be with them today, because he'd loped over the hill to deal with fishermen exploring a high stretch of water whose secrets only he knew. He could guide you to any pool to find the fish you were after, knew exactly how the weather seemed to the trout, and in his tin box of fishing flies could find anything you needed, Greenwell's Glory or Bloody Butcher, producing a favourite March Brown or Invicta at just the right time of day, when he'd had time to watch how the fish were at play. He knew every stone in the burn, and he'd lead you through the woods to show you the paths of the young deer, take you into the jumbled maze of trees that Flemyng had known since boyhood, maybe find signs of a capercaillie or a pine marten's tracks. At night, he and Babble would settle down at the Pole and tell their tales. The old stories. They'd passed them on to the brothers, and Flemyng sometimes wondered if it was the lore, as much as blood, that held them together.

Tiny had left the rods in perfect order. They checked the lines and the reels, found their boots and hats and decided that it wasn't a day when there was a chance of getting wet. The heavy gear could be left behind. Off to the boat, and away.

'What larks, Will,' said Babble. 'What larks.'

Within half an hour they were in the middle of the loch. To the south, they could see the triangular peak of Schiehallion, its top strung with mist, two herds of deer on the side of their own hill, grazing well apart, and behind them the house picked out by the sun, the bow windows catching the light for the first time that morning and the gardens dropping down in a cataract of greenery and red and purple from the rhododendrons and azaleas. The woods on the hill were thick, and from their right they could hear the water in the big burn falling over the rocks, mingling with the soft splashing around the boat and the clatter of Babble's oars as he pulled them out. He paused and stowed them. The boat swayed on the water.

They began to fish. For ten or fifteen minutes at a time they would stay still and quiet, then take the boat to another spot. Mungo stole a smoke after a while, the smell of the rich shag from his pipe hanging over them. Babble produced a couple of bottles of beer about eleven – his joke was that he had waited for opening time – and by then they had pulled in five respectable fish, one of them a substantial two-and-a-half pounder. The brown trout lay in Babble's canvas bag, supper for someone.

There was little conversation. They had taken to the water in order to leave some things on land.

Flemyng absorbed the rhythms of home. He listened to the water gurgling from the burn where it ran into the loch, watched the birds that dipped and crossed from side to side of the glen or fed by the waterside, and breathed in the smells that he had always known. Mungo spotted a straight streak of blue against the high bank on the other side: a kingfisher. Flemyng ran his eyes along the treeline, as if committing it to memory.

As the sun moved overhead, the clouds were dispersing. Babble thought, and the brothers agreed, that the fish had more sense than to rise in that heat. They'd be deep down, sheltering over cool stone. So they turned to the bank, tied the boat up at the little wooden jetty and headed back to the house with their haul, quiet as they took the path home, the brothers abreast with Babble coming on behind with the fish.

Mrs Mackenzie was on hand with tea, greeting Flemyng with warmth. She did well for Mungo, knowing that Babble had first call on the kitchen and that the rest of the house was hers. The brothers had a stroll in the garden, Mungo proud of some of his spring planting that had produced the goods, until Babble said he was leaving for the Pole. 'Anybody for a wee outing?'

Mungo excused himself. 'You'll be coming, Will?' said Babble, and he was.

Escaping to his library, Mungo considered the sadness in always feeling obliged to ask 'why?' when it came to Abel. But there it was. So much of his life was unknown. Mungo had been given a careful insight more than two decades ago, and only a few were so trusted – as with Will, who had gone the same way a little earlier. The discipline determined much of their relationship since.

With Abel, there was the layer of distance produced by his adopted name. Grauber. And with Will, Mungo had an extra difficulty. He knew that during Abel's time in London a decade ago when the sixties were changing everything fast, there had been a breach which had never been explained. Abel's return to Washington and Will's posting to Paris had been simultaneous, directed by different masters, and he had been aware down the years that his two brothers never spoke of that passage in their lives. Through the veil that shrouded their work, which Mungo was obliged never to draw back, he discerned a rupture that he could not explain. He couldn't ask, only wait.

Mungo turned with relief to the papers piled on his desk, and sank himself in the past.

Up at the Pole, Babble and Flemyng were the centre of attention. As a favour with a slight swagger attached, Babble had brought two trout for the kitchen. They were admired, although the two hefty stuffed salmon in dusty glass cases high above the bar seemed to cast dismissive looks at the puny specimens in their wet newspaper shroud. There was a happy crowd in residence, and Flemyng enjoyed a glass or two of beer with Alasdair and Neil, who were about his own age. The talk today had to be about the glen and the hill. They spoke of the need for more rain, the state of the crops, and the prospects for the shooting from August. About the government and its people, not a word. Flemyng appreciated the kindness, recognizing it for what it was. When he and Babble got in the car an hour or so later, he was reinforced in his feeling of restoration.

It only took ten minutes to get to Altnabuie, so he had to be quick. 'Why do you think Abel really rang?' If it had been a family affair, and nothing else, wouldn't he have asked to speak to Mungo? As far as he knew, his elder brother hadn't left the estate all week.

'To tell you the truth, I can't say,' said Babble. 'We spoke about the weather and how things are here, and I asked about the kids – they're capital, by the way – and there wasn't much else apart from the suggestion that he might be here before long.'

'Nothing else?'

Babble thought for a moment as the car breasted the last hill before turning for home. 'Well, he asked after you, of course. Wondered if you were bearing up. If I remember rightly, he said that he wouldn't be surprised if you were a bit distracted – with things as they are. Could have meant anything. Politics,' he sniffed.

'Aye,' said Flemyng, his voice tuned in to home.

Their conversation changed direction. Babble said, 'Why did you want to get away north? If there's something big going on I'd expect you to want to be in the middle of it.'

His defences breached, Flemyng was vulnerable. 'I can't tell you. Everyone thinks I can always handle trouble. I'm known for it, so they say. But it's not really true, old friend. I had to get out for a day or two. You understand.'

In the same tone of voice, without warning of his change of subject, he asked whether any strangers had been in the area in recent days. 'No one poking about? An odd visitor? Just wondering.'

'I worry about you,' said Babble, with a sidelong glance. 'There's been nothing. No one.'

Flemyng nodded. 'Don't worry. It's not serious. Now tell me more about Abel. What time did he ring? I wonder if he might have tried me too.' He looked straight ahead, and gave no sign of the importance he attached to the answer.

'I suppose just before six,' said Babble. 'I was out at the hens.'

There had been no message left in Flemyng's office then; no missed call. Abel had kept his distance. 'I was wondering,' he said, 'if he talked about any troubles. That's all.'

'No. Only one other thing,' said Babble. 'He said it was important that the three of you had some time together.'

They pulled up at the back door and Flemyng went for a stroll in the garden, admiring Mungo's brave efforts with his spindly new fruit trees and the explosion of bloom on the old wall that separated them from the edge of the woods. Back in the house, he said he needed to work through his red box, abandoned the previous night. He went to the study off his bedroom, closed himself in and sat looking out of the window to the glen below, with the box unopened in front of him and his hand on the little pile of poetry books he kept there.

On that still landscape, everything was starting to move, but in his mind there was no pattern to it. Reverting to old habits, he stripped away all the assumptions that his mind might be using to force events into shape, and tried to expunge any false coincidences. Paul Jenner had arranged the opera party in an unusual hurry. Francesca had commented on it. Paul had said that Sassi was a big fish. Berlin was on their lips, and Paul's mind had turned to the Washington embassy, telling Flemyng, unprompted, that he expected him to be pleased with the new ambassador, though he couldn't say why. An uncharacteristic hesitation on his part. And Wherry, as Paul must know, was a-pound-to-a-penny a top house spook in Grosvenor Square. Like the alarm produced by the letter itself, it all resisted explanation. And time, he knew, was short.

The phone rang in the hall downstairs and he ran to it. 'Hello? Will Flemyng.' Then a voice that was familiar, from a long way away. A querulous but welcome word.

'Abel.'

For a moment, Flemyng couldn't speak.

'Hi. I'm here, as you'll know,' Abel said, making it sound as if there was nothing unusual about the call.

'I do,' said Flemyng. 'And not just from Babble.'

They laughed at that, and for a few moments took refuge in family matters, speaking quickly. Wives, Abel's children, Mungo.

Afterwards, Abel recognized the calm that his brother brought to their first conversation for two years. That had been warm enough, in New York, but brief. With the years, the distance had remained. Neither brother wanted to encourage it, but nor was there a reason to break the habit that had taken hold. Each knew that this might be the moment, and that it had been forced on them.

Abel's method was direct, as ever.

'I'm glad to say there's one thing that would suit us both, might help us along. Because we're both aware that we need to talk about my American friend, right?'

'Indeed,' said Flemyng, 'and I'm at your service.'

'I know it, so I'm coming north right now. Tell Babble I'm on the three-fifteen plane. Get my old bedroom ready. I'll be with you for the evening.'

There it was. The years fell away. The front door from the hall was open as Flemyng answered, and he felt the warm flow of the afternoon. 'This makes me glad, you know.'

Abel said goodbye. 'There's work to be done. It always helps.'

When Flemyng had told Mungo, they walked together to the front terrace, watching the ribbons of light on the loch below. They decided not to speak for a few minutes. Mungo lit his pipe again, rare in the afternoon, and Flemyng spent a little time on the path that led towards the river. The bees were in the honeysuckle and he felt the summer warmth from the stone dyke that ran alongside them. After a while they sat together on the bench near the front door, the roses scrambling up the wall behind and the light casting a long shadow from the holly tree beneath the window that had given light to their mother's studio.

'Shall we tell each other what's wrong?' said Mungo. 'Before Abel arrives.' He laughed. 'Maybe that's why he's been sent. By one of the people who run your lives.'

'You were right earlier,' Flemyng said. 'I've been pretending to myself that it's you who's taken the family thing badly. But it's not you, it's me.'

Mungo let him continue.

'Sometimes my mind gets taken over by other things. Held hostage, you might say. Politics, really. It leaves me drained, then emotional stuff hits me harder. I suppose I once believed that my life wouldn't be shaped by other people's problems. I've learned. Listen to me. I've discovered something in the last few days that's been turning me inside out. It may change the game for me. And maybe for ever.' He stopped speaking for a full minute, letting the pause roll.

'You glimpse something by chance,' Flemyng said eventually. 'Maybe something quite small. And you recognize the worm in the apple. The beginning of everything.'

Mungo said nothing, giving him the time he needed, pulled on his pipe, and looked steadily towards the loch.

His brother stood up from the stone bench and took a few steps to the front of the terrace. Rousseau came up from the garden and brushed past him on his way to the door. Bending down to touch the dog's head, he looked up at Mungo.

'I've stumbled on something evil. I do mean evil.

'Someone who's a power in the land is trying to destroy one of my colleagues. I know it now, although I can't be sure who they are. I do mean complete destruction, nothing less. He's trying to drive him mad.

'And I don't know why.'

THIRTEEN

Lucy answered Paul Jenner's summons at a little after three o'clock. It was unusual for her to be in town at the weekend, let alone near the office, and she realized the depth of Paul's distress by the fact that when he had rung that morning he'd made no reference to the awkwardness of the meeting, speaking as if it were one of their regular Tuesday mornings or Thursday afternoons. The crisis had reset his clock, the pattern of his days unrecognizable. She went to his office.

'I have a difficulty,' he told her.

'A new one?' she said, thinking she might get away with that. He was more serious than she had ever known him, the light in his eyes dimmed and the physical sharpness blunted.

'I am going to have to ask you to be very frank with me,' he said. 'That may seem insulting, because you're well aware of the rules and conventions that we all follow, and adhere to them meticulously. I know it, and have no reason to doubt it now. But you're aware that we are afloat on treacherous waters and they could swallow all of us up. For once it's not inflation or trouble in the streets. Something worse. Melodramatic, I know, but there's no point in deceiving you. I need to emphasize that you must be open with me, however much you may feel a countervailing pressure.'

'Countervailing pressure?' she asked, surprised by the phrase and startled by Paul's heavy formality.

'Loyalty to your minister. To Will.'

For the first time, Lucy understood for a certainty that nothing would be the same when the alarm was over. They wouldn't disappear for the summer on a tide of relief and reappear with balance restored and adrenalin running strong. Paul might as well have made an announcement: they'd all be changed by the coming days. Alone with the cabinet secretary, *capo di tutti capi* in her world, watching him in the shadows of an office from which the sun seemed to have been deliberately excluded, she knew that he believed the crisis might, in some way, be the end for him. His eyes said as much.

She spoke steadily, without expressing any alarm. 'So what do you want from me?'

Paul separated two files on his desk, pushing them apart. He left them both closed, and Lucy wondered if they had been placed there as props, to give his hands something to do. A bureaucrat's lifebelts.

He began, still talking with a formality that was unnatural.

'You are aware that I have asked Will Flemyng to assist in handling the difficulties brought on by Thursday's events, because of certain qualities – and knowledge – that he can bring to the task. You are aware of his past experience. This, you will realize, is because of my trust in him.' Paul looked up, as if to check her response. 'He is doing that now, and I'm still hoping we shall all meet – you, me, Gwilym, Will, and maybe one other – tomorrow. I'm expecting to hear from Will later this afternoon with his thoughts. Has he spoken to you today?'

'Nothing from Scotland. Mind you, I wouldn't expect it. He has his speech tomorrow, and he's due down in the afternoon immediately afterwards. He has his box. I made sure it was an unexciting one. He'll have another in the morning. Nothing too onerous, I promise.'

Paul shook his head. 'The speech is off. Make the arrangements. I need him here. I'd be grateful if you could handle that now, with all the usual apologies – ministerial business, and so on. And there's something else.'

Lucy's mind roamed back over the meeting in the same room the day before, and felt the frisson of collective fear.

'Something has come to my attention that troubles me greatly.' He sounds as if he's giving evidence to a parliamentary committee, she thought. 'You should be made aware of that, although there is much in this business I'm afraid you can't be told, even you, because your minister is dealing with exceptionally sensitive matters. You know more than enough from day-to-day business to understand that. What I do need to know now is whether Will is pursuing something else of his own, wandering down another path. Because I am told he is, and that he is very upset as a result.'

Paul was looking down at his desk while he spoke, which Lucy took for a sign of embarrassment.

Before she could answer, he added awkwardly, without looking up, 'I'm afraid I can't tell you how I know this. I'm very sorry.'

The awkward codicil was a painful confession of discomfort. She tried to keep her hair back, and avoided any physical response to his statement, giving no signal of anger, let alone contrition. But they knew that a line had been crossed.

As a consequence, the balance in the room shifted. Paul remained cabinet secretary, master of a rolling domain, with phones that could connect him to anyone he wanted, night and day, and the power to summon or dismiss. But he had revealed a lack of inner conviction, let her glimpse that his heart was not in the interrogation he had begun.

That was enough for Lucy. She took him on.

'No. There's nothing. If you insisted, I could pass on some of his views on certain colleagues, though you know I'd fight not to. They're no more or less spicy than anyone else's in politics, and a good deal more generous than most, as you'd expect. There are confidences that I wouldn't give you – personal ones – and I'd go to the wall with them, resign if I had to. But I assume that's not what you want, because I think I understand your loyalties.'

Emboldened by his hesitation, she held the floor. 'Will's helping you with the business we spoke of in this room yesterday, and I know no more about it now than I knew when I left you two alone. He disappeared yesterday afternoon, on your business, then went to Scotland later on. There's nothing else to report. What do you know that has changed all this? Don't I have a right to know, even if he doesn't?'

Paul sighed. 'Yes, you do.'

She remained straight-backed in the chair opposite him, holding her gaze steady.

'Let me put it like this,' said Paul. 'I've been given a version of his current state that suggests he has developed an obsession with a particular colleague – I know not whom – and that he has become somewhat…'

For the first time in her experience, Paul was lost for the right word.

'… disturbed. That's the talk in certain quarters.'

Lucy took her time replying. Her alarm didn't show, and deciding to deceive him was not difficult. Her task was to defend Will Flemyng.

'If you are suggesting that my minister is veering off the

rails, or starting to talk to himself, you're living on another planet.' She picked up pace. 'Disturbed? Nonsense. He's never been more focused, more interested in analyzing all the things that come across his desk, picking them apart until he understands every detail. If you think his balance has gone, then you're the one who's off the rails.'

She thought she had gone too far. But it produced the first smile from Paul she had seen since arriving in his room. As with her fear, she hid her relief.

'I'm glad you've stonewalled,' he said. 'I hate moments like this – I've had plenty – when people fold up and collapse. I don't know what I'd have done if you had. I'm sorry if I went over the top a moment ago. I need Will, and it's obvious to me that he's firing on most cylinders. But there is talk around here. I can't ignore it. You do understand?'

He waved a hand to show that he could say no more and they should move on.

'We both know how cruel this game is, don't we? Glad you and I are on our side of the fence, rather than theirs?'

She murmured agreement, and waited.

'There are things going on around this place that you wouldn't believe, even you,' he said.

'Do me a favour, Lucy. Talk to Will. Don't mention this conversation, which I'm glad we've had. Tell him about the speech and so on, and get him to ring me tonight. I'll be here, I'm afraid. I'll update him on our late American friend. We'll meet at eight tomorrow evening, come what may.'

Lucy got up and thanked him, with no apology for her forthrightness.

When she had left, Paul opened one of the files on his desk. Before him lay an account of everything that was known about Joe Manson's movements in London after he was tailed to the

Lorimer Hotel. It was thin. On Wednesday night, according to a helpful member of staff, he had left cheerfully for what seemed likely to be a night on the town. No one remembered seeing him again.

But Chief Inspector Osterley himself had returned to the hotel early that morning, alone, in case there might be something more to be gleaned. He had spent some time in the lobby, and had a coffee round the corner with a front desk clerk who had last been on duty on the Wednesday and had therefore not been interviewed after what Osterley now called the second coming, enquiries having been carried out in a routine fashion by local officers. He was rewarded with an intriguing fact.

When Manson was leaving the hotel, mid-evening on Wednesday, he asked at the desk if there was a public phone box nearby. An unusual request. The desk clerk offered him the use of the switchboard. He declined, with the explanation that he had an American calling card that would let him use a box cheaply. The clerk thought nothing of it, knowing that such cards existed, and told him of two telephones within a hundred yards, with the warning that he would be lucky if either was working.

Osterley's note to Paul ended: 'Let's hope one of them was.'

FOURTEEN

Sassi and Abel lunched early and heartily in a Greek restaurant near the Lorimer. Sassi reported that he was making progress and would report that to Maria. 'Bases loaded,' he said, and they raised glasses of rough retsina to success. 'But not home yet,' said Abel, and shook his head. 'Not by a long way. We're asking a lot of them, and there's pride at stake here.' He spoke of his coming visit home, his hopes for his brother, and Sassi said he would ride with him to the airport – in a black cab, not an embassy car, so that they could talk.

Abel knew that he had to answer one question, and it came even before they had manoeuvred their way through the west London football crowds, skirting the beginning of a street fight in Fulham. They were moving slowly along a police line that was preparing for battle when Sassi said, 'How much do you think your brother knows?'

Abel's response involved a gentle deceit. Sassi's store of knowledge did not include the course of the relationship with his brother, let alone the intimation from Mungo of a family drama, so he said that he could be quite sure of his answer because they were still close. 'Not too much. You think Paul Jenner has been discreet, and I think you're right. My brother won't know what went wrong. I'll know for certain by the end of today,' he said. 'I have to ask him straight out whether Manson rang him and spoke about Berlin.'

Sassi nodded.

'I'm assuming, Abel,' he said in return, 'that Paul knows who you are. Your name didn't come up at the opera, but there was no reason why it should. Even we didn't know you were coming. He is aware of you, isn't he?'

Abel's mind went back to another time, before Will chose politics, when they had revelled in the fate, an ocean apart, that had set them on the same path in parallel worlds. His path had crossed Paul's when he was working his way up in the foreign and defence superstructure, which it was Abel's job, in part, to understand. But whether or not Paul knew of the way the brothers had found themselves distanced at that time, he couldn't say. That wasn't for Sassi's ears. 'He knows me all right. Have no doubt of that. He may not know that I'm here – but if I were Paul, I'd be expecting me. Wouldn't you?'

They agreed that they should speak late that evening. Sassi said that he and Wherry were summoning a council of war in a couple of hours. 'Jackson's been pounding the trail all day. He'll have the story straight. You?' Abel said that he planned to make a couple of calls from the airport, and by evening would expect to have some more pieces of the puzzle in hand.

Sassi laughed. 'Well, you have a family dinner to come. Enjoy it. Tomorrow's gonna be a hard day. I'll be reading files, but it should be celebration time for you tonight. It's a homecoming.'

'Truly,' said Abel. 'A homecoming.'

*

Babble was in the kitchen at Altnabuie, wrestling with a leg of lamb. He'd pulled four long sprigs of rosemary from the bushes on either side of the back door leading to his vegetable patch, rubbed the spikes to release a good aroma, and laid them with some of his own carrots round the lamb that would sit in the iron cooking pot for hours, with potatoes from the garden thrown in towards the end. That was all. It was how he and Mungo liked it, the way things were done. He had picked up the lamb at Macdonald's in Pitlochry on Friday and got some fresh salmon at Loch Rannoch, where he'd spent a while at the waterside. He'd poached the fish and it lay in the cold room. Their Sunday lunch had now become Abel's Saturday night welcome home dinner. He'd laid in a haul of cheese and cobbled together a creamy pudding, with the help of generous splashes of his fifteen-year-old Dalwhinnie. It looked to have worked, and it would be a proper meal for the boys. With luck he'd have Abel home from Edinburgh by six, and they'd sit down to a feast at eight. A night of nights. He hummed to himself in the kitchen, and the dogs responded to his lifting mood.

Babble savoured the excitement of Abel's coming arrival, and he sensed its importance for them all. He'd become used to Mungo's habit of talking more about his mother, dead these fifteen years, and knew that he was exploring her history.

Babble had warmed to her from the summer of his arrival here and spent days on the hill at her side, seeing her as the great stabilizer of life at Altnabuie, a fact made more remarkable by her artist's wayward spirit. She had taken the boys on American trips, to her family's old haunts and playgrounds, which had left them exhausted and high for months, speaking of beaches that rolled away for miles and dark woods covering hills where they could disappear for days. Babble's bond was close. Alone of those at Altnabuie, he'd called her Helene in later years. He'd felt her an electric presence in the house and now he knew that she was causing excitement, maybe trouble, from beyond the grave. He cared about Mungo, and had worried on the nights when he retreated for long hours in his study. Now there was Will, in whom he identified an anxiety that ran into the depths.

Mungo and he were planning to spend the next week in London, and both of them were looking forward to a break from the routine they loved. They'd catch the night sleeper from Pitlochry on Sunday, and he wanted nothing to interfere with their plan.

He loved the old house and the hills, and knew he imparted something of his own restless temperament to the place. Life never became too sleepy, nor complacent. Mungo was leading a well-ordered and untroubled life, now that he had given up his university teaching and had rooted himself at Altnabuie full-time. Babble wanted to make sure that there was always bustle around the place, comings and goings. He had a secret terror that visited him sometimes in the night in his rooms on the east side of the house, that it might become a mausoleum, with dustsheets and closed-off rooms. Never.

On his shelves he had a substantial personal library and he read with a youngster's relish, always having a book of poetry on the go, and especially cherishing Dickens, who was his passion. He reckoned that he could re-read the novels comfortably in a regular three-year cycle, although he did enjoy fiddling with the chronological order, just for fun. A copy of *Our Mutual Friend* was lying by his bed.

In the dining room, even by mid-afternoon, the table was ready. The dark blue cloth was well-pressed, with the best glasses perfectly set out, and in the middle stood a silver stag, not tall enough to be overbearing, which had been the invariable adornment when Mungo's father had entertained. Without it, Babble thought the table bare. He had brought up and opened two bottles of good Burgundy, then made it three. The syllabub had set nicely. To help them along there was a pot of honey from the hives that sat down the slope at the end of the garden, close to the carpet of heather that would soon come into purple flower and prolong his bees' summer ecstasy. Altnabuie was ready.

There were flowers in Abel's room again, and Babble knew that the dogs had picked up the quickening in the air, as well as his own exhilaration. They were circling at his feet, and followed him on a walk towards the loch. He checked that he had enough time to get to the airport, and gave himself twenty minutes before setting out. When he had reached the gate where the long path swung away to the loch, he stopped and looked back to the house.

From where he stood it seemed broken-backed, sagging in the middle, because of all the joins that had been made over the years. One corner went back four hundred years, but most of it had been put together much later in fits and starts. It creaked like a ship in the wind and seemed to hold itself upright with a great effort, which was one of the reasons why it stirred up affection. When a pipe cracked, or a slate slid off, everyone clustered around as if they were at the bedside of an old relative, offering support against the coming of the last collapse.

Inside, Altnabuie was well-worn and unmodernized. The plumbing wasn't up to much, although drinking from the taps was a joy because of the cool clear stream that fed them. There were uneven black-and-white diamond tiles on the floor of the hall, and the pictures hanging above were so dark and dense you couldn't identify the faces. The drawing room ahead was a vast space with an assembly of friendly things – paintings and photographs, sofas, books everywhere, and nothing you would be scared to touch. A battered partners' desk stood in one corner and near it the lopsided skeleton of a harp with only two strings.

Babble knew the outline of the shadows on the roof at any time of the day, Altnabuie's every mood. As he watched, a jackdaw took off from the chimney stack above the west gable, and all was still. He gazed on a scene that might have been etched on glass. The dogs broke the spell, turning for home. As they did so, Babble saw Mungo come on to the terrace. He strode up the slope and through the garden to join him.

'I'm glad Abel will see it like this,' said Mungo. They stood together at the front door, Babble in his favourite well-worn, loose blue-and-brown tweed suit, with a dark green open shirt. 'The water's low,' Mungo said. They couldn't hear the rush under the footbridge at the edge of the woods. Although the springs behind the house had never failed in their lifetimes, the long dry spell meant that the trout were fewer than usual this summer. They could do with more rain; it would come. They spoke for a moment with relish about the night sleeper to London on Sunday. Then they sat on the stone bench outside the dining-room window and enjoyed the silence for a few minutes more.

After a little, Mungo said, without any preliminaries, 'We'll need to talk about Mother, you and I.'

And Babble said, 'I know.'

'With Abel here it can't be put off any longer,' Mungo said. The curtain was drawn back a little. Then, as if relieved to postpone the conversation once more, he looked at his watch. 'You'd better be on your way.' He smiled at his old friend. 'You never know, he may be on time.'

When he stood up, Babble noticed that Mungo's colour had risen and his jaw set. It was odd, because Babble considered that of all the boys, Mungo, the first-born, had been closest to her. There had been times of awkwardness – when Abel decided to adopt their mother's family name for settlement in America, there had been a frisson that took a year or two to pass – but he had known it as a placid family. She had been a wilful figure and given to occasional remoteness, but her fire had warmed Altnabuie from start to finish. He knew enough of Helene Grauber's history, wartime secrets that clung to her and imbued her with mystery, to understand how she had come to dominate so many lives.

Babble recalled the times when he would watch her from his window coming up from the loch not long after dawn, her long black coat shining with dew and her eyes bright. She'd have a sketchbook under one arm, and the dogs as outriders in the long grass beyond the garden, and would approach the house with the vigour of the morning in every step.

He couldn't allow his mind to wander. A few minutes later he was in the car and away. Flemyng watched from the wide window of his bedroom as it turned from the house and disappeared in the tunnel of trees that met across the drive. He joined Mungo downstairs, and without anything being said they set off in step through the garden, pausing only when they reached the low stone wall that enclosed the old orchard. There they sat down together.

'It's a good thing,' said Mungo.

Abel's homecoming. Flemyng said, 'We've all been wanting this for a while. But it took something out there' – he waved towards the loch – 'to make it happen. We wouldn't have been together otherwise.'

Mungo said, 'I won't ask what's up. I know better than that. But let's make tonight about other things, too. I've got the letters in my box upstairs. I'll show you them together.' It was the first time he had spoken of them in such a matter-of-fact way.

They would have a grand night, and Babble would be in on it. 'It's his story too,' said Mungo.

His brother nodded at that. 'Of course. The way it should be.' He stood up and stretched. 'Let's take a turn down to the water.'

Mungo said he'd go back to his study. He had some things to arrange. 'See you when you get back.' He walked through the garden, slowly, stopping at a favourite climbing rose and taking some lavender to rub in his hands. Flemyng made for the burn, to the place where he had most often fished as a boy. He knew each rock in the water as if by name.

By the time Abel's plane touched down, they were both back in the house. Mungo was deep in his papers, occasionally raising his head to look through his study window down the glen, towards the hills and the blue-grey line of the mountains far beyond. Flemyng sat at the desk in his bedroom, then went to the hall to ring Sam at home.

'How's the weather in the bonnie highlands, then?' The greeting was cheery enough but Flemyng was alert to the edge in his voice. Sam's voice seemed distant, and Flemyng detected a tremor of irritation somewhere underneath. Could there be anger there?

'Never better,' he said, unconvincingly. 'I'm in heaven here, as you know. How are tricks?'

'When do you get back?' That was all.

'Tomorrow. Not sure when. But I may want to meet.'

'Fine,' Sam said. 'I have something on earlier, but I'll be there if you need me. Just ring.'

Flemyng was conscious of sounding nervous, and kept it short. 'Grand,' he said. They wasted no more time, but Sam said, 'Take care. By which I mean – look after yourself.'

After a moment, he added, 'I mean it.'

Flemyng spent some time in thought. He tried to read some poetry, but found that his mind wouldn't settle. So he rang Paul. 'When do you want me?'

'Eight as planned. I've cancelled your speech and Lucy's putting you on the noon flight,' Paul said. 'I'm not going to say much on this line, but I believe – hope, certainly – that we may be getting somewhere with our American friend. More tomorrow. Enjoy your night at home. And think, Will, think.'

He said that he might make some progress that evening, which was a little test for Paul.

For the rest of the afternoon he and Mungo were alone in their rooms, Flemyng disciplining himself to take an hour's sleep, then turning to his speculations about Manson's purpose in London. He was stuck, and he tried to confront his confusions in the hope that, sometime in the night, they might begin to clear. Leaving the house for his second walk of the afternoon, he strolled as far as the loch, where he sat for a while at the boathouse. The water was flat calm. He watched the reflections, sent some small smooth stones skipping across the surface as he'd done so often before, and thought about his predicament.

He spoke to himself out loud, safe and alone on the side of the loch. 'The only thing I know is that someone killed him.'

*

By six, true to his word, Babble was approaching the house. Sitting bedside him in the car, Abel was absorbing the sights of home, eyes darting from the woods to the high hills ahead of them, then back again, his spirits high. 'Look at the loch,' said Babble as it slid into view. 'See that light? Capital.' He stopped the car for a moment and Abel rolled down the window. He could smell the trees, and hear the faint sounds of the countryside. Nothing was too loud. Tranquillity. Babble waited for a minute or two before driving slowly round the last curve under the sycamore branches, and through the trees Abel saw the house for the first time for long years. When he'd last been here, Will had been winding up his secret life, and thinking of his first election. Only Mungo had been with him on that visit. It had been in high summer, and nothing seemed to have changed since. The shadows were lengthening before dusk, the sky a cobalt grey, but Altnabuie itself was glowing.

As they pulled up, Abel was ready to spring from the car. Babble said, 'Off you go then. You're home.'

Abel got out, and Babble drove round the house and out of sight.

From the gable end, where he stood in a sunny spot, Abel saw his brother on the path leading up from the loch, and caught his profile. Still slim, leaning into the slope, he had kept the lithe ease that Abel had envied in him as a boy. Flemyng was walking slowly towards the house. As if he'd caught some movement by the door, he turned his head.

Abel raised one arm in greeting and he stopped, copied his gesture, and with hardly a pause ran forward to greet him. They met in a haze of relief and after a silent moment fell into each other's arms.

Neither seemed ready to speak first; time passed before they stood back, and Flemyng looked him up and down. 'Welcome home. And healthy as a horse.'

Abel laughed. 'You too, despite it all.'

They walked back together in silence, Abel's arm on Flemyng's shoulder, and there was Mungo in the doorway, a broad smile on his face and arms outstretched. 'A sharpener, I think,' he said. 'We're all here.' He reached for the whisky bottle that he'd placed on the hall table as a sign of welcome. 'Old

Pulteney. We deserve this, for all kinds of reasons. Your very good health.'

For half an hour they caught up with their stories, and settled into each other's company. Mungo announced, 'We're going to sit down at eight, just like the old days. Babble as well, which is important.' Flemyng caught Abel's expression, with its passing hint of surprise.

They went to the orrery, and enjoyed memories of boyhood games, falling under the spell of its shiny mechanism. 'Time for a lunar eclipse before dinner,' said Flemyng, fiddling with the lever. They laughed together. Mungo slipped upstairs. Then Abel, refusing to allow the chance to pass, said, 'I hope we'll have a good catch-up later, apart from the family.' Flemyng nodded. They went to their rooms to prepare themselves for an evening whose course neither of them tried to predict.

After his bath, Flemyng went to the window that looked towards the woods and stood, unclothed, to enjoy the laziness of early evening. The light was softening, the shadows stealthy. As he watched, one of the dogs appeared beneath him and then Mungo, favourite walking stick in hand, setting off with purpose for the orchard where he had planted his saplings. It seemed he had regained some of his old poise; he was straighter and his tread regular. Flemyng's eyes followed his course into the trees, then he turned away.

He heard the phone ring downstairs in the hall, and knew before he picked it up that it would be Paul.

'Sorry to come back so soon, but there are developments.'

Flemyng said, 'Take me through.' No preliminaries.

'No details on this line. But I do want you to know that our friend left more behind than we thought. More messages from the notebook and some intriguing papers. Newspaper cuttings as well, that he managed to winkle out from somewhere. I'll tell you now that they will interest you.'

'Why?' said Flemyng.

'Because they show that you were one of his interests. Maybe a target.'

Flemyng said nothing.

'I wanted to give you fair warning,' said Paul. 'When we see each other we're going to have these complications to sort out. I've put some material in your box. I'll see you at eight tomorrow.'

Flemyng went back to the window. The light had faded. He was being tested. The warmth of the reunion with Abel ebbed as shadows lengthened on the hill. Sam's warning and Paul's message brought a chill. Shaved and changed, he turned his mind to dinner. As he left his room, he told himself that if Paul had planned to put him on edge he could hardly have managed it better. He leaned over the banister, looking down at his mother's pictures on the staircase wall.

Sometimes, alone at Altnabuie with Mungo, Babble enjoyed the gentle absurdity of ringing the Malayan gong that hung in the hall as a call to the table. He would swing the long mallet padded with faded tigerskin as if he were calling a party of a dozen or more from all corners of the garden. Tonight he had good reason. He checked the table, savoured the kitchen smells, and stepped into the hall with the dogs at his feet.

Three mighty beats on the gong summoned the brothers to their table.

FIFTEEN

A ceremony took place before dinner that neither Flemyng nor Abel had expected. Mungo laid on the side table a photograph and a medal with a ribbon attached, and then placed a battered black tin, his deed box, on the floor. At first they were silent. Flemyng inclined his head; Abel had his hands clasped behind his back, schoolboy-style. After a moment Mungo said, 'It seemed appropriate,' gesturing to the black-and-white photograph in its plain silver frame. It showed their mother picnicking on the grass with friends, a long wooden hut visible behind them, its windows open to the sun and doors flung wide. She was laughing, with one arm flung high in the air. Were it not for the two military cars parked end-to-end at the side of the hut, and a uniformed RAF officer striding towards the edge of the frame, it would have seemed a carefree scene.

'Bletchley Park, in the summer of 1943,' said Mungo. 'It's dated on the back. A happy lunch-break, I'd say. What was going on in the hut behind? U-boat chatter, traffic from the eastern front, Goering's troubles, who can say? Both of you were here, home from school. I was on Salisbury Plain, tramping about in a backpack and sodden boots, waiting for something, knowing nothing. And there she was, all the while.'

Abel said, 'I've heard tell of a decoration, but I've never seen it.' He peered down. The silver disc attached to a short green-

207

and-blue ribbon lay against a cushion of purple velvet in a slim leather-covered box.

'From my excavations,' Mungo said. 'The secret medal that she could never wear, for unmentionable services that we can now start to acknowledge.' He turned to them in response to their silence.

'Why are you puzzled?'

'It's odd,' said Flemyng, tapping the table with one finger. 'This photograph. Why was it allowed? Station X was the biggest secret of all. Codebreakers wandering everywhere. Yet somebody was snapping away with a camera.'

Abel laughed. 'You've probably hit the nail on the head, as usual.'

'He has,' said Mungo, taking his seat at the dinner table and drawing them round it before he explained, 'I know who took that picture. The man whose letters are in the deed box over there. Our mother's lover.'

Abel would describe it afterwards as Mungo's finest hour, when he fought off the temptation to slip and slide into his story, trailing loose threads behind him. There would be no false start, no breaks for the brothers out on the terrace to help them avoid the point and take a breather. He had reached his conclusions and would lay them out at his own steady pace, refusing any opportunity to ramble or let random recollections take over. Abel believed that Mungo wanted to set the scene for a memorable tale, properly told. Boldly, with style.

And, in the same way, it was Flemyng's moment. Abel had recognized his troubled spirit from the first phone call and their meeting two hours earlier, despite his happiness at the reunion. His brother's relief at the homecoming gave him a sprightly air, but the strain beneath was obvious to those who had always known him. His shoulders were taut, face grey-tinged in the half-light of the dining room. Abel had noticed earlier that the scar on his neck was rubbed red.

Piecing the story together much later with Maria, he correctly identified Mungo's opening play at dinner on that Saturday as a summons to Flemyng, a private call to arms that was heard and obeyed. Dealing with the family story was the means by which he could beat despair in his other life, and perhaps the fear of failure. A chance for the shadows to lift. So Abel saw it. Describing the change to Maria, when it was all over, he said that on that evening their mother became the alchemist's stone, her magic come back.

Mungo told them that he had felt her presence in recent weeks as he had read the letters he had uncovered. At first there was a single note, lodged by mistake with some family papers in the attic – a puzzling message on one side of the sheet, signed with an initial, and using a nickname that he didn't recognize. But it was an alert, and he was convinced that the letter would lead him to others. He often said that historians believed in hidden treasure because they had to. He checked all the drawers and chests in every corner of Altnabuie, delving into leather suitcases bulging with letters and cartons of family photographs, and one day came upon the deed box, tucked under the eaves at the west end of the house and locked, with a leather belt strapped tight around it. With Babble's help he had gone through the jumble of keys in a wide stone jar in the cellar and found one that could be forced to do the job. In the course of one long Friday afternoon, he started on the journey that led to this dinner table and his brothers.

'I know she would have approved.' He turned to look out of the window, heavy-lidded eyes following the sloping garden towards the loch and the rolling clouds above that would surely bring rain from the west before the night was over, and Abel wondered if he was feeling a shiver of doubt. 'It wasn't spooky,' Mungo said. 'No ghost on the scene. Just a sense that it was right, despite the pain I felt at first. Embarrassment, I suppose.' Abel was watching Flemyng, who had seemed immobile since Mungo's announcement.

But quickly, Flemyng urged him on. 'You told me there was a surprise hidden in her war story,' he said. 'I assumed it was a Bletchley thing, because of what we've found out in the last few years. But you said it was a personal story that could change everything. Then nothing, except that I should pre-pare myself. I have, and I need to know, from the beginning.'

'Me too,' said Abel.

'Lover,' said Flemyng. 'Let's start with that one word.'

'Concise as ever,' Mungo said, turning to face them both. 'I'll give you the story. It seems that Mother' – he waved to sug-gest that he was trying to find a word that eluded him, then found it – '... decided to have an affair. A long one, lasting years and years. Full-blooded, you might say. I found the main cache of letters in the attic, then some that were deposited in the bank in a file with a misleading name, thrown together with other family stuff, and I found that cousin Kirsty over in Blairgowrie had a box that she'd never opened. Sure enough, there was another bundle inside. I've now been through them, and I've got them all here. Believe it or not, there are hundreds of them. Hundreds.'

Mungo took a sip of wine and passed the bottle, to let the revelation sink in. Babble dropped in a question of his own. 'You used a funny word. "Decided". I always thought affairs were things you just fell into. They're accidents, generally speaking.' That had certainly been his experience, the remoteness of Altnabuie having proved no barrier to his passions down the years.

'I used the word deliberately,' Mungo said. 'Let me tell it in my own way.' They were eating cold salmon and cucumber as he spoke, and the conversation was punctuated by periods of silence. To Abel, it seemed as if they were all glad that there were opportunities to pause.

Mungo said, 'I was putting the other family papers in order for my own researches. I've been through the far past – I've got the Jacobite business all wrapped up – and in the last few weeks I've been trying to work out the story of the various things that were done to the house over the years, how the estate expanded and all that kind of thing, the story of the shipbuilding years, and then this came along.

'I should say that I was a bit slow at first, and didn't recognize them for what they were. Maybe naïve. But they soon became clear, and when I looked at them chronologically, well, everything took shape. They tell her story. It's not there yet in every detail – not by a long chalk – but I know a good deal more than I knew three months ago about my own mother.

'Our mother, I should say.'

The letters were now in order and covered a period of many years. There were dozens written by the man with whom she had certainly been in love, but many more written by her. At some point, Mungo said, it was clear that they had been returned to her. He assumed, from their level of intimacy, that no one else had read them all before.

'You can imagine that I was quite knocked out by the discovery at first,' he said, and looked to them. 'Not in the head, mind you.' He looked up for reassurance.

'Were we meant to find them?' Flemyng asked. 'Did she want this?'

Mungo shook his head. 'I can't say, except that she didn't burn them.'

'Which means the answer is yes, and she knew they'd be found,' said Abel. 'And I'll bet they've been edited. But I'll be quiet for the moment. Keep going.'

'Now we come to the big question, the first one anyway. Who?'

Mungo drummed his fingers on the table edge. 'I'm going to have to ask you to wait, because the truth is I'm not sure. I know that sounds strange.' He got up and walked to the window, leaving them at the table, so that he could turn away for a minute. 'I want to come back to the word that puzzled you, Babble. *Decided.* It's the key, I think. She loved Father, as we know, although he had quite a few years on her. And this place was everything to her. But there was something else at play, and I think I have worked out what it was.

'She wanted to escape. Safely. The affair was her way.' He was back in his seat, frowning a little.

'Escape,' Babble said. 'From what?'

Mungo didn't answer directly. 'That's what moves me. It wasn't some silly… dalliance. I'll explain in a moment.'

The natural pause brought Abel in. 'I should say to you all,' he began, looking at his brothers and then Babble, 'that I'm a little farther ahead in this game than you are.' Everyone was aware of a tightening in the atmosphere. 'When you wrote to me with the one or two facts you had, Mungo, I didn't say. But I knew more than you did.'

Babble murmured that the lamb would be ready and left the room – his timing at such moments never failed – and Abel was ready to change tack. 'Let's begin with the fact that shapes everything.'

He hunched forward, the youngest child, bearer of her surname by a choice made in adulthood, the one who had always cherished most the visceral thrill of rolling American beaches and snug log cabins, fiery barbecues in the dark and adventures in the mountains when the family had crossed the ocean for the first time. His concentration kicked in, the famous strength that had carried him through the shadows and been his protector.

'Her lover was an American,' he announced.

Mungo nodded, and said, 'Exactly.'

Flemyng leaned back in his seat, and for the first time his astonishment became obvious.

'Back to you,' Abel said, with his broadest, most dimpled smile.

Mungo said he would come back to the question of identity in due course. 'It's been a slow business,' he admitted, as if he'd wanted to speed it up. 'There are more than three hundred letters. Gaps in the dates, of course. Whether we'll find others, I can't be sure.' He had sorted them out chronologically and there were sequences covering two or three years at a time. 'I was helped by the fact that there is not much in them about us. At first that upset me, a good deal if I'm honest with you. But I found as time went by that I was grateful for it. We were a different part of her life, but no less precious because of that.'

Turning to Abel, he confirmed he had learned quickly that the lover was American. There was the language used in the letters, then the family references. He had found one or two episodes in New York when she had taken the long sea trip to visit her own mother's family in New England, the Graubers, whom they had all known. At least once, the lovers had met when the three brothers had been with her in post-war America, when Mungo was in his early twenties, on a journey that they would never forget. It was the trip that Abel believed had changed the course of his life. Mungo said it had been an opportunity for one of the lovers' last meetings. But he'd discovered that mostly they met in London.

Mungo had now recovered from his hesitation. 'As I read myself into the relationship it made sense, remembering the way Mother taught us years afterwards about America and her family, and gave us such an exotic picture. The thing began to seem quite natural to me. It fitted her.

'The letters reveal, but they also conceal. And, Abel, you're right. They've been weeded, I think, to keep his identity obscure. There are no envelopes. I don't know how she received them. She was meticulous about covering that up, and successful.'

Mungo said the strength of the affair was clear from the endearments exchanged between the lovers from the start. But, and he emphasized how important this was to him, he was convinced that the man had never come to Altnabuie. She would have thought about him as she sat in the bedroom that was her studio and looked down to the loch – must have, night after night – but the letters made it obvious that right to the end he had never seen the place. It had flourished in his imagination.

'He longed for it, knowing that he would never see it. That was their pact, the pain that they accepted would always run through the affair. She says as much in some of the earlier letters that I've got. Wartime ones. He has to stay away, and she says later that it wasn't for Father's sake – though surely it must have been, in large part – but for hers. She had to be able to keep her two lives apart. I don't know whether that was kind or cruel. Who's to say?'

There was a period of silence while they ate, and Mungo left them with that thought while Babble made a circuit of the table to refill their glasses.

Flemyng opened the next phase. He said that they could leave the speculation for later. There were facts to be established.

'Dates,' he said, quite loudly, so that the word was slapped on the table.

Abel looked to Mungo, who still showed no sign of agitation, although he had risen from the table once again. No lights had been lit in the dining room, and with his back to the bow window he had taken on the appearance of a silhouette against the dusky landscape. The last flicker of daylight was disappearing. Babble had returned and the four men enjoyed the silent intimacy of the table. Flemyng let his question lie, and waited.

'About the end of the affair, I can be specific. But I am afraid there is no such certainty about the beginning. If you read the letters in that box, you only pick up the story after the relationship is established and up and running. When it began, I can't say.'

'Which means,' said Abel, 'that our journey has hardly started.'

Mungo pointed to the photograph on the side table. He described a letter telling the story of the day the picture was taken at Bletchley. Her lover was serving in the American forces' liaison office in London, flitting from one clandestine world to another, and had reason to visit Station X from time to time. 'He was one of the few Yanks who knew its real purpose,' said Mungo, 'and I wonder if it was through his connections that she was picked for secret service in the first place.' The letters had hints of that. They'd met regularly, in Bletchley and in London, and Mungo suspected that it was in those years that the affair was at its zenith. 'It continued for some years afterwards, before it tailed away. They were ageing.

The end is heartbreaking, in its way.' He found himself unable to continue. 'I'm sorry.'

Flemyng picked up, and led Mungo back on to difficult terrain. 'If you have reason to believe that his connections may have led to her recruitment, then we know something for certain.'

'I'm afraid we do,' said Mungo.

'That they knew each other before the war,' Flemyng continued, 'so maybe they were lovers at that time. The question is – when precisely did it start? Before we came along, or afterwards?'

Abel smiled. 'It rather matters, doesn't it?'

When they had come to the table, Flemyng had appeared the most serious, without his usual sparkle. Mungo was in charge and confident in his story, Abel alert and smiling. Now Mungo was feeling the weight of his revelations, and as he lost some of his poise he seemed to shrink. Flemyng, by contrast, was alive with interest. Abel was watching every gesture, his face a mirror of Flemyng's excitement. Faced with uncertainty, perhaps a discovery that would oblige them to question their own identities, the two youngest brothers had found new energy. Flemyng was leaning in, his hands flat on the table. The tiredness on his face had gone, and his eyes were eager.

He turned deliberately to Babble, and his eyes widened. 'Can you help?'

'Maybe I can,' he said, every eye upon him.

Flemyng smiled at the confirmation. 'You knew.'

'Oh aye, I knew.'

Mungo turned away again, and Abel saw the physical response as evidence that he was re-entering the state of shock that had come on him when he first delved into the letters, on his own. He had to find something to do because he didn't want to speak. He moved from the window to the side of the room and found the switch beside the table where the picture lay. Two wall lights on either side of the fire threw a soft yellow glow across the table. Babble was illuminated in profile, and Abel thought it was as if he was being picked out on-stage by a light from the wings. He was waiting for Mungo to return to his chair. 'I'm sorry,' said Babble as he sat down. 'I've kept it to myself.'

Mungo had known this man nearly all his life, and as a boy had been a companion to the cockney with thick auburn hair and a bark of a laugh, a ragamuffin in his twenties bent on adventure when he'd become part of the household. The streetwise boy without a city to play in, let loose in the hills. Pot boy, apprentice gamekeeper, jack of everything. So close had they become in the endless summers of Mungo's early years, in long walks through the woods and lost days on the hill, and so much of what he knew about the place had been discovered alongside Babble as they mapped their world, that the friendship was inseparable for him from family memories. It remained a pillar to which he could cling on lonely nights. Warm evenings on the loch; late-summer harvest days at the home farm when they fed the threshing mill with corn and barley into the dusk for a solid week; cool early mornings on the burn before the mist had risen, when he might catch a trout in the shallows with his hands. Together they lived the working out of the year.

Now, a secret that divided them was opening up. Babble addressed his boys.

'I did know. It wasn't a dark secret – more a gift. It was precious then, and still is, because she trusted me. It meant deceiving your father, of course, and I never enjoyed that. I had to choose. Whether to keep your mother's trust or to tell your father, which would have doubled the deception, if you think about it. So I didn't.'

He lifted his glass as if to make a silent toast and the others did the same, obliged to follow his lead.

Flemyng spoke first. 'When?'

Abel never forgot, in the days that followed, the smile that Babble gave them then. His face was only half lit and his hair was a rich bronze, with the overhanging eyebrows dark outcrops on his face. He raised his hands, palms out. 'I saw a letter by accident, after the war, and she told me everything. I think she wanted to. There was trust, and I helped her. I burned the envelopes, put some of the letters away. She was careful which ones she kept. As for dates, what can I say? They had known each other before she went away in the hush-hush time – definitely – but as for when it began exactly, I can't be sure.'

Flemyng then steered them back to Mungo's tale, as if to give Babble's intervention time to bed down before they questioned him further. Mungo spoke with relief, and Abel suspected he had felt embarrassment that verged on panic. 'I said I had reached some conclusions about what the affair meant to her. Can I go back to that?'

He spoke. 'I began with a feeling of weariness, sadness. At first it made me feel sad… weary… to read about it. A burst of anger, too. Now, I confess, I'm more taken by the colour of the thing, its sheen and its verve. That's the odd thing. The vivacity is so attractive. If it had been seedy, I'm not sure I would have coped, being honest with you. Is that a wee bit precious? Perhaps.'

Flemyng said he knew why his brother was able to accept what had happened. Mungo raised his eyebrows with a touch of theatricality, and said, 'Go on. I knew you'd understand.' He leaned back.

Flemyng said, 'You're convinced that without this secret side to her, Mother couldn't have been what she was, to all of us.'

'Precisely.'

Abel intervened then. 'What do you know of him?'

'Very little,' Mungo said. There were mysteries, despite the stories told in the letters. The man's first name was not uncommon – Lewis – but he'd never seen a surname. 'As Babble says, the envelopes have been destroyed.' Abel wondered how many had turned to smoke in the Altnabuie fireplace with dogs asleep on either side and the boys sleeping upstairs.

'They're intimate letters. Of course. I'll leave you to read them for yourselves. But they had a physical relationship that was evidently... fulfilling. There's more to it, though. A better side to it than that.' Flemyng smiled – dear Mungo. 'He painted too. That's clear. They spoke about the world of their imaginations, and she told him, often, how much she loved Father.' His voice faltered for a moment. 'And us.'

For the first time, Mungo's eyes filled up. 'I've come to realize that without this we might not have had such a happy time. And that goes for Father, too. A difficult thought to accept, turning everything upside down as it does. But I have.'

And Abel said, 'So have I.' Before he spoke, while his brothers waited, he brought his mother to mind. She was on the stairs, clattering back from the henhouse and through the kitchen door carrying a pail with fresh eggs sitting on a high nest of straw. Her long black hair, with the natural grey streaks that had come early, her thin pianist's hands and high bearing, all contributed to an imperious demeanour that was at odds with her character, which was – in her own favourite phrase – as warm as pie. She painted in the first-floor room at the far end of the house, where her oils and varnishes gave the place an odour that he liked to think had never evaporated. A place full of light.

There were some easels still leaning against a wall in the cellar, a few tubes of sticky paint thrown together in an old potato sack, and three pictures on the staircase. Two were of their own glen, one showing it in the depths of a famously hard winter, and the other of a Maine seashore where she'd introduced them all to the rough touch of the Atlantic and the first frontier. Each bedroom held a little portrait of a member of the family. Flemyng's had his father – dark and alive, and smiling.

Abel imagined he was hearing sounds from the gunroom on a damp October morning when they were heading for the hill, or the splash of the first fish of the day. Maybe his mother straight-backed at her easel, wrapped in folds of violet and red and whispering to herself as she reached for the palette and looked out of the window towards the high places. Sometimes the boys would hear singing while she painted, her voice carrying along the long bedroom corridor.

He spoke up. 'You've got it, Mungo. There's a completeness in this that we all understand. Without this, she'd have been a different person and not the one we knew. Think of the paintings, and the life in them. The fulfilment.'

Then his own revelation. 'I've known for a while. There's one of her pictures in my club in New York. I recognized it about three years ago when they took it out of store and hung it in a big sitting room – the style was so obvious, it hit me like a rocket. There are two paintings, in fact – one's not on display. I took the trouble to trace their history. One's signed, the other not. The archivist was interested, he's a sharp guy, and it helped that I bear her name.' His brothers smiled. 'I learned of their life together. The lover was a member and the pictures came from him. Left to the club when he died. I'm still following the story backwards. More later.'

And then it was obvious that they had gone far enough for one evening. It was time to pause.

Mungo's relief was obvious. The deed box stayed shut; the letters would be examined another day. Like exhausted lovers, Abel thought, they knew it was time to rest.

Babble responded to the atmosphere and raised his glass – 'Your mother.' Mungo stood, falling back on formality, and his brothers followed suit. It was a natural break. 'Let's draw the line there for tonight,' Mungo said. 'There's just too much.'

Flemyng said he understood. It was time to breathe.

He put a hand on Mungo's shoulder, and felt it steady. 'We'll settle it, never you fear. For now, you need to feel happy that this is all out. We're with you. Babble too.'

He poured whisky for all of them, and they moved outside. The heat of the day was gone, and a breeze floated up from the loch. They could feel its moisture on their faces. 'Rain on the way,' said Babble.

Flemyng felt a pang at the thought of leaving Mungo to climb the stairs to bed alone, but he had to talk to Abel in private. Babble understood. He took Mungo's arm. 'Let's go down the garden and take the air before the rain.' They left.

Abel said, 'They know we need to be alone.'

Moving to the stone bench outside the window, glasses in hand, Flemyng began, 'After all that, we can speak more frankly, don't you think?' In the light cast from the drawing room, Abel's eyes were bright against the deepening darkness as his brother made his leap.

'I need to know why Manson came here,' he said with no preamble, watching Abel's face in profile.

'All I can tell you right now,' he said, untroubled by the abruptness, 'is that it was private enterprise on his part, and dangerous. Maria Cooney didn't know. She was angry – fit to be tied – and that makes her more distraught now. He wanted to confront a certain individual, and we don't know who. That's the truth. You're telling me you know nothing more?'

'Almost nothing,' said Flemyng. 'A confrontation?' he went on. 'About what?' Abel had avoided the question of motive.

'Personal,' said his brother sharply, giving a signal that there would be no more.

'Personal?' Flemyng picked up. 'Nothing's personal in our game. Outside the family, away from here and all this, we can't afford the personal, can we?'

Abel agreed. Fear of the personal had caused them to drift apart years before, and it need never have happened. 'Why did we get worked up about that rivalry, operations we couldn't share, just because we were playing the same game for different people?' It shouldn't have stopped them, he said, but it had. They had realized too late that their paths had taken them away from each other.

'We needed time to grow up, that's all,' Flemyng said. 'But it cost us.'

And politics poisoned the personal, he said, sometimes killed it. 'I'm watching it happen now, day by bloody day.'

A quietness came on them, and the mood changed. Against all Flemyng's instincts he had opened up a secret corner of his mind. Now, instinctively, Abel and he were contemplating their lives, and they felt the grip of competition.

'It's all going to come to a head in the next few days,' Abel said after a minute or two. 'We're agreed on that, I think?' Flemyng nodded. 'What I'm able to say – from Maria, who salutes you from afar, by the way – is that our worry isn't what brought Joe here – a personal obsession, we think. It's what he might have said about other matters in chasing it that worries us.'

He showed no surprise when Flemyng answered this with, 'Berlin.' But it wasn't the time to answer.

Instead, silence. Abel shook his head. Then, dropped into the awkwardness, the question, 'Did Manson call you?'

Flemyng was emphatic in his reply. 'No. I was unaware. He didn't try to get to me, as far as anyone knows. I mentioned Berlin, just so you know, because that came from elsewhere.' It was a challenge, and his brother ducked it.

Drawing back from intimacy as quickly as they had rediscovered it, Abel took charge with a question of his own. 'The Washington embassy. Brieve said at dinner last night that there's been no decision.'

'Brieve?' Flemyng's eyes flashed. He slapped his thigh. 'Something's gone wrong. I don't know what.' Another admission of ignorance from the minister who knew nothing. 'But that's got nothing to do with Manson, has it?' his eyes coming up. Abel was still and quiet, so he pressed on. 'Where did you see Brieve?'

'A dinner thing.' Abel tossed his head, added, 'Wherry,' and threw in another quick question, piling it on. 'You're troubled about something else, on top of that. Who cares about ambassadors? And don't forget how well I still know you. Tonight's been a reminder of that.'

Flemyng said, 'You're right. There is some trouble. I'm feeling battered.'

'Is it everything here? Mungo's treasure hunt? Mother?' Abel gestured into the dusk, where Mungo had disappeared with Babble on their walk towards the loch. 'It churns me up too.'

Flemyng shook his head. 'No, a different thing. But I've found myself using the family stuff as cover with Francesca. She's worried. And it's maybe cover for me too. Keeping panic at bay, I suppose. A family crisis is always the trump card. I can't decide if that's what I've done or whether it's true that this is taking over, because of what we're learning. Maybe I'm using it as a diversion from another problem I've got, and have to see through. They're inseparable, and one covers for the other.'

'Inevitable,' said Abel. 'Part of the choice we made, the two of us.'

Flemyng said he'd grown aware of something else. 'You don't shed emotions as time goes by. They multiply.'

They had reached a natural break in their conversation and, after a few moments in the silence of the darkening landscape in front of them, turned together towards the door. Approaching the threshold, Flemyng was lost in thought, but Abel was ready to exploit the moment. He had a story to finish.

'There's more,' he said simply.

Flemyng turned with his back to the hall. His arms were folded. 'I assumed from what you said that there was something else about the American end. Not for Mungo's ears?'

'Until later. It's about how I came into the game. How and why, I suppose. You know I was spotted at Princeton. Twenty-two, I suppose I was, on that graduate programme. What you don't know is that it was Mother's lover who managed it, through one of his people.' There was little light, and his face was a happy jigsaw of shadows.

'He'd come back from London towards the end of the war with a reputation, and I've learned since what he did with it. You'll laugh.'

'Try me,' said Flemyng, and Abel laid it out, seizing the quiet moment towards the end of the day to produce a climax.

'He invented Maria's outfit, became the godfather of the network. Lent it spirit and lustre, I'm told. And, early on, he wanted some people who might make whoopee in London. I was a natural. You'd already signed up here. Mother knew all about that; must have told him. So I got the tap on the shoulder, and jumped.'

Flemyng, sounding calm, asked if Abel had met the man. No. He had turned into legend before Abel arrived, after careful preparation in his last two semesters at Princeton and a learning stint in London. By then the maestro had gone. Judging by Mungo's timeline, Abel said, the affair was over by then too, before the sixties had been dreamed of. But there were now clues to the completion of the story. Even Abel's decision to take their mother's family name when he made the American move had been encouraged by her. He now recognized that as part of the plan, an element of her contentment. There must be letters, he said, that would show how they'd spoken about it, how it was done, and how pleased they had been when he followed the script. Had they gone on the fire, he wondered aloud, or were they in the box?

'I know it now: I do this because of him. They must have loved the sight of us, both in the family business.' Abel laughed.

It was natural that at such a juncture they should pause. His brother's revelation was a spur to Flemyng's imagination, but he needed time in which to reflect. Moving closer, he said, 'It will take a while to sink in. Coincidences often do.'

Mungo and Babble were coming up from the garden, their faces splashed with light as they came through the door from the dark, and they joined them in the hall. Mungo stopped at the long barometer, and tapped it hard. 'The glass is falling. Good.'

They lingered for a moment, reached towards each other, and said their goodnights.

In his bedroom, he looked at his father's portrait, and went to the window. At night, there was not a light in the whole world that he could see from his room, as if the house had drawn a cloak around itself. He could follow the shape of the hills, but there was no moon and no glint from the loch below. As he undressed, he heard the creak of a floorboard. Abel was pacing his room along the corridor. On his bed, a book of poetry in his hand, he heard the boards creak once again.

Downstairs, Babble switched off the last lamps in the dining room, and stood at the front door for a moment to enjoy the approach of the freshening rain. The dampness touched him. Eventually, he turned towards the west end of the house, his books and his bed, casting Altnabuie into darkness as he went.

'The brothers,' he said to himself half aloud as he closed his door behind him, 'together again.'

Sunday

Sixteen

Flemyng's locked red box was one of five dispatched northwards on Saturday afternoon, secured together in a train that arrived in Edinburgh late in the evening. Three were taken immediately to the homes of ministers living in the city, another delivered to a country house an hour away to the south where one of Flemyng's colleagues was spending a short weekend. The instructions accompanying his own – they were Lucy's, but originated with Paul – were that it should arrive at Altnabuie as early as possible on Sunday. As the first colours of the morning appeared on the hills, a government driver was leaving the main road and relishing the winding route through the trees, the box lying safe and secure on the seat behind him.

He had left a wet city. Now the rain had gone and the eastern sky was bright behind him.

At the house, rivulets of water had poured from the roof all night, and when Babble went to his window an hour before dawn he heard the rough splashing of the downpour on the gravel behind the house. Through it, he caught the sound of the burn as if it had burst into action in a gesture of thanks for the deluge. The air was fresh again, with the cooling lift they had all missed. As familiar as sea spray to a sailor, it would come from stony grey skies that lingered stubbornly for days and then broke, or from the softer rain that crept in from nowhere and turned to mist, coaxing the greenery on the hills and in the woods into life, so that there was a trickle from every branch on the dark pines, their needles fattening with the water, and a shine on the leaves of the larch and the holly.

He could hear little streams of water falling from the overhang outside his window and a steady, heavy drip from the stone lintel above the back door. By mid-morning the garden would be full of colour and plumped up, parched places soft and damp and the blooms turning towards the sun. Lifted by the thought, he felt an exhilaration that he attributed in part to the difficulties of the previous night. Emotions in the house were high, and Flemyng sometimes told him that he was the most romantic man he knew.

At the other end of the house, Flemyng was awake too. He was listening for the car.

He planned his morning, stretched out under a single sheet, and relaxed himself deliberately, limb by limb. After the box had been delivered into his hands, by old rules that he knew the driver would follow to the letter, he would walk in the early light, taking the dogs up the hill for a scramble through the heather. He would go to a spot high above the back of the house where the landscape opened up to every point of the compass, and when the last of the rain clouds had gone his reward would be a fresh panorama of hill and moorland stretching into the far distance, washed in pastels, with trails of mist on the shoulders of the crags and a diamond sparkle on the loch below.

He didn't expect to see another human soul.

While Flemyng made his plans, Babble was reading. He pulled his favourite armchair to the window, picked up Dickens and took himself to London. On his rare solo expeditions, he would visit an old girlfriend who lived near Southwark Bridge, because for him that was close to London's beating heart, the old Babb home standing only a mile or two away, and still the hub of a throbbing network of cousins and their broods. Wandering around Borough High Street, Babble was in the city to which he returned again and again in the pages on his shelves, walking the streets of his imagination. The Marshalsea prison where Little Dorritt's father was banged up, Jacob's Island not far away where Bill Sykes met his end, the old city across the water with its dark tangle of passages and alleys that had once teemed with rough life, the river itself with its barges and lightermen and all the secrets that were revealed when the tide fell back and the mud banks lay exposed. His private playground.

He held close the vision of that London gone, a place of fables and violent rumour, the tumbling fairground of thrills and sadness that moved him still. It was lost, and he knew that was why he had come to love the empty places around him. He could dream there, and remember that which he'd never known but wished for. He had created a second life.

Picking up *Our Mutual Friend* he left Altnabuie behind for the dark fantasy that lured him back. '*The white face of the winter day came sluggishly on, veiled in a frosty mist; and the shadowy ships in the river slowly changed to black substances; and the sun, blood-red on the eastern marshes behind dark masts and yards, seemed filled with the ruins of a forest it had set on fire.*' He floated off.

Mungo was stirring upstairs, and aware of the water all around. He lay for a while and listened. He had been awake twice in the night, and the patter on the roof and the soft rattle of his window in the wind gave him pleasure. His greatest satisfaction was home. For a few minutes he considered the difficulties of the last few weeks. He ran through the table talk of the night before, and the openness the brothers had tried to find as they edged into their past, remembering the shades of darkness that had sometimes touched Abel's face and the pulse that had quickened in Will as he began to relish a secret that he thought had scared him. Mungo was relieved, and surprised. He had expected his brother's journey to take him in the other direction, from confidence to doubt.

He wondered if their discussions in the coming days might be easier than he had imagined, and turned his mind to the papers he'd assembled in his library, ready to go south on the night sleeper. The black tin box had been prepared with special care. Inside, the selection of letters was tied with pink ribbon – he'd unconsciously bundled them up in lawyer's style, as if for a courtroom – and they would be worked through again in the week ahead, carried alongside the old leather suitcase that Babble had taken from the cellar in preparation for their expedition, buckles and straps buffed up for the journey that they loved, rolling south from the hills through the dark.

As Mungo prepared in his mind for the day ahead, he settled on a course that had come to him in the last moments before sleep. After his brother had left, he would make a call to London, to someone who might understand his anxiety, and to whom he could talk with frankness. He had the number stored away, although he had never used it before. The moment had come.

Sleep was over. He got up, let Rousseau through the door and down the stairs, and dressed without any hurry. He took the bottle of water which he always kept by his bed, drawn from the spring on the hill behind the house, and went directly to his library. He climbed the short spiral staircase and sat at his desk with his papers in front of him. He was looking west, and saw that the first patches of light from behind the house were giving a pale wash to the shadows on the hills. Soon the water in the loch would pick up the sun, and Altnabuie would be awake.

He opened his deed box, the black tin lid squeaking as he eased it up, undid the ribbon on the letters, and began to read them again.

'The boys are well. I wish you could see them...'

'Let me describe this place to you, when the spring comes...'

'I have your painting in the room where I work. No one else knows.'

'Tell me how it looks in New York right now...'

For more than an hour, the house was quiet. The dogs were anxious for the hill, but they responded to the atmosphere of a morning that would be precious, thanks to the departing rain. He read for a little, taking time over a short story he'd loved from boyhood. When he came down to the kitchen, the animals were at his feet in an instant but made little noise. Mungo fed them, made a few preparations for the breakfast that everyone would share in an hour or so, and got his boots on.

*

Flemyng was ready. A few minutes later he heard the car on the drive.

'A fine morning, sir.' He knew the driver, who'd done the run from Edinburgh often enough before, and offered him tea. They stood outside and enjoyed the coming warmth. 'Freedom, don't you think,' said Flemyng, making it a statement. Taking the leather-covered box from the driver's hand, he said he'd work through it immediately, before leaving for London. The driver smiled, knowing ministers' ways and innocent pretences. Babble would give him some breakfast, and he could sit in the garden or take a drive into the hills, for the views. They'd meet again in two hours. Flemyng would be driven to the airport, and deal with any unfinished papers in the car. They would be delivered safely to his office by the next morning. He went to his room, climbing the stair as quietly as he could with the lead-lined red box in his hand.

Unlocking it with his own key, he saw a collection of Lucy's familiar files. Green for parliamentary business, red for office telegrams, blue for correspondence. There were two sheaves of papers tagged with pink ribbons that separated them from the ordinary, although he knew that the intelligence assessments they contained would have been sanitized before being put in his box. If he wanted more, he'd have to ask. Halfway down the pile was a large white envelope, firmly sealed, bearing his name handwritten.

He went to the window to open it, as if he needed all the light he could find. The note from Paul, in his own hand, was clipped to some photocopied sheets. '*Will: These are items from our friend's belongings – one is a newspaper cutting, as you will see. The other is a copy of one page of his notebook – there are others, which you will see later. I wanted you to have time to consider these before we meet, but you will understand that I didn't want to discuss them on the telephone. Please give me your thoughts when we convene this evening. P.*'

He placed the two pages side by side on the small table under the window.

The newspaper cutting was familiar, and Flemyng almost laughed. The headline read *Gang of the Future*, and above the text was a photographic montage of faces. It was a cutting from a Sunday newspaper dating from October the previous year, an article which he remembered well because it had irritated him. 'We're stuffed now,' Ruskin had said when it appeared. 'Everyone's after us,' although he smiled as he spread the word. And there they were, Flemyng and Forbes, Ruskin and Sorley, McIvor at the Treasury with his swot's spectacles, even flaky little Sparger at the Home Office, pink-faced and done up in his stripes. And for good measure Brieve was part of the team, tagged as the invisible fixer and photographed at an angle that showed his mouth as tight as a zip. Ruskin was laughing, Forbes seemed about to speak, and Flemyng himself wore a lazy smile that he had thought at the time held a touch of arrogance. They were labelled as the coming men. Sorley had been especially pleased.

On the photocopy, someone had drawn circles in thick red marker pen around the heads of Ruskin, Forbes, Sorley, Brieve and Flemyng himself.

He looked at the other photocopied page, from Manson's notebook. There was one handwritten line, and an indecipherable doodle underneath.

It read, *Friend Flemyng knows.*

He stood for a few minutes at the window, conscious of the sunlight bringing the loch to life, and thought of the question Paul would ask in the evening. Whose friend?

There was no better time to walk. He placed the sheets in Paul's envelope, put them at the bottom of the papers in the box, and locked it. As he went downstairs he heard nothing in the house, and stepped quietly through the kitchen. The car had gone: the driver must have taken to the high road to enjoy an hour in the hills. Flemyng took the glass case from the orrery and set it going, with the cheerful guilt of a schoolboy wasting time. In the quiet, he heard the sound of the mechanism pushing the planets on their trajectory and hauling them back, and for a few minutes the years fell away. When the spindle stopped turning and the brass arms were at rest, the cycle complete and everything still, he didn't replace the top – he knew that Abel would be drawn to the orrery again and let it take him on a journey – and stepped through the connecting door to the kitchen, closing it gently behind him. From the back door he could see the light streaming over the hill, looked to the clear skies and decided that he needed neither coat nor jacket. He got his favourite stick, a shepherd's crook with a curved ewe's horn at the business end, and set off with the dogs, who jumped at his heels and then charged on ahead.

In a few minutes he was through the lower trees and out on the hill, following the wandering track through the heather that would take them to the top. The dogs put up some birds from a copse and sniffed for rabbits around the trees. As Flemyng bent himself to the climb, though it was neither hard nor long, they disappeared in the bracken, the only evidence of their scampering being a movement in the long sun-browned fronds that shook with their passage, making an undulating wave that raced up the hill.

He called the dogs to him as they reached the top and they burst from the bracken. He was fit and on his game, his senses stirred. There was a little cairn of stones when he stopped at the highest point of the hill, where the ground fell away to the south before it rose sharply in a rocky slope and offered a steep climb to a higher summit about a mile away. All around him, the landscape opened up and allowed him to turn like a weather vane and survey the land in every direction, point by point. He looked northeastwards towards Blair Atholl and the rounded mass of Beinn Dearg, south to the hills that lay beyond Loch Rannoch, and in the west he could see the jagged line on the horizon that was the grey fringe of Glen Coe. The clouds were thin, evaporating in the blue. Within an hour there would be a clear sky and a sharp landscape of sudden peaks and long ridges, guarding the glens that ran away from him west and north towards the highest mountains of all.

For a few minutes he leaned against the cairn and took in the smells of summer carried on the lightest of winds. He was breathing easily, the tension gone, and a feeling of loosening spread through his limbs as he took in the scene. Below him, on the eastern side of the hill looking away from Altnabuie, a few deer were huddled in a shallow corrie. They were living statues. He'd missed them when he first took in the landscape. Letting his gaze run slowly across the hillside, he stopped when he sensed their presence, and after a few seconds he was able to focus on the stag and his entourage, perfectly blended with the colours of the hill so that they almost disappeared into its folds and shadows. Even with a stalker's spyglass he would have taken time to pick them out.

They were watching him, having caught the first hint of his scent on the breeze, and he knew that at one movement from him they'd be off like the wind.

He had time to think. For a little while he was as still as the deer. He felt the calm of the morning, but knew he must break it.

*

Back at the house, Babble was spooling the events of the weekend through his mind. Abel had asked him on the drive from the airport on Saturday if he would keep to himself the news that his visit was not a matter of family duty alone: he had to talk to Will. Babble knew he was being asked to keep the fact from Mungo for good reason, not as an act of deceit. It was well meant. But he was unsettled, and worried that he was engaged in a tricky manoeuvre which would interfere with their plans. He put the two warnings together, naturally. Abel was involved, and, to put the tin lid on it, he'd been compelled at the dinner table to reveal the deception of his own that had lasted so many years. Mungo had been gracious, although Babble knew he was shaken.

Flemyng had spoken as they rose from the table of all the complications crowding in, and Babble remembered his own reply. 'You never wanted it any other way, Will. Never.'

Before Mungo's revelation, they had gossiped about some of Flemyng's colleagues. Babble had never met Brieve, the spiky one, and had heard enough not to want to. He had once spent a happy evening in Edinburgh in Ruskin's company, when he had been reminded of the sheer exhilaration in some of those who surrendered themselves to political life. Babble wouldn't easily forget Ruskin's impersonation of the mysterious Brieve, nor the warmth of his bond with Will. They'd spoken of boyish adventures together, and Ruskin had quoted Kipling with zest. Babble remembered the light that had come into his blue eyes as the words rolled out. He'd thought that Ruskin and Will seemed to read each other's minds, conversing in a vivid shorthand that had become a language of their own.

Forbes came to mind, too. He'd spent a day and a night at Altnabuie the previous year in the course of an official trip to Scotland, and attracted mixed reviews. He'd entertained well at table, even played the piano without being asked, and Mungo had enjoyed his relish for political history. They had talked of whigs and covenanters late into the night. Outside, it was a different story. Tiny believed that Forbes imagined he could shoot just because he was a defence minister, and on the evidence of one day's long stalk he had concluded that the armed forces could do better than have this man trying to run them.

Forbes had also boasted about hunting stags with dogs on Exmoor, and Tiny was appalled. By trade he was himself a killer on the river and the hill, but thought it barbaric to set dogs on deer.

Flemyng had defended his friend but enjoyed passing on a Ruskin observation on Forbes that had entered the folklore of the gang: 'Jay dreams that some day they'll name a missile system after him.'

Babble replayed in his head the conversation from the previous night. He knew that Flemyng was troubled at the start of the evening, because he had an uncommonly careworn look for someone who'd just been fishing, and his scar seemed to Babble to be nagging him again. But, like Mungo, he'd noticed a change for the better as they talked of their mother, which surprised him because secrets were supposed to be troubling things. Flemyng's response went against the flow.

In a mood of expectation about the collective mood, Babble thought of the journey ahead and the next few days in London. He'd meet some old friends as well as having fun with the boys. There was *The Tablet*'s summer party at the Travellers' Club that was tickling Mungo's fancy because of the article he'd written for the magazine – and first a promised lunch in a pub that was an old Babble haunt.

He'd be packed up by lunchtime. There was a hotpot sitting in the low oven, and they would spend the afternoon in the garden. Then Pitlochry, and the train. Babble was ready for anything. The streaming sun turned his bronze hair into a glow.

Out on the hill, Flemyng was making his way down. Turning westwards he took in the house and the loch beyond, where he thought he could see Tiny bent over a fence near the boathouse. He stepped forward, the dogs ahead of him, bounding down the hill, Rousseau with a long tassel of sticky willow attached to his tail, flying behind him like a streamer at a party.

They all stumbled and jumped their way down, leaving Flemyng breathless as he took a detour round the house to visit a favourite pool in the burn. Mungo was talking to Babble in the kitchen, and had the kettle on the range.

'Well, we'll soon be on our way.' It was many a long year since they had used names for each other when they were alone, and they were perfectly fitted to each other's company. At Altnabuie they had found a pace that suited them both, and after Mungo stopped teaching he was relieved to find that his permanent presence in the house didn't disturb Babble. Three or four times a day they'd sit down together, to eat or talk, and they'd often walk side by side to the woods or the hill, or fish quietly in the burn or on the loch. For the rest of the time they'd go about their business, Mungo in the library or the little estate office at the back of the house, Babble on his domestic rounds. In the evenings they'd usually spend some time together after they had eaten, and in the winter they'd have a hand of cards by the fire as often as not.

Mungo said, 'Last night was a surprise. But I know you've not tried to deceive us, not meaningfully. I'm aware of that.' Babble said he was grateful for the assurance. Everyone had behaved properly. Life was complicated; that was all there was to it. 'We'll talk,' said Mungo, raising both his hands as if he might clap, and without acknowledging any awkwardness, they jumped ahead.

'I'm going to have a look up on the roof at the back, there,' Babble said, to emphasize domestic continuity. 'I want to make sure we haven't got a leak, and I'll give the gutters a going-over when I'm up there, before I take Abel to the plane.'

Mungo said he should be careful on the ladder. He himself would be going over to Inverlaggan where Father Aeneas would celebrate mass later in the morning. 'He's a grand man, you know. And he's got a Gaelic singer coming. We don't often have that pleasure. A link to our story in these parts.' There was a hint of invitation there. The Flemyngs had stuck with the old religion, and Mungo liked the idea of the family's stubbornness down the years, clinging to a thread that connected them to a distant time.

Babble did make regular appearances at church, although he was no Catholic, and he was all for Aeneas. 'Aye, he's grand, right enough. But there's a lot to take care of. Will has a driver somewhere about the place, and I'll look after his breakfast if he wants it. And make sure everything is right for Mrs Mac. Just so. Tiny's having the dogs as usual. They've been on the hill with Will. Lizzie has a new lease of life.'

But Mungo, helping to clear up, stuck to his theme. 'You know why I like Aeneas so much?'

'Why would that be?' said Babble, busying himself with the dogs' bowls.

'He's more interested in questions than answers. Much prefers them.'

With that, Mungo got himself ready for a walk. He smoothed down his rich green tweed jacket with a pat on each side, checked that there was enough in his pocket for the collection plate and hung it behind the door in readiness. He slipped on a pair of boots and disappeared for the burn, stick in hand. He met Flemyng on his way back, and they spoke for a minute or two.

Soon Abel was in the kitchen with them, the only one with tiredness in his eyes. Flemyng was preparing to leave, wondering if his brother had slept. 'I'll have to be off in less than an hour.' Abel gestured, without speaking, and led him through the passageway to the front door. They stood on the terrace. No one was near them, but Abel leaned into him as he spoke, and kept his voice low.

'What can you tell me?' He looked his brother in the eye, and fashioned a moment of perfect stillness. Flemyng's face was motionless, dark eyes unblinking.

'Almost nothing,' he said. 'I was going to ask the same of you. I need to put the pieces together. Help me.' Abel said nothing, and Flemyng added, 'It's not my game, it's yours.' His brother's expression changed. He smiled into the light. 'You think so? I'm not sure.'

'Come on, Abel.' Flemyng realized it was the first time that he had used his brother's name since he'd arrived. 'I'm caught up in a string of accidents.'

Accidents galore, Abel said, but who could make more sense of them? 'That's who owns the game. You learned that a long time ago.'

Then he spoke quickly, as if he'd been prompted by the sound of a hidden alarm. 'You met Sassi at the opera, I'm told – what a nice life. He's the lead man in all this, and you two should talk again. You'll realize that my worry is my dead friend Joe. Not why he came, but what he said after he blew into town. You say he didn't call you. Did he contact any of your friends that you're aware of? Anyone been a little knocked off balance of late?'

Flemyng shook his head. 'As for others, what do I know?' He pulled back and looked away from the garden to the slopes beyond. The family intimacy of the previous evening had gone, whether they liked it or not. Each was drawing back into himself. Babble broke their silence. 'There's a call, Will. London. It's a colleague of yours.' He sounded disapproving. Flemyng left Abel.

Back together ten minutes later, and with no explanation from Flemyng about the phone call, Abel said straightaway that he should see Sassi face to face. 'Start with him. I'm flying down in the afternoon, and I'll be back in the hotel this evening. You're seeing Paul Jenner later?'

Abel was now in charge, and Flemyng was giving more than he was getting, elder brother or not. So his tone sharpened as he tried to assert himself.

'Yeah, at eight. He says he has more on Manson.' Abel's eyes were on him, and Flemyng reacted with an abrupt change of tack. He stiffened, showing something of the tension that Abel had felt on Saturday before dinner, and his voice rose. 'Can I ask you something?'

For Flemyng, who had spent the time before sleep calculating when he should make his enquiry and precisely how it should be worded, the stillness in the air was a bonus and an encouragement. He was ready.

'I got a bit of a warning from an old friend that there's a worry over someone. A minister. Could even be me.' A chill settled over the conversation, as he'd known it would. Flemyng tossed his head in a show of amusement, but didn't laugh.

'That's not a question,' Abel said.

'Don't avoid the point,' his brother said, and shook his head again. A disturbing current ran between them for a moment, and they both felt the shock of it. Lines appeared on Flemyng's brow. 'Have you heard anything about me? That's definitely a question.'

'I haven't. And that's an answer.'

'Quite sure?' Flemyng said, making it certain that the edginess would remain.

'Positive. I'd tell you otherwise. And you can take it from me that I do know a few things about what goes on around you. But others know more.'

'Quite,' Flemyng said. 'I'm told there's a watch on.'

'Not on you.'

'So you've picked something up?'

Abel said, 'Second-hand. Maybe third. But if it's true, which I can't say it is one way or the other, you aren't the target.'

Flemyng, a flash of anger shot through his embarrassment, said he didn't know whether or not to be grateful to his brother. 'If I were you,' Abel said, 'I'd take it as an unexpected homecoming gift. That's all.' Before Flemyng could reply, he moved on.

'What have you learned? Last night, you didn't say much. Almost nothing,' Abel pressed.

Flemyng steadied himself, aware of the danger of being caught off balance, and held back his knowledge of the first discovery of Manson's body. 'The police who found Manson have come up with some stuff that wasn't found at the scene.'

Abel looked surprised. 'Why only now?'

A stab in the dark. 'He'd put it in the hotel safe, and it was checked later on, after the first panic.' And, for all Flemyng knew, it might even be true.

'OK. And this is what, exactly?'

'I don't know,' said Flemyng, slipping back happily behind the veil. 'I'll find out from Paul. And you?' Abel said he'd be meeting Jackson Wherry, and they found common ground again. With a speed that was becoming familiar to Flemyng, the mood changed.

'A good guy,' said Abel. 'I hope you found that out at the

opera. Decency is his business, especially when it's in short supply. If anything comes up, I'll say. And you talk to Guy, OK? Then we can move.' With unspoken understanding they entered the house together. Each of them found something to do in the kitchen, and they moved apart. Flemyng fiddled with the line of boots and shoes inside the back door, and Abel washed his hands.

Babble arrived. He'd driven a mile to the shop to get the newspapers, a Sunday ritual when there were guests. 'All quiet on the western front,' Flemyng said, glancing at the front pages. He delved inside a paper at the table and smiled at Abel as if nothing of significance had occurred between them, opening a new scene. 'Jay Forbes is in full flow here – end-of-term interview. Great stuff.'

He was pictured beaming, pulling on his beard. Even in a black-and-white picture, they could see the glistening of his moist, full lips. A caption referred to the generosity that was still to be found in politics. 'We're going to get away this week ready to be refreshed. All of us, and the opposition too. That's important, isn't it? I hope people will be able to forget about politics for a while.' Perfectly judged, Flemyng said. Forbes had listed the books he would read on holiday in the wilds of Crete, and said he had told his office only to ring in the event of catastrophe or war.

'I guess that's the way to do it,' said Abel.

Time to go. Flemyng joked about Abel's promise to attend mass with Mungo. He knew that in New York his brother's only religious oblations involved a happy acquiescence in Jewish holidays with Hannah and a cultural absorption in their Friday night suppers which gave him a mysterious joy. To his brothers' surprise, he'd come to look forward to Passover. 'I'll be supporting Mungo, never you fear,' he said. The driver had returned, knocking quietly on the open back door to suggest that it was time to be off. In the spirit of a weekend of atmospheres that changed in the blink of an eye, the two brothers clasped hands, and Flemyng got his bag ready for the car, giving the red box to the driver first. It was placed in the boot like a trophy. He caught up with Mungo in the garden to wish him well.

'See you in London tomorrow.' Their eyes met, and Mungo raised an arm in farewell as his brother turned back towards the house. 'Please don't worry.' A few minutes later Flemyng left, watching Abel waving from the front door as the car rounded the bend in the drive.

*

The church door was open because the day was fine. Looking west from inside the porch, where the marbled granite kept the atmosphere cool and the sun never had a chance to work on the dusty, musky smell of the place, a loch stretched away ahead between two steep hillsides – one rocky and topped by overhanging crags, the other wooded from lochside to summit, the water fringed with birch, hazel, larch and fir. Looking from inside, the doorway framed a wild but settled landscape. The loch was flat calm, the trees still on a wind-free morning, yet the scale of the hills and the sweep of the water into the distance, towards the soft outline of the mountains beyond, hinted at a rampant energy lying underneath, forces that had once split the land and left for all time a majestic landlocked fjord.

A picture of peace, free from any trace of hurry.

From inside the church, and carrying down to the lochside on the stillness, came a single voice, carrying an old tune.

'Is e an Tighearna mo bhuachaille
Cha bhi mi ann an dìth...'

The Lord is my shepherd, I shall not want...

As it started a new line, one or two other singers joined in behind, quavering and soft at first, but carrying through the doorway of the little church, a gentle sound that soon melted into silence. There was no organ, only the words.

'Ann an cluaintean uaine bheir E orm laighe sìos
Làimh ri uisgeachan ciùine treòraichidh mi...'

He makes me to lie down in green pastures
He leads me beside the still waters...

In the midst of a mostly silent congregation could be heard some voices let loose in the old style still practised in a few of the Scottish islands, in improbable improvisations that an old blues man might have recognized, or an Appalachian fiddler who'd picked up tunes his forebears had carried from the old country. Abel, sitting in the back row, the door open behind him, was electrified. He couldn't remember when he had last been so stirred. Mungo, beside him, was quiet, but Abel could sense the power of his response to the setting and the sound. For a few minutes they felt the old ties restored, to each other and to home. Abel also recognized in himself a surge of envy, and Mungo, sitting so close to him in the pew that they touched, could feel it.

The church was full, which meant there were a mere ninety people, and they had come from a long way round about because Aeneas MacNeil had spread the word about a singer and some friends visiting from his home island of Barra. Preceding mass they would sing, and sing they did, in the language that held the echo of old times in these glens, reviving the past. No one else in the church was a native Gaelic speaker, generations having grown up without it, but they enjoyed the backward journey.

Aeneas was priest to a string of tiny communities across the central highlands, rattling from one to another in his elderly Land Rover, which the congregations had clubbed together to buy for him, second-hand, as an act of appreciation to a man who carried his burden across the high hills. Alms for their history.

Mungo loved the story that was conjured up every time he came through the church door. The Catholic line among the locals was sustained by a handful of families who could trace themselves back to the days when the hills around were the last redoubts of the Jacobite cause, echoing to the hopeless call of Bonnie Prince Charlie and his raggle-taggle army. He'd been writing about the Flemyngs' loyalties in that tumult, and their subsequent travails, and was surprised at *The Tablet*'s interest. He enjoyed its questioning tone, and had recently been adopted to its advisory board.

The ritual over, he shook hands with Aeneas after the blessing and benediction, when the last rhythmic responses in the mass had died away. 'Well, wasn't that some cracking singing?' said the priest.

'I loved it from start to finish. Mind you I only got one word in ten, even with the book,' said Mungo. 'My brother Abel.'

Aeneas greeted him warmly. 'Ah, the American one.' Abel bowed and put out his hand.

'There's something interesting coming up in *The Tablet* for you,' said Mungo. 'In this coming week's issue. I've written it just the way you suggested, and I think it's a good tale. I've tried not to sound too archaic.'

They stopped outside the west door of the church, a broken plaster saint on his side poking out from behind a bench in the porch, under a poster for last year's nativity play still pinned to the wooden notice board alongside the times of the masses (Sunday 11 a.m. Vigil, third Saturday of the month, 6 p.m.). For a moment they were completely still, although the first puff of wind was starting to disturb the loch below them and the silver birches and the alder around the church were stirring a little. Mungo began to move through the chattering crowd at the door, exchanging greetings as he went, knowing quite a few of them but realizing that others had come from far afield, up hill and down glen.

They talked about the weather, enjoyed the peace of the day, and opened themselves to their landscape, which this morning had agreed to look its best. Mungo was not over-dressed, but smart in his light tweed jacket and golden yellow tie, his sharp silver hair swept back neatly on each side and curled behind, still full for a man in his mid-fifties. His broad features were welcoming, cheerful on a day like this and he was apple-cheeked. 'Hello, Alasdair. That's some fine barley you've got over at Balnagask. Fine indeed.' The farmer acknowledged the compliment with a deep nod. 'Ah, well. The weather has helped, for once.'

Mungo turned to Aeneas and said, 'We need to have our little talk. I'll see you at the house when you're done.'

After a few minutes more, he eased himself away from the crowd – 'Business at home, I'm afraid' – and drove his car up the slope through a corridor of yellow broom to join the road that would take him over the hill. At the top, he stopped for a few moments and looked back over his shoulder. Abel did the same. The sun was high now, and the loch a sheet of light.

They said little on the short drive to Altnabuie, but Abel confessed, 'I was moved. D'you know what hit me? How ordinary it was, which made me wonder why it ran so deep. To be honest, I'd expected to be repelled, because it's too far back for me.' He laughed. 'You'll be glad to hear that I wasn't put off. I found it strangely natural.'

Mungo smiled. 'Let me tell you something. Sometime in the night – last night – I felt a wave of relief. And then I was cast down again with sadness. Perplexity. I feel there's something I must do for Will, but I don't know what. He's so up and down.' Abel shook his head.

'He's working through it. He's always at his best when he's faced difficulties, dragons in the woods. I know that. There's been danger sometimes, as you well know.'

'I hope you're right.'

They were quiet again on the last run down the hill towards Altnabuie. Babble would soon have a lunch ready. The hotpot, and some crumbly sheep's cheese. Before that, Mungo and Abel would take a glass of warm beer on the terrace. Aeneas would join them in half an hour or so, and Mungo intended to tell him that the family silence had been broken on the subject on which he and the priest had shared thoughts over many months.

Talking to Abel of Aeneas, he said, 'This is my rock, you know, still. What's yours?' Abel smiled.

For the last two miles they stayed quiet, Abel rolling down his window and letting a warm breeze fill the car.

*

As they swung round the long curve of the drive to the house, Flemyng was preparing to board his plane in Edinburgh.

Home was behind him, but he felt as if he was carrying a box of secrets wherever he went. He had time for phone calls at the airport, quick ones to Lucy and to Sam, whom he would try to see in the afternoon. He avoided the lounge, where there might be friends lurking, even on a Sunday, and stood at the payphone in the corner of the departures area, back to the wall and eyes on the thin morning crowd. There was no one he knew. His conversations were brief, and quiet. He'd see Lucy before Paul. 'I need you here,' she said in response, and that was nearly all. 'Lots of stuff. Too much.' She knew better than to say much more. With Sam, he made a quick date. 'Why don't we look at your favourite painting?' he said, not even identifying himself. 'At about four.' Nothing more. 'Yes,' said Sam, and hung up.

Flemyng stood at the phone when he had finished, and barely moved. He had taken the sun, and his tan had deepened, so that the hollows in his cheeks were more obvious. He was wearing a loose shirt in white linen and dark blue cords, and held a light jacket in his hand. A passer-by would put him down as a man at ease, relaxed and in no hurry. In the time he spent at the payphone he didn't look once at his watch. His face spoke of contentment not alarm, and there was no patina of fear. He watched the doors, and scanned the clusters of passengers at each gate, smiling at a mother scampering after a runaway child, running a hand through his hair. Then, in a quick movement as if the silent phone behind him had rung, he turned and picked up the receiver, coins ready in his other hand.

He dialled. Francesca was in the garden, and Schubert was coming through the French windows from the radio. Despite the sun, she wanted to go on a melancholy journey and was listening to *Winterreise*, which spoke of a lover's pain. She looked at her watch when she heard the phone ring over the singing, and went quickly inside.

'It's me. I've made a decision.'

'Will, darling?'

'I'm going to tell you the whole story.'

Her voice was cool. 'Thank you.'

'As far as I can,' he said.

Seventeen

A quartet of latecomers to the plane recognized Flemyng. He was in the window seat in the front row where ministers were always placed, unless they wanted to make a point and move back or there was a posse of them on the early Monday flight that had to be dispersed, and although at first his face was turned away he missed none of the greetings. A couple nodded at him and seemed about to speak, but he interrupted smoothly with a confident smile and waved them on their way down the aisle with an easy gesture. A man who might have been an acquaintance arrived immediately behind them and gave a slight bow that was more formal and might have had an ironic edge – hadn't he worked in the office, long ago? Flemyng bobbed his head without speaking, as if joining in a mime, and watched him move without another pause towards his seat, four rows behind. Reaching across for the newspapers on the seat beside him, he was greeted finally by one of his outer circle of friends, an Edinburgh lawyer named MacGillivray, who stopped for a word, conscious that the passengers round about were watching and listening, and barely lowering his voice.

'Will. How's that government of yours? God knows, they need the likes of you. Keep it up.' He waved away an answer, to demonstrate that he had no intention of invading his privacy, and caught everyone's eye as he went to his seat. When he flopped down he gave a satisfied gasp that was heard by a dozen passengers, and loosened his tie in a quick fumble that suggested that he might have been about to choke.

Later, MacGillivray would report to his wife that Flemyng had seemed to be in a summer reverie. 'He'd no papers, not like him. But on the way to London, so work no doubt. A moment of freedom on the plane, I'd say. From events. Who knows?'

A flight attendant who knew Flemyng as a regular and a public man offered him a drink, but she did so with a silent gesture that acknowledged the answer would probably be no and that on this day she need say nothing. She left him alone, and passed on.

Had the separate witnesses been called upon afterwards to assemble a composite mosaic of his mood, even the state of his mind, it would have been accurate. He was alert, missing none of the comings and goings that might touch him, and had abandoned none of the obligatory politeness of his trade. Yet MacGillivray as he blundered past had picked up with his cold, practised eye the nervous shiver underneath. He had never seen Flemyng display a tic or a tremble in his cheek, but told Mrs MacGillivray in their bedtime phone call that he had detected an edginess that startled him. And the passenger sitting four rows behind Flemyng, who had not expected to see him and who spent the rest of the flight trying to remember where and when they had last met, recognized an alertness that he associated with high excitement, because that's how it had been when he and Flemyng had ploughed the same furrow, mostly on different continents, an age ago.

Left alone after take-off, Flemyng deliberately put the other passengers out of his mind and turned to his family. In his hour of solitude on the hill that morning, he had accepted that Mungo's concern for him was justified. Abel had known the secret, to a degree that had startled him, and Mungo was protected by the security blanket of the historian: even his mother was fair game, because the truth must out. And Flemyng, of the three of them, had known least. That awareness cut deep. Mungo knew it, and Abel too. But with the acceptance of fragility, a tenderness that was being touched, he had felt a frisson of confidence running through him, just enough to raise him up. A challenge. He had tried on the drive to Edinburgh to identify its origin, and failed. Something had been said, a connection had been made, but the source eluded him. It would come, he told himself. It always did.

He stretched out his hand towards the flight attendant as she passed, and she understood. One drink. Lawrence would be waiting to take him straight to the office. Flemyng sipped his wine, put his seat back, and prepared for the afternoon in studied relaxation, thinking all the while.

*

Jackson Wherry had spent the morning in the office, Sunday or no Sunday. He was the first man in his post to have worn shorts there on such days, and the bravura was an inspiration to the boys he led. He bulged and waddled, and they loved him for it. To work. Three months in London and already he had done enough favours to be able to start to call them in, even on the Sabbath. He'd learned one more fact about the Manson investigation and composed a message for Maria, which he sent himself. It would have reached her at breakfast time. Two of his new friends in town turned out to be in their own offices, which did not surprise him on this weekend, and he exchanged a few thoughts. A name or two. On his way home for lunch and a snooze in the garden, he wondered about Sam Malachy.

Safely stretched on his sun lounger, a Bloody Mary to hand and a rumpled heap of newspapers on the grass, he saw Betsy coming through the garden doors with the extension phone in her hand. 'Here, baby.' He didn't have to rise. She handed him the phone and blew him a kiss.

'Jackson… Will Flemyng. I'm terribly sorry to ring you on a Sunday.'

The response held no hint of caution. 'Will! My pleasure. I'm afraid I'm half naked in my garden, but you'll be relieved to hear that we don't run to a pool. I'm enjoying what I'm told is going to be the last of the summer. How're tricks?' He knew Flemyng would enjoy the friendly shamelessness of his greeting, as if nothing was disturbing the Wherry weekend.

And in turn he would enjoy the artifice of their conversation. Knowing some of what Flemyng must conceal, and aware that there would be much more of which he knew nothing, Wherry relished the game. 'I'm all yours, Will.' Then, upping the pace, 'Where are you?'

Flemyng said he was back in town from Scotland, though he left it at that, and his weekend was a mess. Wherry knew that he'd stop there. He waited.

'Look, Jackson, it's simple. Turns out that Guy and I – Sassi – have a couple of mutual friends in DC. I didn't make the connection when we spoke at Covent Garden. I'm in the States in September – your embassy folk know that – so I want to try to put something together with us all personally. Not through the office – more informally than that. So forgive a Sunday call. Can you help? He's not on my radar – Guy.'

Wherry said happily, 'He's not on most people's.'

Flemyng continued, despite the risk of clumsiness, even farce. 'Is he still around... or...?'

Wherry teased. Having spun yarns all his life, he cherished them. 'He's still in Europe. Maybe here, maybe elsewhere. Not sure. "They seek him here, they seek him there..." I'm stuck with other things this weekend... it was just good for him to have a friend at the opera.' He didn't blush as he said it, as Flemyng would realize, and their little dance went on.

But Wherry then changed tack. 'Would you like to talk?'

And, with hardly a pause, 'Now?'

'Yes.'

Done. Their fan dance over, Wherry asked where Flemyng would be in the course of the afternoon, and got the number of his private line at the office. He said he'd pass the message before he got on with turning his turkey-red scorch marks into a real tan. 'I'm here now,' Flemyng said. They laughed, rounding off their exchange with the happy pretence that it hadn't happened.

'Drink, soon,' said Wherry, and added with glee, 'when everything is over.'

Flemyng sat at his desk, aware that he wouldn't have to wait long. Unlocking his drawer, he removed the photocopied letter. He recalled Lucy's questions, and read it again, wondering why he was still convinced that it lay at the centre of things. His mind turned naturally to Mungo and his box of recovered letters, and he realized with the sharpness of a mild electric shock that he hadn't taken time that morning to start on them, or even to ask his brother to provide him with just one that would give him the full flavour. There would be time, but he was startled by the ability of the single sheet that lay in front of him to cast the rest of his life into shadow, even the part that touched his mother. Its secrecy was all-consuming, telling him that until the spell was broken nothing would resume its rightful place and his world would remain unbalanced and perplexing. He considered the puzzles that tormented him and felt again the approach of the enlightenment that had excited him in the course of his flight two hours earlier, only for it to evaporate before he could give it meaning, and leave him tantalized. It was very close.

The private line rang.

'Hey, Will, good to hear from you again.' Sassi. They hadn't spoken since Thursday night, but never mind.

'Guy. I'm afraid I was less than entirely open with Jackson a few minutes ago.' The only way.

'I assumed that.' Then, to take the wind out of Flemyng's sails, he said without warning, 'Let's talk about Joe Manson.'

Flemyng, almost forgetting that his conversations with Abel hadn't involved Sassi directly, hesitated for a moment and got the second blast.

'And Abel, my friend.'

There was nothing for it now but to say, 'Where are you?'

Flemyng was unsurprised by the reply. 'Not far away from your office, as a matter of fact. Near Sloane Square,' said Sassi. Well, they could meet that afternoon: Flemyng thought he could make it in an hour. Done.

St James's Park played its customary role as comforter and bringer of calm when Flemyng left the office, having promised Francesca that he'd try to drop home about six. The canopy of willows over the water and the little bridge, with a long flotilla of water lilies winding under its arch, was a picture of innocence and simplicity. He lingered on the way as he struck out west, making detours to avoid the posses of tourists and a few drunks sleeping off the afternoon, pigeons scavenging their picnics as they snoozed.

It took him half an hour at a gentle pace, with a stop or two along the way just in case, to reach Sloane Square. He had seen nothing that aroused his suspicion, no familiar face nor a fellow-stroller who appeared more than once. They'd arranged to meet in the café next to the Royal Court, and Flemyng admired Sassi's style in dropping another theatrical hint for their meeting, in which each would play a part that had stagecraft as well as truth in it. He went into the back room, and from the gloom came Guy's soft greeting – 'Hi, Will,' a whisper that was just loud enough.

There was almost no one else in the place. Far too sunny outside. They were able to huddle in a corner, Flemyng with his back to the entrance so that his face couldn't be seen. Sassi surprised him, yet again, by suggesting that they have a glass of wine in a pub. Most un-American in mid-afternoon.

'You're forgetting our licensing laws. No booze until evening. Watery coffee or Coke. That's it.'

Sassi laughed. He wore jeans and a midnight blue sweatshirt, with scuffed sneakers, but his hair was smooth. He looked as suave as he had in his suit, and showed no sign of suffering from the heat. Flemyng thought his olive skin had darkened in two days. He was sharply groomed, with a faint shadow of stubble.

They exchanged smiles and Sassi said straight out, 'So you know Maria.'

From his point of view, the arrow was perfectly aimed. Flemyng hadn't yet settled, and it was a question he hadn't expected.

'Sure. Paris, an age ago, or so it seems. We enjoyed those streets, the mayhem. Had long nights out and she often spoke about her family. I feel I knew them. She always said she could hear them singing, somewhere in Connemara.'

Sassi said, 'I know it. A great girl. Apart from all this, in good shape, though we all know the seventies haven't been so much fun. But the outfit survives. Let's hope it stays that way.' His eyes widened a little, but Flemyng played a defensive stroke.

'To be honest, I've got little idea about life in the undergrowth nowadays. You'll know that I'm not the minister in my office dealing with it day-to-day – they thought it would be wrong for me, for obvious reasons way back. So I'm not up with the ins and outs in DC. Occasional talk, no more.' So his past was laid out on the table.

'I've been working with her on a matter,' Sassi kicked off. 'Let's call it a channel that needs to be opened. Something of that kind.' Their mutual fishing expedition began. 'It's been a difficult one for you guys, and us too.' He gazed at Flemyng, brown eyes under long black lashes drawing him in once again, and Will could do nothing but shake his head. The challenge had to be declined.

'Let's be frank,' he said. 'I'm not in the loop on this. Just not.' He added a line. 'Ministers are often a bit detached; left on their own. You'd be surprised, or maybe not.'

'I thought as much,' Sassi said. Flemyng almost said – you mean you knew all along.

Sassi changed tack. They spoke of Maria's instinct for survival, her capacity for steering a more or less steady course through the chaos of recent times. 'We've been in a tumble dryer, Will. Wild, round and round. Never know which way up you are and you're squeezed and rung out before you know it. Agency? Screwed. CIA not the place it was. Our own little outfit? One day they say we've changed the world; next day they're pissed that we haven't got the goods on somebody they've found in an attic in Munich that they hadn't heard of last week. Or a marine with too many funny friends. They say it'll all be done from the sky some day, but they'll still need us. That's what we say, anyway.' Sassi was a man who smiled a good deal, but for a moment he became more serious than Flemyng had seen him. 'It's been bad, man. Too many scandals, and that means too much politics. No way to do business.'

But Maria was as good as it got, he said, and showed no sign of losing it. 'She makes her choice. Then she plays one off against the other. Always been her way.' Flemyng felt his concentration kick in and Sassi springing into sharper focus in the dim light. He and Sam had always been told that watching was as important as listening. It had been his first controller's daily refrain. So his eyes were fixed on Sassi's face as the American said, 'She chooses her allies carefully. The ones who matter.

'They're all supposed to be on the same side – but she sees the openings, where to aim to the advantage of her people. And gets there.'

Flemyng was sitting very still, weighing each word, watching Sassi sit with one hand pressed to his chest as if to preserve his balance. Flemyng was aware of making progress, and thought of Sam, and Empress. A matter of pride. He could see some light seeping in.

Sassi was still speaking. 'She turns them inside out, and afterwards they think she's still their friend. They haven't noticed what she's done.' He laughed. 'Classy dame.'

Flemyng's principal skill, so important to him at this moment, was to display no sign of dawning revelation. Later he would take time to think about friends and allies, trust and deceit. No pattern was emerging yet, but there was some movement in the fog, even a patch of sunlight visible. The day was beginning to make sense.

He picked up from Sassi's homily about Maria with a chirpy question that struck a fair balance between openness and enquiry. 'So you and Abel?' There was no way round it.

'Never on the road together, but the same team, more or less.' Then the most improbable question of all from Sassi. 'And how far back do you two go?' delivered with a wink.

'I've known him for a long time.' And Sassi laughed. Good enough for the game.

'Joe Manson,' said Flemyng. 'You mentioned him on the phone. I'm sorry about his death.'

Sassi said thank you, and explained that he had a difficulty that he wanted to lay out for Flemyng. The start of a deal.

'Here's what I can say. I may know why he came, but I need to know what he said when he was here. You?'

Flemyng gave the smile of the innocent. 'I'm clean. I don't know why he came, nor what he said to anyone when he was here. But, Guy, I'm grateful already because I think you've cast light on something for me. Why he came and what he might have talked about are two different things. Right?'

Sassi raised his glass. 'Thank you,' said Flemyng.

Then, 'I'll try my best. Everyone has a back story, and it explains everything. Nearly.'

He inclined his head towards Sassi. 'I've been thinking a lot about my mother of late – she was American – and a story she used to tell us. She knew a guy called Patsy O'Donnell. Boston politics in his blood. Face like raw rumpsteak and white candyfloss hair – in the boiler room in every campaign. They say he knew every ballot box by name. Election year there was some whispered scandal that never got out; then a candidate quit the mayor's race at a useful moment and Patsy's man won the primary. Somebody congratulated him on a happy coincidence. You know what he said?'

Sassi smiled, inviting the pay-off.

'There are no coincidences in Boston.'

Sassi loved it. 'Sure aren't!'

Flemyng was astonished at that moment to realize how much he had allowed to slip away. His obsession with what he didn't know and his anxiety to provide food for Paul, his worries about how far to push Abel, had diverted him from the bare facts of Joe's death. Maybe Sassi was opening the door.

'I know this will sound very odd coming from me,' he said. 'I'm in the government, after all, and supposed to know things. Sometimes before they become public, if they ever do.' He smiled at Sassi, hoping that his recurring embarrassment was under control. 'For me, there's something that seems to run through this thing. Or maybe it's a distraction, a false trail. I need to ask you. One word: Berlin.'

Sassi's expression didn't change. He placed two hands together, and because his elbows were on the table adopted for a few seconds an attitude of prayer as he looked straight at Flemyng, through the arch. The pause he left was deliberately long. 'City of secrets. You put me in great difficulty. I can't take you there yet, Will. You understand compartments, Chinese walls. And I know, if it's any help' – a practised, patronizing touch – 'that on your side this thing is as tight as it gets. We've known nothing like it before. In any case, I might mislead you – suggest something's happening with your people that isn't. Because I don't have it all yet.'

Each knew there was no more to say. They had reached a bend in the road and would go about their business separately. Sassi went into action first. 'Let's talk tomorrow. I think I'll still be here.'

'OK,' Flemyng said, and laughed at that. 'Things may have settled a little by then. Let's hope.'

'Fine,' said Sassi. They left the café together and Flemyng was relieved when they parted. Time to think. He'd see Sam in an hour, and might make more progress there.

As they shook hands, Sassi hesitated, the first time Flemyng had seen him uncertain. 'This may be more sensitive for us than for you,' he said. 'Believe me.'

*

Sam's favourite picture was a theatrical scene that hung in the Tate. It showed a curtain closing on-stage, and the outline of a ruined face, curved in terror and caught in the limelight like a crescent moon. Flemyng had known there was a helpful Sunday opening for the end of a Pre-Raphaelite exhibition – a week ago, before the convulsions began, he and Francesca had spoken of spending the afternoon in the gallery. He and Sam could make use of it.

He arrived on time, and cut away from the foyer and the queue for the exhibition, entering a side gallery where he found himself almost alone. He stood in front of a Walter Sickert canvas for a minute or two, another picture that led him into the theatrical shadows, before he strolled down the long room. Without warning, Sam was at his shoulder. He was wearing a suit and tie, his hair temporarily in place and his expression gloomy. 'Sorry about all this.' He jerked at his tie. 'I've been at a christening. Godfather.' Flemyng knew Sam as a colleague who lightened his load with a carefree demeanour, and saw at a glance that his impression from the phone call was right. His old friend didn't try to smile and all his jauntiness had gone.

'Let's hear it,' said Flemyng.

Sam passed through an arch into the next room, which was empty of visitors, and moved close as he steered them along a wall of pictures. 'The first thing you need to know is that I've had the heavies put on me. Don't ask me how, but they know we're talking and they don't like it. I've been warned off because you're trouble.'

If Flemyng was cast down by this, feeling betrayed, nothing showed. He had to help Sam along. 'We can do this quickly,' he said. 'We'll talk about everything else another time, when this is over.'

Sam's eyes met his, and Flemyng saw that they were filled with fear. His pupils were dilated and they flicked along the gallery walls, as if the pictures were returning his gaze. His breathing was uneven. 'I can help you a little, but I don't have everything. Only the beginning, but still enough to have the dogs set on me.'

Flemyng moved closer. 'Come on, Sam. Open a door for me.' His nerve strengthened as his friend's faltered.

So Sam rose to the occasion, telling his short story with gusto, and in language that sometimes overtook him with bursts of excitement. He spoke of an operation, buried deep in the office and out of sight of the likes of him. A long game had come good, he said. 'We like 'em long, you and me, don't we? Always have.'

He would take Flemyng back, he said, to the time when they were young blades together. Days when they searched for a flash of light in the dark, an opening that might let them step through the curtain – for someone who might become a friend.

'They found one, the boys,' Sam said. 'Long ago. Helped him, didn't rush, told him there was all the time in the world, and let him grow.'

It was the catch of all their lifetimes, so Sam said. Years passed, but no one panicked. They waited. He ripened. Now it was harvest-time.

Flemyng was staring at a picture in front of him, unaware of what it was. His eyes seemed darker, his cheeks drawn in.

'One of our best ever, Will. Someone looking east and west – don't ask me how, that's beyond me. Someone told me it was like he was sat on the bloody wall itself, looking both ways at once. A rare bird. The one we've waited for. When the end game comes and they run for the hills, one fine day, he's our man. Knows all the people, the good and the bad. And he's ours alone.'

'Alone?' said Flemyng, looking round.

'That's my Will. You got it in one. Alone.'

So precious a source, Sam said, that he was handled in London by only two or three people, and almost none of his material found its way to the rest of government, fed anonymously into the daily rations like the rest of the bits and pieces, the low-grade kind. 'This gold is kept back for the boys alone. And it's valuable enough, I'm told, for us to have done big deals, got ahead in difficult places, dream of more to come.' They were still walking through the gallery, but now Sam stopped. 'So why do I say that he's ours alone?'

The source came with a twist. 'A proviso written in blood – that none of the raw stuff goes down the tube to Washington. None. Why? I hear you ask. How often does that happen? Never, in my experience.'

Flemyng didn't have to ask him to carry on; Sam wasn't stopping now.

'As you know, none better, we have interests involving neighbours, and sometimes, more often than we say, they're quite different from the interests of our other ally. The big one across the pond. This particular stuff is ours, not theirs, and for an excellent reason. We have been learning a good deal about how our Big Ally is operating on both sides of the great divide. Sometimes against our interests. All right so far?' And after he'd looked at Flemyng, he added, 'Sure?'

Flemyng's gaze was steady, and his voice quiet. 'I'm fine Sam. Just fine. I want you to finish.'

'Sod's law, Will, our American friends discovered a bit of a problem in that very same part of the forest. A leak. And to what I might fairly call the mighty consternation of everyone in your old office who knew, they revealed to us in the midst of the brouhaha that they were aware we had the perfect source in place to help. They knew. Shit all over the walls. Sorry.'

Flemyng said quickly, 'They want to use him?'

The Americans were turning the screw, said Sam, because they had the secret. 'The price is high, Will, very high. They need us – the loyal ally – to use our asset to feed stuff to their dodgy guy and trace the leak, watching how it travels, where it ends up.'

'A barium meal,' said Flemyng, who had veered away.

'Exactly,' Sam said. 'We've served up a few in our time, you and I. Down it goes, and we watch it all the way.'

'And he has no choice but to take it,' Flemyng said, and then it seemed to Sam that he drew an invisible curtain around himself and disappeared from view. For a few moments he was removed from the scene.

'That's right,' Sam said. Silence.

Flemyng was looking at a picture, stock still. After a long pause, he asked, 'Are you sure?'

'Certain. Does it help?' Sam steered him firmly into another room to kick start the conversation after the awkward pause, and walked quickly. 'But that's where my story comes to an end. I'm sorry.' He made an actor's pause, and turned. 'Except for this.'

There was a shake of anxiety in the hand that he put out to Flemyng. 'It's gone wrong. The thing has turned upside down or back to front or something. There's panic. It's Finzi and the Turks all over again, only worse.' He gazed at Flemyng's face, watching for the reaction. 'And no sooner had I picked that up, just a whisper, than I'm rumbled and sent packing. I tell you, Will, in certain quarters you are now "the bastard Flemyng", minister or no minister, and as for me, I'm being kicked out of town, pronto. Long-running thing in Athens and they need a spare bagman. To shovel crap through the night, in other words, and maybe never come back.'

Flemyng held him for a moment in a friend's grip. 'Stay steady, Sam. You'll survive. Promise.'

'And you?' Sam said. 'I don't like the look of you.'

Then he stepped back and spoke slowly. 'Somebody wants to get you,' he said. 'Don't ask me why, but watch it, old friend.' With that, Sam left the room and joined the crowd heading for the Pre-Raphaelites, a catalogue for the exhibition appearing in his hand.

Flemyng saw him disappear, walked out of the gallery and crossed the road. The afternoon was still hot, and he swung his jacket over a shoulder. Turning left along the embankment he watched the river glitter with sunlight, and saw that he was following the ebbing tide as he walked.

His step was quick and he ignored the heat. He could reach his office in ten minutes if he kept up the pace, and Sam would give him time to be well away before he left the gallery. No one recognized Flemyng as he walked, his head being down now. He exchanged a word or two with the door-keepers in the office courtyard and took the stairs to his office. There was no sign of life in the corridor, nothing to disturb the dusty beams from the high skylight that laid squares of light in a row on the wall. The outer rooms of his office were empty. On Lucy's desk there were two high piles of papers: they looked undisturbed, and he concluded that she had not made one of her quiet Sunday visits. He went to the inner room and, unusually, turned the key once more before he went to his desk, locking himself in.

He sat for a full five minutes without moving, arms crossed and his eyes on the picture straight ahead of him. Then he stood up, unlocked the lowest drawer of a filing cabinet in the corner of the room and removed a long grey metal box which was also locked. Selecting a tiny key on the ring in his pocket he opened it, and removed two thin notebooks. They lay side by side on the desk, scuffed and dog-eared relics from a past life. He turned each of the covers and the books fell open. There was no identification on either front page, and the contents were a mixture of numbers, some strings of letters and a few short sentences. Most of the pages were blank. To anyone else, the pages would have been mystifying. There was no pattern, no evident logic in the entries. Flemyng fingered the sheets in the books like a man without sight feeling his way, and looked at the few initials scattered here and there. He found what he was looking for, a set of letters that would mean nothing to anyone else.

Writing carefully on a sheet of office newspaper, he created a phone number from the notes on the next page. Using a pen to touch the figures one by one in a pattern that he remembered, he soon extracted what he wanted. He ran the pen underneath the string of numbers and felt the jerk of recognition in his mind. It was time.

But first he let stillness take hold again. A few minutes passed before he pulled the phone towards him and dialled on his private line. The first attempt failed, and he waited before he tried again. The connection was slow, the clicks echoing in a background of static.

There was silence, then the soft voice of a woman far away.

Flemyng was ready. He spoke slowly, although his German flowed as easily as ever.

He gave a name, not his own, and asked if he might leave a message.

Eighteen

On Sunday evening, the fourth day of the crisis, they gathered a few minutes before eight. Paul was back in his casual suit, tieless and apparently relaxed, almost suggesting that they were off-duty, but Gwilym showed signs of wear and tear. He sagged as if he had been knocked askew by a hidden blow and might topple over at any minute. His face was livid and Flemyng thought the tremor in one hand was getting worse. His stage cheerfulness was summoned up for their first greeting, with evident effort, but his voice had lost much of its rich timbre and he sat down quickly to avoid crumpling into his chair in a heap. 'Will. Ah, Will…' he said, inconsequentially.

Paul had three files in front of him, differently coloured, and Gwilym had brought some official papers in a bundle as a stage prop, or perhaps a comfort toy. Flemyng prepared himself, aware that his researches had led him into territory whose promises and inducements had drawn him on, stirred his senses, but left him with few of the answers Paul had asked him to seek out. To the others, he appeared untroubled, and ready to lead.

They began, knowing that they were approaching a decisive moment when the whole business might tip one way or the other, wrap itself up in a puzzling configuration or start to unravel. Paul's serenity made a contrast with Gwilym's constant restlessness, his posture straight and his hands placed neatly side by side as he welcomed Flemyng quietly. Their intimacy, buttressed by a shared fear, had the effect of introducing a strange formality to proceedings. Flemyng felt as if he were in a doctor's consulting room, with an old friend across the table who knew everything about him.

He took his cue, and said that he had learned a little about Joe Manson's last movements – pushing it a good deal – and added that he had begun to put together a pattern that might help them make sense of the disparate pieces of the pattern that was confusing them. About Sam and Berlin, nothing.

'I hope I can take you forward,' said Paul. 'I have another teaser for us. It will require some thinking through.'

Gwilym had resumed his sighing role from Friday, now with both hands clutching at his head, which was streaked with sweat, leaving his straw hair matted and spiky. He rubbed his hands across his blotched red forehead. Flemyng suspected that he hadn't slept for more than a few hours since he had last seen him.

'Will,' said Paul. 'Something very funny has come up. A few things, in these papers.' He flapped the beige file in front of him, sliding it away from the others. 'But first, you. What do you know?'

Flemyng looked him in the eye, trying to identify suspicion, bewilderment, trust. It was clear, however, that the path now led away from the room where they sat and straight to Abel, who could no longer remain an offstage presence and must be introduced, Gwilym notwithstanding. Looking across the table, Flemyng realized it was not going to be difficult. Gwilym was all over the place, tuning in and out. He made his decision.

'I've been to the place where Manson was found – I spent a little time there on Friday, and I have some thoughts. But first,

I can tell you how my phone number got into Manson's pocket. That's the proper place to start.' He glanced to the side of Paul, and spoke slowly.

'Gwilym, I have a brother.'

He grinned back. 'Don't we all? Many of us, anyway.'

'Mine's called Abel,' said Flemyng with a smile.

'I hope he's still with us,' said Gwilym, and hooted. 'Do you bear the mark of Cain?'

Flemyng laughed dutifully. 'He's living and working in America. He has – had, I should say – some connection with Manson through government service – maybe distant, I can't be sure – and I've established that he gave him my number in case he needed a contact here. Some time ago, when Manson was coming to London on official business. Kind of thing my brother would do for a colleague. I spoke to him about it this weekend.'

He stopped. Then added, 'In Scotland.'

Paul took his hands from the files in front of him, where they had been resting, put them behind his head and leaned back, his whole body relaxing. He was able to smile. 'And where is he now?'

Flemyng glanced at his watch. 'Probably on his way back to London.'

'I take it...' Gwilym began, looking at Flemyng, and at a glance from Paul he desisted.

'I can arrange to talk to him later tonight, or tomorrow. Or for you, Paul...' Having opened the path, Flemyng could let it lie clear. 'Obviously not here.'

Paul took his cue and fished a folded piece of paper from the pink file in front of him. 'We mustn't overlook one quite obvious fact. This is what Joe Manson had in his pocket, the number written down in his own hand. There's no name attached. Assume for now that he didn't know whose number it was when your brother gave it to him' – he looked at Flemyng, received a nod in return – 'some time ago. For emergencies only. But this was surely a crisis for Manson. Why not use it?'

They couldn't escape the question, Paul said. 'What was it that he came to London to find out, and why didn't he use this number to try to get to it?' He was watching Flemyng's every movement. 'Any of us would use a helpful contact, wouldn't we?'

Flemyng said, 'I'd go at it the other way round. I'm interested in what he knew already. Because I think that's what is scaring our American friends, even more than what Manson wanted to find out.'

Paul thought about this for a few moments. 'Let's run through it. Joe Manson dropped in here in a hurry, for purposes unknown. He met a friend from the American embassy, Halloran from Wherry's outfit. There are dozens of them these days, as you'll know. Within twenty-four hours of that lunch he was dead, having gone to parliament in the meantime for some reason we can't fathom and then succumbed to an overdose.

'Before we leave this room we're going to find the thread that connects these events. Maybe I should start with what I have here.' This time the beige file, flapped apart, stayed open.

He produced several sheets of paper, which he said had come from Osterley, a copy of the magazine article that Flemyng had been sent in his overnight box, and a notebook. They were laid on the desk, with a hint of ceremony.

They had been found at the Lorimer. 'Where exactly?' said Flemyng.

Paul's embarrassment welled up at revisiting the story. 'The team on Thursday missed these things. They didn't want to hang around. As I indicated to you on the phone in Scotland, Will, the police who were called after the discovery of the body found them in the course of subsequent enquiries.' He paused. 'They were in the hotel safe-deposit box.'

Flemyng laughed out loud. 'Glory be,' he said. 'I haven't lost the old touch after all.'

Paul cast him a puzzled look. 'The most interesting item is probably this.' He picked up a sheaf of papers, roughly stapled together. Flemyng could see they had been annotated in red ink.

'They're the transatlantic travel histories of four ministers in the government, and one official who sits not far from this room,' said Paul. 'Going all the way back to a time when they weren't in politics. Two decades, a little more.

'And, Will, you are one of them.'

He sank back in his chair. 'Why? Why in God's name would anyone want that? All my government trips are public and I've been coming and going from the States all my life. My mother and so on. She was American, as you know. What's this about?'

Paul shrugged. They agreed that they were coming at the conundrum from the wrong angle, and couldn't know where the right one lay. Somewhere in these sheets lay the answer. 'The trouble is that we don't have the faintest damned idea what it means without knowing the question we're trying to answer,' said Gwilym, demonstrating that his instinct still lived. 'We're stuffed and skewered. Yet again.'

Paul slipped the pages quickly back into his file, and said that there was nothing obviously suspicious about the patterns revealed in the itemized journeys – no quick in-and-outs, no odd one-way passages, nothing noted as peculiar against any name. Although, he said, there was a good deal of underlining. They reminded him of a balance sheet that had been through

the hands of a pernickety accountant. But as Gwilym had said
– Paul nodded in his direction – they were meaningless without access to the question to which they were meant to provide
an answer. So he wouldn't say who else was on the list.

'It must have taken Manson some effort to get all this,' he
said, 'from the bowels of various offices. Why?'

The theory was that he had got some of the details, at least,
from Halloran, his embassy friend. Paul said they would sweat
him, via Wherry, at the right moment.

But not all had come from that source. 'We can infer from
these,' he said, 'that Manson set about getting the details before
he left Washington. Records on these people wouldn't have
been pulled together in one morning, even with the American
embassy's resources – visa records, and so on. This is personal
and sensitive. Manson has been determined, and careful. There
is evidence here of hard work.' He waved the sheets.

Flemyng had felt a strong tide of excitement in the air at the
start of their meeting, perhaps expectation, something even
Gwilym's flagging spirits couldn't disguise. Yet they seemed to
be stuck again, perhaps doomed to sink. The atmosphere in
the room had become heavy with the waning of the day and he
felt a pressing need for air. Paul did the sensible thing, and
called a break.

They poured a drink, and when Gwilym excused himself
for a moment, Paul took the chance to zoom in on Abel. 'You
must ask your brother directly. There's no alternative. I have no
idea where this corpse is leading us, if you don't mind my putting it like that. And I have to know quickly.'

For the first time, Flemyng realized how shaken Paul was,
as he ran through the difficulties. 'There's the law, apart from
anything else...' He was white and downcast. 'Imagine where
this might lead, God save us.'

Flemyng had taken a place by the fireplace, standing where Paul had on the first night, and commanded the room for the first time. 'I'll have to ask something of you, Paul, in return. You know that Abel's position here is sensitive almost beyond my capacity to describe it. You know – Gwilym doesn't, and almost nobody else does – and even you, I'd suggest, don't know as much as you think. If you want me to break this open for benefits that I agree with you are valuable, I've got to be able to ask some awkward questions of you in return.'

They were both on their feet, Paul over by the window, drawing the curtains. 'Of course,' he said. 'What about?' A deal. The nature of their business.

'I'll come back to what I need from you in a moment,' Flemyng said. 'First, Abel. He did help a little. Manson angered Maria Cooney' – he raised his eyebrows to Paul, who nodded in return – 'by coming over here. It was his own thing, and she knew it was personal. Off limits. Something that may have involved a confrontation with someone, but I don't know why. She doesn't know who that person was and nor does Abel, so he tells me.

'The problem is that Maria thought Manson might have talked about something else while he was here, and that's what's got her into such a state. That's where I want your help.'

Alongside Flemyng's hand on the mantelpiece, the clock struck one chime for the half-hour and broke the tension. 'I've just thought of something,' he said, looking up and smiling. 'The Inverness train will be on its way in a few minutes.'

Paul's brow was creased. 'Inverness?'

'Mungo, my other brother, is on his way to Pitlochry, and then south from there.' Flemyng drew the scene – Babble carrying the leather suitcase up to the platform, his hunter's watch in hand, the sleeper from the north leaning round the long bend, with all the folk who got on at Aviemore and Kingussie settling into their bunks or sliding along to the bar. The night train still rolled into the dark with some remnants of style. There were even kippers in the morning, if someone had remembered to load them at Inverness. 'And tomorrow,' he said, 'we'll all be together in London.'

Paul smiled. 'I like your brother Mungo, and I know how close you all are.' He exchanged a look with Flemyng that caused them both to linger on that thought. Gwilym still hadn't returned.

They could both see humour in the plight of a family caught in a story that was tying two brothers in painful knots, but energized by the knowledge that the participants were flocking together, drawn by forces whose origin they couldn't know. They enjoyed the moment and sat down again. Gwilym hadn't returned.

'Answer me this,' Flemyng said. 'Why were you happy for me to be in Scotland?'

Paul smiled. He toyed with the file and kept his eyes on it. 'What I prize in you is the talent for feeling out the connections we can't prove. They're there, and we know it. You're someone who watches the way people behave. That's how you were trained – to watch, and to know that it's sometimes more important than listening. Correct?'

'And?' said Flemyng.

'I assumed that Abel would go home,' Paul said. 'Wouldn't you?'

Flemyng raised a hand in acknowledgement. Retaining his calm, he said, 'Somewhere in the middle of this mess is a political game for high stakes. A price that's too much for someone, and a lot of hurt pride. I want to know if that stuff on your desk can help us.' He gestured to the newspaper cutting lying in the open file on the desk. 'I'm glad you put that in my box.'

'We can take it that Manson's target was in there some-where, can't we?' said Paul. 'It's obvious.' He pointed to the rings round the heads of Ruskin, Forbes, Brieve, Sorley and Flemyng himself. 'Which brings me,' he said, reaching across the desk, 'to the notebook and the message I copied for you. *Friend Flemyng knows.*

'You see my problem.'

Manson had written in an old-fashioned hand, with gener-ous loops and each *F* carefully formed. 'It could only have been written by an American,' said Flemyng, reading it again. 'That's obvious. But there's a trap here. What's the question it raises in your mind?'

'Whose friend?' said Paul.

'Of course,' said Flemyng. 'But where?'

'In Washington, I assume,' said Paul.

That, said Flemyng, was where he was wrong. Having thrown Paul for a moment, he seized the conversation. 'I'll come back to that, but I have something else I have to raise, which may be just as serious.

'There are rumours.'

Paul's expression didn't change.

'About me.' Flemyng paused to invite a reaction. None came.

'They are worrying, because they touch on loyalty, or seem to.'

Still nothing.

'Paul, I can't put it more bluntly than this. Am I being watched?'

He moved his head to look at Flemyng from a different angle, as if he wanted to hear the question repeated in another way. His mouth was open, grey eyes wider than ever. He didn't speak for a few moments. Then, 'Are you serious?'

Flemyng turned away. 'I've never been more serious in my

life. Is it true?' He was speaking over his shoulder. 'I haven't seen any signs. But that may just mean I've lost my touch.'

Paul moved back to his desk, to speak from a place of safety. He sat down behind it. 'You force me to confront something rather disturbing.'

'That I am being spied on?'

Paul hit the desk with his fist. 'No.' He was bending forward so that he spoke towards the papers in front of him, avoiding Flemyng's gaze. 'For me, something even worse. That I may not know what's going on; that your assumption – and mine – about this office, these files, all this paraphernalia, the bloody red light on this phone, is wrong. They're illusions. Or delusions, I should say. Telling a story that's not true. A fiction. You understand what I mean. It's not a question of whether this rumour you've heard is true or not – and God help us, I can't believe you think for a moment it might be – so much as the fact that I can't tell you one way or the other. D'you see what that means for me?'

The confession had cost him his balance, and the relaxation with which he had convened the gathering had turned quickly to dishevelment. He flopped back in his chair. When he looked up, he seemed to be pleading.

Flemyng pressed on. He asked, calmly, whether Paul had ever heard such talk.

'No. Not a whisper. Nothing. But you must have something to go on. A reliable person? A friend?'

Flemyng shook his head. There was no point in going further, he said. Paul's bewilderment was convincing. If something was happening it was without his sanction, and cause for a different kind of fear. Perhaps in them both. 'Let's put it down to gossip. A crossed wire.' Paul said nothing more.

In a tone that betrayed none of the disturbance he felt,

Flemyng returned to the question of friendship. 'Manson thought I could help because I was someone's friend.'

So it seemed, Paul agreed.

'And you assumed that friend to be in Washington,' Flemyng went on. Paul said that seemed the logical conclusion because it was a friendship that Manson thought might help him and it was surely on his patch.

'I disagree,' Flemyng said, shaking his head. 'Look at it from the other end of the telescope. Then we might find ourselves getting somewhere in this whole business, for the first time.' Lifting the atmosphere that had sapped their spirits in the last few minutes, he smiled. 'That would make a change, wouldn't it?'

Paul leaned back. 'I'm waiting.'

'Manson thought I might help because of a friendship of mine. One here, in London. That's my conclusion.' He approached the desk and came close to Paul. 'I have many friends, you among them. But one of them can get us to the heart of this business.

'Who it is I have no idea. A political friendship – one of the men with a ring round his head in that cutting on your desk, or someone else in government? Maybe someone closer to me in another way? Who knows? But whoever it is knows something that can explain this madness.'

Their exchange seemed to have drained Paul of energy. 'Another bloody secret,' he said in a voice that was not far above a whisper.

'Of course,' said Flemyng. 'There's always one more.'

Nineteen

As the train pulled out of Pitlochry, Babble let the whisky in his glass on the tabletop pick up the swaying of the coach and watched his drink slide from side to side. That satisfying motion marked the happy start of a journey he always loved, slipping and rattling into the night. They watched the dying light on the hills, the last of the sun lending life to the colours for a few minutes before the landscape became a shadow and no more. He said to Mungo, without looking away from the darkening window, 'All right?'

They were together in a bar in which every place at the tables, and the two banquettes at the end of the carriage, was occupied. The regulars knew that the last part of the journey before darkness was precious – and on a summer's night, a golden hour – so they had come for a nightcap before settling down in their berths. The steward was an amiable and twinkle-toed host, though his face shone with the purple polish of a lifelong whisky man and the fiery red of his Royal Stewart tartan jacket had long since faded to dusky maroon. His hair was oiled down, and glistened. The company rolled along hap-pily, with Mungo and Babble as comfortable and secure as they might feel at home, together on the rowing boat on their loch or on the hillside. They had been keeping a contented silence since they sat down, broken by Babble's question.

He spoke again. 'All right? After last night.' The question, repeated, demanded an answer.

'Fine, surprisingly. I'm wondering why.'

Mungo's wistful air had gone and the boisterous spirit was back, the one that had been evident during the preparations at home. His previous mood of introspection, which had visited him so often in recent weeks, had lifted. Now he turned to Babble, as if to make the point.

'We're going to have a grand time delving around. But I'd be telling fibs if I didn't admit that your contribution to the story has come as a bit of a shaker. There has been pain. No doubt about it. You saw Will.' This held enough weight to hang in the air for a little, and to draw Babble's eyes towards his old friend's.

'Uncertainty for you,' he said, with a directness that made a point about their friendship. 'But Will has taken it harder.'

'That's true,' Mungo said, taking a sip. 'You know him so well.' Behind Flemyng's mask of confidence there was emotional tenderness, a vulnerability, that would surprise those who thought he skated through his public life with the ease of a chosen one. 'You know the truth as well as I do,' Mungo said. 'Will takes things to heart. You'd think his trade might have changed that – not just politics, but the other one in days gone by.'

Babble didn't wait for the next question that he'd known would come after the revelations at dinner. From Mungo it would be polite and considerate, but would still need an answer. 'I'll tell you as much as I know,' he said. 'The first thing to say is, I never met him. You're right – he never came north. But your mother spoke about him. She trusted me, I suppose. Sometimes when we were alone in the boat, or in the car – the old Rover that saw us through the fifties – she'd pick up the story, say a little about what he meant to her. I remember when she first told me.'

Mungo said nothing, determined not to stop the flow.

'It was after the war. Maybe a year or two. Your father was away on business. She took me into the drawing room – I remember sitting with the orrery on an autumn night – and out it came, all in a rush. She was in love with a man, though she still adored your father, and had been for years. There was nothing to be done – she would never leave home, but she loved the other man too. Nothing to be done, except to tell someone. And it was me. I saw some of the letters, looked after them when they arrived and kept them for her. Organized a few deceptions, I suppose, though they seemed innocent enough. At the end he sent back her letters – it was what she wanted – and I helped with them too.'

Mungo said that he had to ask a question on the brothers' behalf. 'Did she ever indicate to you that there was anything different about any of us?' His face was turned to the window, and Babble watched the reflection on the glass.

He said, 'No. Never. I didn't ask, and she didn't say. I'm sure she would have, if there was anything to tell.'

'Do you think so?' said Mungo.

'Probably,' Babble said, placing a limit on his certainty.

And they sat for a while in silence, Mungo remembering days on the hill and the smell of paint and turpentine in the room where she painted, the picnics at the lochside and the bramble-picking along the side of the burn. The letters in the deed box could take none of that away. When they both thought it was time to speak again, he said to Babble, 'You're part of the journey we're all going to take. But I don't find it a frightening one. Not at all.

'Whatever lies ahead – I suppose there might be blood tests or something, God help me, to settle our minds if it gets that far – there's no darkness attached, only a mystery. What Will calls a veil. It needn't be destructive. There's no way of avoiding the question, though. Are we who we seem, the people we have always imagined ourselves to be?'

For the first time out loud, he put it another way. 'Are we Flemyngs, after all?'

Babble said that seemed to him to be just about the biggest question you could ask.

'It may be for Will above all. He's depended on a certain kind of confidence all his life – to help him through difficult things – and he must feel it threatened,' said Mungo. 'His underpinning gone. That's not true, of course, but he can't see it. Remember, I've known him all his life.'

Babble waited, and Mungo went on. 'I realize – maybe Will hasn't got there yet – that becoming older doesn't mean you solve questions more easily. You relish them more. Things don't become more certain as you get older, they throw up more doubt. I'm learning to enjoy that, because it has come as a surprise. Would it change what I've been, the way I've lived, if I discovered that I had a different father? Mother is still Mother. I've realized in the last few weeks – I know I've been preoccupied and you've been worrying about me – that my relationship with Will and Abel is the one that we've made for ourselves. It's not only a gift of blood. It's man-made. That's Aeneas's view too, by the way. An enlightened man, to my way of thinking.'

He returned to his whisky. 'Our own decisions are the making of us.'

Babble raised his glass high in agreement.

The whole story was travelling southwards with them. Mungo had stowed the black deed box carefully on the shelf above the narrow bunk in his compartment, and tucked the key in the pocket of his green tweed waistcoat, which he touched as he spoke. 'This is going to affect Will quite a bit. Must do.'

Babble said, 'And Abel.' He allowed a pause. 'Why do you think he's over here? Not just family, I'm assuming.'

'It's work, right enough,' Mungo said. 'Funny the way we're all holding things back at the moment. The other boys are having to keep silence, on this and that, I suspect. I feel freer now.'

Babble nodded, and lifted his dram.

'It's lovely, really, for me. The piece I've written for this week's *Tablet* – it's quite long by their standards – takes us all back through the earlier history of the family, the eighteenth-century mess, the religion and blood, heroism, the hollow triumph and the fall. Betrayal. And running through, it, old friend, is a strong thread. An adherence, a refusal to bend to the wind. Whatever I turn out to be – who I am – I feel connected to that. So I'm confident enough to wonder.

'My problem is that I've always been most interested in what we don't know.'

Babble raised his glass again.

'I used to think of it as a weakness. Now I think it may be making me strong. People believe we cling in panic to our personal histories, and especially to religion, to settle on a simple answer. Often, and Aeneas and I speak about this all the time, it's the other way round. I want the freedom to doubt.'

Which brought them back to the family, the deed box, and Flemyng and Abel. 'Now I find that just where I thought I'd established the most obvious, ordered part of my life – Altnabuie, the hill and the loch, the dogs and the deer… you, for God's sake! – everything changes. I find I want the unknown, and… do you know? … it doesn't scare me after all. I never expected that, and it excites me. I hope it might be the same for Will and Abel.'

Mungo lifted his glass as he said it, and signalled to the steward with a raised finger. 'Maybe not. Funny, when they're the ones who're supposed to be good with secrets. Your very good health.'

Babble was moved by the conversation, because it touched on territory they avoided in their daily round. The cycle of their week was generally untroubled, interrupted by nothing more serious than the weather, or a little bit of Altnabuie tumbling to the ground, or marauding deer, maybe local gossip taking off for a day or two and spreading as far as Pitlochry. Tranquillity would always be restored. Now Mungo's discovery and his reflections suggested a turning point he hadn't expected. With the other brothers in attendance in London it would, thought Babble, be like flying towards a hairpin bend at high speed. He was braced for fun, despite everything.

They recovered the silence that they'd first enjoyed getting on to the train, and Mungo produced a book. Babble, in his turn, made a few notes in his diary, where he kept dates and reminders and little sketches of moments that seemed significant. He had two dozen volumes of notes on his shelves. He scribbled a favourite line: *the wing of friendship never moults a feather!* And, in keeping with his long habit, made a notation in brackets afterwards (Dick Swiveller, *The Old Curiosity Shop*) before taking another glass.

Each lost himself in words and memories, and let the night come on.

Twenty minutes later they began to weave their way along the narrow corridor to their compartments, next to each other, squeezing past posses of heavy-booted walkers and a line of Scandinavian boy scouts. 'Sleep well, old friend,' said Mungo. Their arms locked. Each closed and locked his door, and got ready to slide into the hard bed, feet to the window. Mungo eased his blind up for a few moments, and saw nothing but blackness outside. His face was reflected on the glass, and his eyes were bright. They must be in the Borders. There were no clusters of lights to be seen, only some distant pinpricks on an invisible hillside, and he felt the presence of the undulating landscape in the dark. There were five hours of rest ahead.

*

Flemyng was leaving Paul's office, light-headed and distracted, aware that he should be sunk in seriousness but perplexed by a feeling that came close to exhilaration, a reaction against the chaos he felt around him. There were snares on every pathway, it seemed, and whenever it looked as if he might break free he was pulled back. Paul was now sunk in alarm, and his habit of massaging the right side of his nose when disturbed was a feature of almost every conversation. Flemyng knew that he was the subject of anxious enquiry in Paul's own mind.

Paul would be obliged to wonder if Flemyng was concealing a link with Manson. Then there was Sam's tip off about 'the bastard Flemyng', and Manson's note about *Friend Flemyng*, who knew something, Abel's unknown game and Flemyng's own suggestion that there might be a surveillance operation of which Paul was humiliatingly unaware.

Yet considering the alarm running through him, he felt the return of a sense of bravado, long-buried, that had troubled him by its absence. When he made his first move – was it only on Thursday? – he had in part been trying to recover some of the old verve, knowing that it had drained away in recent times. Now it was back, and he could think.

He ran through the observations lodged in his mind in the course of the day: Sam's knowledge that behind one locked door there was another, Maria's way with allies, the role of pride, and Sassi's startling suggestion that he had as much to lose as anyone in London.

Walking from Whitehall back through the courtyard from King Charles Street, he surprised the night-time security guards. But they nodded him through with no trouble, and when he went up the great staircase he could understand why. There was a light in his office and the door to the corridor was ajar.

He checked the time, and saw that it was nearly midnight.

Pushing back the door with two fingers he stepped quietly into the outer office. From the inner room he could hear the clicking of typewriter keys. Walking carefully to the door, he looked in.

Lucy.

He laughed, she gave a start, put her head in her hands. There was embarrassment, a touch of concern on his part, but his mood of strange lightness was enough to ease the atmosphere.

'What on earth are you up to?'

She sighed, and pointed to a heap of files on the floor beside her. 'I've been here for a while. I just had to get through all this stuff, because it will be wild later in the week when they all get back from Paris. Mad catching up and everything. And… I had to write something personal, too.' He let that pass.

'I might ask the same question of you,' she said, turning it round as quickly as ever.

He motioned her into his own office and took one of the dark green armchairs, giving her the other. 'This business is moving very fast.' She noticed that he was smiling. 'This, as it happens, is a very fortuitous encounter. Let's talk about something we've let slip in the last day or two. It's time.'

'The letter?'

'Of course,' said Flemyng. 'Where has it taken you?'

Lucy understood that he wanted no preamble. 'I tried to think who fitted the bill, mentally.'

'And?' He was at attention.

Shifting sideways in her seat, Lucy slung both legs over one of the arms. She was in jeans and a loose pink shirt, and threw her head back so that her hair hung down from the other arm of the chair. 'All that self-examination... the pleading... you name it. It's peculiar.'

He asked her to think back to their conversation after he'd shown her the letter for the first time. 'I asked you to read it very carefully, to think about why it was written, and you seemed puzzled from the start.'

Lucy said, 'I was. At first sight it seemed straightforward. He was complaining about being betrayed, and floundering in self-pity. I told you I had wondered at first if it might be sex, but thought that it wasn't – for some reason I can't quite identify I still don't, to be honest. But something else has occurred to me in the last day or so – I was thinking about it only about an hour ago – that makes it seem very strange indeed.'

Flemyng's eyes were shining. 'So?'

Lucy said she'd gone over the thing in her head a dozen times, and had begun to think that, far from being an outpouring of emotion straight from the depths, it was a concoction. 'I don't know anything about furniture,' she said, out of the blue, 'but I suppose it must be like coming across a perfect Chippendale chair or something and then having a suspicion that it's a fake. Once you get the idea, there's no stopping. You can't go back. The thing becomes an obvious piece of invention, a kind of insult.'

Flemyng nodded, and waited because he knew that she would take the next step, too.

'It brings us back to the fact that whoever wrote it, copied it. Assuming that he did that himself. Incidentally, I'm sure he did – I now think that fits with everything else. When you told me, I said I thought it was mad and I still do in a way, though you could also argue that it's consistent. That's the point, isn't it? Put the copying together with what I've just said about its... sentiments, and you get something that's really strange. A cry of pain that's been... managed, created... for a purpose. And that is where I thought I was stuck. Because we don't know who was going to receive it. No name at the top.'

'Can you guess?'

Their eyes had met now, for the first time in the conversation, and he waited for Lucy.

'No.'

He nodded. 'I share your ignorance, but I think I know *why* it was written. Out of rivalry that turned to obsession. The letter wasn't written to an enemy, but to a friend.

'That's the thing about this letter. It isn't passive – a cry of pain. It's active – a weapon. As sharp as a knife, and deadly too.'

He took his own copy from his briefcase. 'Listen.

I have come to the conclusion that you are bent on a cruel destruction of our relationship. This can't be happening by chance. I would beg you to stop, but it may be too late. Is this inevitable in our lives? Did you always know?

'I think it's a lesson in how to drive somebody mad.'

Lucy said they'd both identified cruelty in it, but couldn't be sure they were right. 'The letter could be genuine, just as it stands. We think it's the opposite of what it seems, but there's no way of proving it isn't a cry for help but an attack.'

Then, as was her habit, she asked the simplest and most important question. 'Why?'

Flemyng found that he could recite from memory the sentences that spoke of death for one or both of them. 'There's no reason I can see. That's why I use the word mad, useless though it is. I think that's what he is, whatever the word means. He's ambitious, no doubt. But it runs deeper in this person, and makes him dangerous. We're both assuming it's a man, I notice.'

'Definitely,' Lucy said. 'If I did this, it would be quite different.' She smiled.

Flemyng said, 'You see my difficulty. To tell or not to tell.'

Lucy was nodding, keeping up with every thought, ahead of him at times. He laid out his problem. 'The complications are terrible. Here's an obvious one. Imagine he is one of the people who may be sent to Washington as ambassador. Possible. I say nothing and he's sent, a glorious fanfare with him, safely out of government and off the stage. This nonsense goes away. For all I know, he gets over it and rebalances himself. Normal service resumes and everyone is happier, especially his victim. Or, by contrast, catastrophe. It all turns very ugly. And it's my fault, for saying nothing.'

He went on, 'So I have a duty, don't I? He may well be off his rocker. That seems the best way to put it. Seriously, can I stay quiet? The trouble is that if I show it to Paul, we can't know what might happen. A leak, it goes public. Anything. We're lighting a fuse. Bang, and all of us are burned up.'

She said, 'You're sure of what we're dealing with, aren't you?'

'No. But... maybe I'm getting close.' He smiled at her.

Flemyng asked her to think about it overnight. In the morning they had to decide together what was to be done.

'Think?' she said. 'You said that's what Paul wants you to do. Not rake around like a policeman, but think. You turned this letter round in your head. You've done what he wanted. Isn't that your answer? Tell him what you believe. I think you're nearly there.'

Flemyng saw that it was after midnight, and realized he hadn't heard Big Ben. His eyes rested on her for a few seconds; they were bright and black and full of life. 'I had a call to make. It's too late.' He didn't mention Abel. 'We should go. The next day or two are going to be…'

'Fun?'

'I was going to say…'

'Testing?'

'I'm sorry, was I?' said Flemyng. The meeting with Paul and Gwilym now seemed hours away, its gloom and edginess superseded by the energy and even gaiety of the last hour. There was a death, a crisis, maybe the horror of a confrontation with a friend, unknown. No way back.

He realized, sitting at his desk with the letter in front of him, that the exhilaration disguised an exhaustion underneath that was rising like a tide on the turn and would have its way. Suddenly he wanted to get away.

'Time to go,' he said.

Lucy got up. 'Thanks for telling me everything,' she said. 'It's been good of you. I hope I've helped. I'll do everything I can in the next day or two. We'll get through all this. Don't worry.'

Flemyng said, 'I wish it was everything. I'm afraid it isn't the half of it.'

He had his jacket on, and had locked his briefcase in the desk, straightened his papers and switched off the overhanging reading light beside him. 'I'm going to leave my overnight box here. I'll try to work through it early tomorrow. I know we'll survive but don't doubt how difficult it's going to be. I may have to do something that destroys someone. Deceive others. Have you considered that?'

He went to the door. 'And there's some awful complicating stuff from the American end. Not to mention…'

'… a body?' she said, and Flemyng didn't reply. She knew it all now, almost.

Lucy got up and straightened her clothes. She slipped on the sandals with wooden soles that she'd left under her desk, patted her tower of papers, clicked off her own desk light and moved to the office door beside him. 'I'm afraid I'm enjoying this. Sorry.'

He laughed in relief.

Then, his last surprise of the day.

Lucy took his hand. She squeezed.

Oh, no, he thought to himself. Please, no.

MONDAY

TWENTY

In his room at the Lorimer, Abel prepared for the end game. It was his alone to begin, his own loyalty that he was about to test. His brother would understand when the time was right. Abel was confident, and placid in his own mind. He prepared with care, falling into a routine that in his mind was associated with every moment like this. He assumed that there was no physical danger attached, but he gave it the same respect that would be due to an enterprise in which caution governed every move, and where he was always aware of the darkness round the corner.

His message to Maria overnight had explained what he proposed to do, having judged that the moment had come. He had waited a long hour for the reply, sitting in the dark with just enough light from his bedside lamp to read the novel he had packed for the journey. He never left home without one, and a spare at the bottom of the bag in case he needed a change of scene. When the hotel put through the call from Washington, just before 3 a.m. in London, she spoke softly but with no hesitation. 'You're right. It's time. Good luck.'

From habit, he laid out his things with care as he prepared to leave, just as he would if it was a room to which he knew he would never return. There was nothing that would identify him easily, and his few clothes were neatly stacked, the badge of the traveller who rarely stays long. Exercising for his standard ten minutes, he then indulged in a leisurely wet shave, taking care to find every tuft of stubble, and showered with vigour. He thought of Mungo and Will. The weekend had restored some of their closeness, and he wondered whether it would survive the events around them.

The trick was to make sure that nothing interfered with the openness they had rediscovered in the course of the family revelations; that it could survive the business that must be done. They could recover their intimacy without undoing everything that had made them who they were, each balancing the two lives that they cherished. He had his secrets, so had Will, and they were part of the brothers, as much as the texture of the old life Abel had been able to touch and savour at home, and which had moved him unexpectedly once again.

He was in Room 431 and passed Joe's resting place on the way to the lift, offering a silent promise to his friend.

Abel was wearing a tan summer suit and light green cotton shirt, carrying no bag. Passing through the narrow lobby he seemed a traveller bound for an easy morning walk, with nothing pressing on his mind. He picked up a *Times* from the old paper seller on the corner and walked to South Kensington tube station to find his way to Victoria. His mind turned to the man with whom he would have breakfast. They had shared some merry times over the years, but their meetings were rare. Abel enjoyed his humour and understood his ruthlessness, which was what had drawn them together and offered them both an opportunity. He was confident of his ground, although the two had not talked face to face for a year or two. So it went. In his mind, he sketched out the delicate message that he would compose afterwards, which would require Jackson Wherry's help.

Maria would be waiting. In his overnight message he had let her know his plans by using a name whose significance only she understood. In her phone call to send him on his way, she hadn't asked him to take care, nor played the controller with advice, only reminding him gently that this encounter might decide the game. It was now the pre-dawn hour in Washington, and Abel doubted that she would be sleeping.

From the underground at Victoria, he walked two hundred yards to the red-and-white brick fastness of one of the 1890s mansion blocks that cocooned Westminster Cathedral. He remembered Mungo and Aeneas as he passed the Catholic church, and paused near the steps. But he had a timetable. Knowing precisely where he was bound, he identified the building and the bell with no trouble. Easing past a housekeeper polishing the thick glass windows on the front door and wishing her good morning, he rose in a clattering brass cage to the third floor where he knew he would have an hour. They began, as they always did when they met, with talk of Maria.

'How's my favourite Irishwoman?'

'In the rudest health,' said Abel. 'Fighting the good fight.'

'Aren't we all?' They sat on either side of a table set in a window bay, with coffee and orange juice, some pastries and a banana lying on each of their side plates like imitation weapons with which they might fight a children's duel. They felt each other out, trying to judge the other's mood. 'Abel, you don't age,' his host said as they gossiped about government, elections, the people of politics and their foibles. An ambassador had been caught with his trousers down in Helsinki, a mutual friend in France had troubles that might be terminal. Abel learned little, but wasn't pressing.

After a little while, he laid his wares on the table. 'I wanted to see you alone, and here, because I have information to pass on. It will be useful to you, I hope, in the way that you've often helped me. Your people must learn about this. They need to know, but indirectly. That's why I wanted to come here. You know I don't often ask.'

The reply was quick. 'Does it affect me directly?' Nothing else. Abel had expected it, because he knew his man.

'Maybe, but I can't know. That's a matter for you. Let me tell it in my own way. There is a guy from Washington whom I have no reason to believe you have met. He's in town – or may be coming, I'm not sure – and I think he may contact you. You need to know that if he has done that, or is about to, it's not at my request.' Abel was alert for the slightest symptom of discomfort. There was none, only a hungry look.

'Has anyone tried to reach you, privately, in the last few days? I'll tell you why in a moment. Any American, using any name? A phone call to the office? An intermediary trying to arrange a meeting with you? A mention of my name, perhaps. Someone hanging around here, even?'

The answer was emphatic. 'No.'

'You're sure?'

'Yes.'

Abel painted a picture of Joe, stripped of any glamour and even his name. There was enough to establish the importance of the episode, but not enough to adorn it with too much significance. He couched it in the context of Joe's psychology, making it a mystery and not a thesis. 'He has some knowledge that your people don't have, but would benefit from.' Abel, the agent of generosity. There was no mention of Joe's death; he might have been cavorting down Victoria Street outside the flat for all Abel's companion knew.

As he spoke, Abel was unable to resist the thought that his brother would have admired him at that moment.

The relationship between the two men at the breakfast table was marked by bursts of obvious camaraderie, because of the stakes for which they played, and moments of calm in which they appeared to be probing each other. His host disappeared to the small kitchen to make another pot of coffee, and broke the flow with some gossip while he was on his feet: a chance to draw breath. He spoke of summer storms and febrile parliamentarians. A shrinking budget and angry unions. A jumpy press. Back at the table, they resumed, in the more serious mood they had both adopted simultaneously, knowing that the purpose of the encounter must be revealed.

'We think a little storm is coming your way, building up,' Abel said. He thought of Maria's hurricane and how much more danger it posed than his friend could know. 'It's a very British one, if I may say so. Sex.'

His friend leaned back and sighed, 'Carry on. I can't wait.' They laughed together.

'It's old, but alive. There is talk in Washington of an affair that has sprung back to life after years. No names for you, because I don't have them, but there's a suggestion – no more – that it touches your government at its heart.' He continued for five full minutes, mingling the few facts that poor Joe had carried to his death with a few speculations of his own to muddy the waters. When he finished, satisfied that he'd spun a beguiling yarn, he said, 'I'm telling you this because we've exchanged a few favours over the years' – his friend smiled – 'and I think this is one where I can help you. I don't expect to hear any more about it, incidentally, because it's not my business. For what it's worth, it's all yours.' A gift.

Across the table, he detected relish and amusement. No agitation, but the beginning of excitement.

Abel knew these moments well. He had planned to get one question answered on his visit, and one alone, after he had handed over his polished gemstone, and took the temperature to decide when was the right moment to cast his fly. After nearly an hour, his story told and some mild gossip offered in return, he moved.

'One of you is coming to Washington, we know. Is it you?'

His directness was evidently no surprise. But the answer had a regretful tone. 'As things stand, seemingly not. But the deal isn't done. You never know. Will Flemyng's in the frame, I hear. Not what he wants, and I know there are those who'll do their best to stop him if it's in the works. Maybe they're busy already. Can't quite believe in Flemyng myself – you do know him, don't you?' Abel shrugged. 'I'm still trying as best I can. I may still be in play. Just.'

'Good luck,' said Abel, leaning in close. 'It would be fun, wouldn't it?'

'Pity you can't help,' was the response. It was almost pleading.

'Wrong government,' said Abel. They both laughed, and it was time to go.

They parted at the lift, his host raising an arm in farewell as the grille clanked shut and the cage slipped down.

Abel noticed outside, as he walked towards the station, a government car drawing up outside the door of the block he had just left. Just made it, he thought. Like Lawrence, all the drivers were on time.

TWENTY-ONE

'Time to tell?'

Francesca's first words, when he'd arrived home from Paul's office after midnight, but they had agreed that he needn't begin his story until the morning, and she'd made the offer of a drink instead. A peace offering. They opened the garden windows and sat outside, enjoying the lingering warmth and speaking quietly in the dark. She talked of the coming end-of-season performances at the opera house, their plans for Scotland in August, and there was no politics, save mention of a phone call that afternoon to her from Jonathan Ruskin. 'Nothing to bother you with if you were late, he said. We had a long gossip. Fun, as usual. But poor Harry Sorley's in a mess, Jonathan says. Wife in meltdown.' Then she steered away again, knowing that Flemyng might begin to sink into a troubled mood again. 'Let's carve out some time together next weekend. OK?'

He said he would.

'I'm still a little angry.'

'I know.'

They went to bed, each aware that the morning would bring revelation. As the night took hold she was aware that he was awake, and didn't say a word. Then, around two o'clock, the phone rang. Flemyng was out of bed and downstairs as if he had been waiting for the call. Francesca lay still, wondering if she should go to the stairs in the hope of hearing something. She resisted when she heard him close the living room door.

Flemyng, sitting in the corner by the front window near his bookcase, was speaking quietly. Picking up the receiver, he had heard a voice from long ago. 'Old friend,' it said, in English. 'Thank you for thinking of me at a difficult time.'

They spoke for fifteen minutes. As the conversation ended, Flemyng said, 'I'm so sorry.'

Upstairs, he told Francesca that he couldn't discuss the call, only that it was business. She understood, she said, and they tried to sleep.

When they were awake, just after six, and lying in the bright light that streamed through the window, he accepted that the time had come.

'I'm going to start with home,' he said. 'The business that Mungo wrote to me about is more complicated than I'd thought. Terribly simple, too. Our mother had an affair for years and years. He was an American, and we don't know when it started, which means there may be a lot we don't know about ourselves.' There it was.

She put an arm round him. 'My poor Will.'

He rolled over in bed to face her. 'But that's not why I've been so down. In fact, it's lifted me up in a strange kind of way. I'm awake again. You've noticed how I've been, haven't you?'

She laughed at him for the first time in days. 'Noticed? I've never known you like you've been in the last two or three weeks. I think it's only fair that I hear why. I've been worried silly. So, please, tell me.'

'It's a puzzle, but I'll try to explain it,' he said. 'And I'll give you one word to start with, the one you heard at the opera house. Berlin. It's a good beginning, because that's the strangest place I know. You've never been, and I've never explained properly what it feels like – frozen in time but still the most unstable thing you'll ever touch.' He spoke of a place boiling with politics and intrigue, never stopping, not just the wall and the wire and the scars, armies staring each other down, the thumping hangover of unsettled business. 'All of us saying we want it to come to an end, although most of the time we believe it never will, and feeling relief because we can't imagine anything else. We don't like the unknown, but we should.'

He turned to face her. 'Something has happened there that's causing troubles. I feel them all around, but I don't know how they began. I want an inkling of the kind of trouble it might be. The other problem is that Paul wants me to stop the convulsions – but he can't tell me what he knows. Just as I can't tell him everything.'

'Why not?' she asked.

'Because I know there's personal stuff going on in the government that could rip us all apart. Politics, I mean, not you and me. And I'm scared to tell him what I've found out. He's got enough to worry about without me dumping another crisis on his doorstep.'

'And why doesn't he level with you?'

'Because he's as scared as I am, for a different reason.'

'Give me a clue.'

'Survival.'

'There's something else, isn't there?' she said.

'Things I can't say. A death. Troubles with Washington that feed on themselves. But there is something that'll make you happy. I should have told you sooner. Abel's here.'

She didn't smile. 'Why?'

'He's in the middle of it, with me. And I can't work out how, or why. We love each other, but there are limits we've set for each other, I suppose. Things we can't say.'

They lay quiet for a while, and she realized that she could hardly hear him breathing. Eventually, she said, 'You're worried because you think all this stuff is connected and you can't understand how. But you know it is. That's what's stirring you up. It's obvious.'

'Of course.'

'You said you were lifted up by the Mungo business. Why?'

'Because he was right about something he said about Mother. That this other side of her life was what made her what she was to us. So we should be glad, and even grateful. A generous observation.'

'Will, I think that tells you something.'

He got out of bed to pour two glasses of water. 'Go on.'

'That when you talk about politics, events, deals and all the rest of the stuff, you and the gang forget that emotion drives your world too. It's not a machine that sometimes gets out of kilter, it's run by people. They're moved by feelings, deep ones, mostly hidden. The most interesting ones are. Mungo's letting you understand your family better, painful though it is. That's because he's discovered what made it function. An accident, but he's got to the core.'

Flemyng said, 'The heart of things.' He stopped talking for a while, then said, 'I'm going to ask you a favour, darling. Let's leave it there. I want to think for a while. Let me go into the garden on my own, before Lawrence picks me up. OK?'

'Of course.'

'Thank you.'

*

An hour later, Flemyng's office day began with a silent acknowledgement between him and Lucy that nothing had happened at
their midnight encounter. Nothing. She knew that he was
relieved that her advance had been declined. Declined. And
although she was sorry it had been made – she'd hardly slept
afterwards – she had decided that an apology would make it
worse. He was determined that office business should proceed
briskly, and she accepted it as the least awkward solution. They
went about their morning with a surface amiability, and in a
way that carried no hint of difficulty. It helped that his night-
time phone call was preoccupying him, and he knew that was
a story he couldn't share. As for Lucy, they'd simply try to
forget what might have happened. There would be no gossip, no
oily trace of trouble for the office to sniff and savour. She
compared it in her mind to the placid political landscape that
had become the happy talk of government, at least among those
outside Flemyng's circle – an end of term drawing to its close
with fewer alarms than usual, Sorley's coming climbdown so
exquisitely leaked to the Monday papers that its sting was
already drawn. She marvelled because they knew the truth:
that the calm was one of the greatest illusions they'd known.

He had a pile of papers to get through and four meetings
that consumed three hours. Just before noon he crossed the
street to Paul's office, leaving Lucy behind.

Gwilym was managing the coffee cups. Paul picked up a
file. 'This is a summary of the post-mortem report that has
come from Osterley. Naturally, I haven't seen the original.' He
managed a smile. 'After all, it has nothing to do with any of us.'

Nonetheless, his hand shook as he read the report. Post-
mortems on dead spooks should have nothing to do with him.

However, he said that they could be sure that, despite every
tribulation, one blessing had come their way. This was a death

whose cause was known, beyond doubt. He gathered strength from that fact. 'Let's remember, just because an event is odd and shocking, it doesn't mean that we have to fall apart. There is every reason not to.'

Manson's death seemed straightforward enough, despite the circumstances. A heavy overdose, a mixture of unmentionable things that were familiar to the medics, and had guaranteed that some day, it just happened to be last Thursday, he'd come to a horrible end. 'There is evidence of prolonged abuse. He's almost certainly had previous seizures, probably a while back. Interestingly enough, they don't think he'd used needles before. They're surprised, but apparently that's often how it goes. You can't tell when they'll try something new. He's been on and off the stuff for years – every cocktail you can imagine. From our point of view, that's good news, if you see what I mean. It may have been an unnatural death in one sense, but it will not warrant, in official minds, a criminal investigation. As far as we can tell at this stage.'

Paul would be cautious to the end, Flemyng thought, until the last trump sounded.

'Where he got it, and when, we don't know. In the depths of Wednesday night, it's assumed. They always know the places to go. In the little envelopes found in his room there was enough for our people to know what he'd taken. With some extra ingredients in the syringe, they say, for luck. Not good at all, obviously.'

They all leaned back. Flemyng noticed that Paul was tensing up again.

'That, I suppose, counts as the good news.'

Now for the rest. Paul first.

'You will remember that we had some bits and pieces here, produced by our friend Osterley. The notebook and the papers.

This is considerably trickier, and not good news at all, I'm afraid.'

Flemyng was stiffening, absorbing the alarm that he could see had settled in Paul so that it had become something like a permanent state. He watched as Paul picked up a blue file, the one that had remained unopened the night before.

'Think about the message, *Friend Flemying knows*. I imagine you've been trying to work it out.'

'You could say that,' Flemyng said.

'Any thoughts?'

'I wonder if "knows" is a more important word than "friend".' He left it there.

'Our people have been quite busy, and productive,' Paul said. There were some American numbers listed in Manson's notebook, and they had been traced. 'I may say more about those later,' he said. But first there was one page of the notebook in which Manson had used a crude code to conceal four numbers, jumbling them up with a formula that various clever people – Paul's phrase – had been able to crack easily.

'If I were in a flippant mood I would ask you to guess those numbers,' he said. 'They are in addition to Brieve's, which was written without a code on another page.'

'Here we go again,' said Flemyng. 'Forbes, Ruskin, Sorley, and me.'

Paul spread his hands in a gesture of congratulation. Not difficult to win the prize. He said, 'Back to our questions. Whose friend am I supposed to be? And what am I supposed to know?'

Paul made a small gesture of understanding. He said he could not have given an answer to that question the night before, which was why he had decided to keep the blue file's contents to himself, but light was beginning to dawn. 'Not that it will help us. At least, not if we want this to get easier.'

He waved an arm as if to settle them down for a long story. His listeners saw a change in him. Flemyng thought his voice took on a distant quality; and he noticed that Gwilym, for the first time since the start of the crisis, appeared expectant. His political senses had quickened again, aware that the game was approaching a climax. 'I have a very strange tale to tell,' Paul began.

Flemyng was in the wide chair by the window, with Gwilym on the other side of the room. He had one hand on his scar, massaging it through his light blue shirt. Anyone might have thought it an absent-minded gesture; but in the last few moments he had felt his concentration kick in, the old gear change he loved. He knew for a certainty that the end game was beginning.

And Paul delivered.

A couple of hours before they arrived in his office, he said, he'd had a visit in that very room from one of their colleagues. 'Out of the blue.'

'A colleague?' said Flemyng.

'That is an accurate description,' said Paul, giving no more.

He said he had been surprised by his visitor, because the person concerned had no troublesome business that might bring him to the cabinet office at that hour, let alone into Paul's sanctum. Usual end-of-term arguments flying around Whitehall, but nothing out of the ordinary. There had been no trouble in the air, no warning of an urgent meeting. He had simply arrived.

Unusually, his visitor had used the underground passage in Whitehall that was a useful back way into the office for avoiding prying eyes, or cameras. They had been alone in his room and, said Paul, he had been told an extraordinary story.

'My problem, as you will learn in a moment, is whether to believe this. I have no reason not to. On the other hand, if I do believe it, I'm aware of the consequences. I have no choice about whether this complicates matters or makes them easier. I can't pretend I didn't hear it. The first thing is, I couldn't send him away. I had to listen. So do you.'

Paul cupped his hands behind his head, and looked upwards.

'Our colleague has been told – he wouldn't say how it came to him, but he was determined that I should hear, so I didn't waste time with questions – that there has been American… concern… about someone in this government. He wasn't clear whether it was a minister or an official somewhere around here who was the source, but someone of substance, and considerable alarm.

'He had no name for me, and I wasn't going to get into a guessing game, for reasons that will become apparent to you – or maybe they are already.' He looked up at Flemyng. 'When he began, I realized that I should let him talk. Whether he was speaking the truth or not, he had to get it out.

'According to him, it would be wrong to say this worry is about security as we usually think of it. More accurate to call it personal. But sadly, we may not be able to separate the two. Given what we have been discussing these last few days, that will not surprise you. I did feel, I should say, as if I was being patronized just a little. But never mind.

'He has learned, from his own source, or sources, why Manson came to London.'

Gwilym leaned forward at the words. Flemyng was perfectly still.

'But – and this is very important, and helpful to us I think – he knows nothing about Manson's demise, unless he is a better actor than I can imagine. I am fairly certain he does not even know Manson's name. I need hardly say what a relief that is. I was able to play the daft laddie up to a point – thank the good Lord, I didn't let anything slip too soon – and it was clear that he knew only that there might be someone poking around who was interested in what Manson was interested in, if you follow me. He was also given no indication by me that I had heard anything about such a person. We might have been talking about a ghost.'

The story the visitor brought with him was clear enough, said Paul, and appalling.

There was a sexual accusation, private at the moment, but potentially public and embarrassing, not only to the individual involved, but to the government as a whole. 'Catastrophic' had been the colleague's word.

'Not to put too fine a point on it, the story is about a rape. Apparently – as with all these stories – the truth would be more or less impossible to establish, but the evidence would be a sensation, and that's all that matters. The aggressor was someone in this government. There was a child – a young man now – and it all happened about twenty years ago, or a little more. Ancient history, but come back to haunt us.'

Flemyng brought to mind the travel itineraries that Paul had produced the night before, still lying in his beige file. It was a natural connection for him; Gwilym would just have to catch up.

'I repeat. He has no idea against whom this accusation is being made, or might be made. None. Doesn't know whether it has already been made, or has yet to happen. He is not working to our timetable, I'm glad to say.

'But he said he did know that some person of an intelligence kind' – a strangely touching phrase to Flemyng's ears – 'might be dispatched, or perhaps had been sent already, to dig around in London, and that I needed to know, as well as your old friends across the river, Will. I have no doubt that he has passed it in that direction too, as a matter of duty.

'And that was the sum total of the story. I expressed natural concern, thanked him with some warmth, said I would make my own enquiries, established that he understood the sensitivities, would swear silence, and he left. Whether he will respect that request or not, I'm afraid I can't say.'

Paul said he had been struck by his visitor's sobriety, untouched by any skittishness or relish. His mood had been serious, even dark, and there had not been one sardonic note in the conversation.

'It fits,' he said. And turning his hands out, palms upward he said, 'Agreed?'

Flemyng looked out to Horseguards Parade and the park beyond, knowing that he was at the point at which all pretence vanished, the curtains were drawn back and they gazed on the ugly truth that lay before them, the knowledge that there was no escape from a man-to-man confrontation with someone as yet unknown, with consequences that were uncertain but fraught with menace.

'So, in a way, it's an affair of the heart,' he said. 'The whole business.'

Paul said, 'I think we are clear where we now stand,' as if absorbing his thought. 'Manson had these numbers in his notebook for a purpose. He had taken steps to get them in the hours before he left Washington. He also made a note of your name separately – *Friend Flemyng knows* – and carried your phone number in his pocket.

'The information I have just received fits all that. We know that Manson rang Tom Brieve, though he didn't manage to speak to him directly. At least on that occasion. He may have made calls to others, too. He had a purpose, after all, and didn't come here by accident.' Realizing what he had said, he stopped, as if making a silent apology to Joe's shade.

'Will, this may be the most awkward question I have ever had to ask anyone in your position. You see my difficulty. We have been given a glimpse of Manson's mission, and names. One of them is yours.'

Flemyng said that he quite understood, but he could be clear. There was nothing in his past that would fit the story. Nothing. 'I realize you know how often I've travelled across the pond over the years' – he remembered Manson's records, carefully annotated – 'and I don't know about the others on that list. You'll just have to take my word. It isn't me.'

He looked at them both, smiling for the first time since Paul began speaking. 'You do believe me?'

Paul said that he had already come to that conclusion, although he had been obliged to think it through in the course of the preceding hour after the departure of his visitor. 'I do think I know you well enough, but I've been surprised so often in this office.'

Flemyng's behaviour when he'd seen the travel logs in the file, Paul had decided, simply didn't match the reaction of someone carrying that kind of burden. A guilty man would have cracked.

'But there is something in those lists, and we have to find it.' Paul was on his feet again, trying to follow a story that was moving too fast. His hands clutched at the air, trying to grasp the invisible.

'I suspect the reason Manson leaped on a plane wasn't because somebody here was going to be embarrassed. That happens all the time, as we know, and Washington wouldn't care at all. It was because of something we had decided to do – the way we're playing the game. That must have been the reason for the hurry. There are complicating matters of another kind as well.' He glanced at Flemyng.

'Let's start with them. It was planned – until this morning – that this week a new ambassador was going to be named for Washington. It hasn't been finalized – won't be until the big chiefs get back from Paris – but I can tell you that in all probability it is one of the names on that list. Well, let's forget probably. A final choice, I should say, has not – I repeat not – been made.'

He caught Flemyng's eye, and even Gwilym noticed the depth of the glance.

'That's obviously on hold now, but remember this. The embassy was not mentioned to me by my unexpected visitor this morning. He made no connection with the appointment of an ambassador. Didn't suggest the link.'

Flemyng muttered, 'Very clever,' and Paul heard him.

The problem was, said Paul, that if they were connected in some way, disaster beckoned.

'Well,' said Flemyng, 'you have to talk to everyone. I'm spoken for, I hope. Brieve's not far away, unless he's left for Paris. Forbes, I assume, is over the road in his office. Sorley? Is Jonathan in the building?'

Paul shook his head. 'He's just left for Oxford to make a speech. The reason I'm smiling is that I've read the advance text. It's all about the calm that's descended on the government.'

He couldn't help a nervous laugh. 'He's promoting a new phrase, ahead of Paris. He calls it "The Politics of Optimism". '

Gwilym had found himself in recent hours retreating to his schooldays, his natural escapist trick at moments of crisis, and had slipped easily out of the moment. 'I've got a better title,' he said. '*Sunt Lacrimae Rerum.*'

'*The Aeneid,*' he continued, into the silence that followed.

Paul and Flemyng waited for more. 'Aeneas is crying, it's quite a moment. I'm a great one for loose translations, and there's an especially good one – *the tears of all the world.*'

Flemyng, one hand stroking his cheek, said that Gwilym probably remembered the rest of the line, and smiled at him as he gave it.

'*Our mortality cuts to the heart.*'

TWENTY-TWO

The brothers would meet in the afternoon. Mungo had sent word around that he might be something of a minor star at the *Tablet* summer party, which happily coincided with the weekly's publication of his account of the eighteenth-century Flemyngs, their bloody travails and the adventures of their first descendants. At the party the brothers would arrange their dinner plans for the next night. So in the little clusters of guests that came both ways along Pall Mall and up the steep steps of the Travellers' Club, Flemyng and Abel made separate appearances, one having walked through the teatime crowds in the park and the other dropped off by cab. They climbed the stairs to the library, about ten minutes apart, and found Mungo in his element, framed by bookshelves and warm leather chairs, a few shafts of evening sunshine illuminating a cheerful tableau.

Abel watched his brothers together – tossed into uncertainty, imagining that they might be loosened by an accident of birth from the family they'd thought was theirs, but beaming, and feeding happily on the energy generated by their crisis. Abel was still able to picture himself as an observer of the scene, and smiled at the eldest brother, in his element: it proved Mungo was one of them, after all. At the centre of the crowd, and glowing.

For Flemyng, order was being restored for a moment. He moved and spoke easily, comfortable with the choreography of party talk. There was a mixture of Catholic grandees, a good sprinkling of pick-and-mix hangers-on who were limbering up for the French embassy garden soirée a little later, and a couple of wizened and talkative priests, stooped and smiling, one of them wearing, to Flemyng's amusement, a soup-plate hat of the kind he thought the Vatican had long since banned. They held court in a corner like two presiding aunts at a family funeral, sizing up the crowd, watching for an exciting social *faux pas*, and willing the tide of gossip to lap around them.

Abel hugged Mungo with a warmth that was evident to everyone. He whispered in his brother's ear, 'Can't wait to talk some more.'

Mungo's article in the latest issue was passed around and admired for its story-telling. Abel scanned it. 'There are parts I still can't get. You'll have to explain – at greater length.' He waved the magazine. Mungo roared with laughter. 'And keep the family story going,' said Abel. 'Will you put sex in the next one?' And raised his eyes.

At that Mungo heaved another laugh and, to Abel's astonishment, winked.

They were interrupted. A figure emerged from the crowd that had swarmed to the high open windows to catch the air, and took Mungo's hand. 'May I introduce myself? I admire your piece very much, and I'm also new on the *Tablet* advisory board so I'll be seeing a bit of you. They pull us in, from wherever they can. I'm Archie Chester.' They began to talk.

Standing just within earshot, Flemyng was more startled than anyone noticed. The atmosphere in the room had not changed – the heat was high, the conversation loud and rising. Trays of drinks were being ferried from corner to corner at increasing speed, but Abel alone spotted the change in him. Perhaps he recognized the shiver of excitement that passed through his brother: Flemyng himself gave no outward sign, except that he took himself into a corner to gather his thoughts before the conversation that was now inevitable. Standing behind a pillar near an old revolving globe and a table piled high with nineteenth-century travelogues, he made cheerful conversation with a civil servant whom he knew and a couple of journalists. He was playing for time.

To almost everyone around him, nothing seemed to have changed, although Flemyng had just been visited by the first piece of luck to come his way since the affair began. For him, it might be the turning point. He became more talkative, brightened a little more, seemed to become a bigger figure in the crowd. His eyes were dancing. With Abel following every move, he detached himself after a few minutes from the conversation and set a course for the opposite corner of the library. Rounding a pillar, he approached his target and they faced each other.

The figure standing with Mungo turned his head. He was jovial, sported a loosely knotted purple bow tie at his neck and, although he was quite tall, seemed spherical. Points of light danced on the high planes of his cheeks, and his bald dome made him look older than he was. It was surrounded by a fringe of rich white hair. He put out his hand and lowered his head. It gleamed.

'Mr Flemyng – the third of the evening! Delighted to meet you. Archie Chester's my name.' Abel could see no sign that they had met before. He did not catch the words, but noted the warmth of his brother's greeting.

'You wrote me a note,' said Chester, dropping his voice and moving out of the crowd in an easy fashion, with one hand placed lightly in the small of Flemyng's back. Abel could hear nothing from where he stood. They slipped easily away from the others, and Chester came close to Will. He spoke quietly, and his warm brown eyes were hypnotic. 'In quite a hurry, if I may say so, or that's how it looked to me, and with an accompanying letter. Would you like to talk?'

'Shall we step outside for a moment?'

'Good idea.' Chester gestured to the door and followed him out.

They stood at the top of the grand staircase leading up from the lobby, and moved along the corridor to be alone. A copy of a classical statue looked down, offering to strew grapes on them. 'Before we speak,' said Chester, 'let me give you my card.'

Archie Chester
Consultant Psychiatrist
6 Mansfield Mews
London W1A 2XL

'I should explain my presence. I've been recruited to the advisory board of the magazine, as perhaps you heard over there, because it's an enthusiasm of mine. A Catholic cabal, of course.' He beamed. 'I've read your brother's piece this week and like it very much. He's fascinating about your family, you know. Where you spring from, how you came to be what you are.' His eyes were widening as he spoke.

'I suppose I should be grateful for that,' said Flemyng. 'Happy chance.' He smiled. 'I suspect we are very fortunate to have met like this. To be honest, it gets me out of the awkwardness of ringing you up.'

There was a moment of silence. Chester was waiting.

'Should I explain things?' said Flemyng.

'If you are happy to speak here, by all means go ahead.'

He began. 'I sent you a copy of a letter, with my own note attached, because I got the chance. In that sense it wasn't a plan – I just took advantage of an opportunity that presented itself. I used the good offices of a friend in government service who is familiar with your consulting rooms. I hope this doesn't sound too convoluted.' Chester said that, on the contrary, he found it admirably clear.

'My purpose was simple. I wanted an opinion on this letter, because I had come to the conclusion that it was important, and dangerous. I went to Mansfield Mews to meet my friend whom I knew to have visited you before, and asked him to be my messenger because I'm afraid I didn't want to deliver it personally. I take it you understand my nervousness.' He was still smiling.

'Very well indeed,' Chester said. 'Carry on.'

'I am sorry I haven't been in touch since. I've been held up by other matters. Much is going on.' Chester acknowledged the explanation with a wave of his hand. Flemyng said that he had also been in Mansfield Mews the day before the delivery of the letter, and was deliberately precise, underlining the point. 'That was on Thursday, just after mid-day.' He stopped, apparently to invite a response.

Chester's expression was hard to read. He spoke without changing expression. 'You know something of my history, then?'

Flemyng said he knew from friends in government that Chester was trusted as a man of medicine whose discretion was absolute and who had proved useful in many delicate cases, with those needing help of the most discreet kind. 'I'm told you have done the state some service, if I may put it like that.'

Chester said, 'That's true, I suppose. It doesn't mean I'm any good, of course, just useful.' His smile broadened, and he added, 'I'm interested in your reference to the day before you had the letter delivered – the Thursday. Why do you stress that? And what brought you to my front door, so to speak, in the first place.'

Flemyng said, 'I had a rendezvous with my friend there on Thursday' – he'd keep Sam's name out of the conversation – 'and when we arranged another meeting the next day at the same spot, I realized that I could have the letter delivered by him. So I made a copy for you.'

'What you mean is you planned it that way,' said Chester. 'Let's go back to Thursday. That seems to be just as important to you, and I'm intrigued. Why?'

Flemyng didn't pause before he answered. He was in his stride. 'I left the street – after the first meeting with my friend – when I realized there was probably someone in your office whom I didn't want to meet. A government car was waiting outside.'

'I see. That's not an uncommon experience. You'd be surprised.' He spoke to Flemyng now as if they were old acquaintances. 'I realized from your note that you were disturbed. Fearful, I would say.'

Then he added, 'And has that feeling lessened?'

'Quite the reverse.'

'In that case, please come if you feel it would help. I'm always available.' Chester turned side-on so that his next words could be whispered. 'I should say, although this is neither the time nor the place, that you did the right thing in seeking advice – and rather ingeniously, if I may say so. I have no doubt about that. The letter is disturbing, and very curious. Revealing, to me. We must talk properly, and soon.'

Flemyng's gaze encouraged him to say more. 'You wouldn't

have sent this to me in the way that you did, leaving me to speculate on its origin, unless you felt that it was important to the life of one of your friends or colleagues in government. May I assume that?'

'Of course,' said Flemyng. 'And there's the question of time. Urgency.'

'Quite,' said Chester. 'I remember a phrase – was it the penultimate line of the letter? – "*We may not have long*". That did alarm me a good deal.'

Flemyng was expectant now, but Chester drew back, reasserting a professional distance. 'Now let me go and say farewell to your brother. I look forward to our next meeting. You have a most interesting family, by the way. The historical piece makes that clear. Quite an inheritance. You have my card. We'll talk, and soon, I hope, because I do think it's really quite important. If it helps, remember I can come to you.'

Flemyng stayed outside the party for a few minutes more and composed himself, although he was used to the lightning speed of such exchanges. He was alone at the top of the stairs, having said goodbye to a couple of departing friends who were taking the evening at a placid pace, when the hall porter approached from below. 'Mr Flemyng, sir, a message for you. Please ring Mr Jenner in his office as soon as you can. Thank you, sir.'

He went to say goodbye to his hosts and his brothers and gave Archie Chester a wave. The priests were still in the corner, reddened with refreshment and their eyes flickering across the crowd. They gave him separate little bows as he passed.

He took the stairs quickly and rang Paul's secretary from the porter's lodge and then Lucy, still at her desk. 'Do me a favour, please. There's an envelope in my desk drawer with "Private" written on it. It's the letter. Could you bring it down and meet me in the courtyard in ten minutes? I'm on my way to Paul's. Thanks.'

As he turned the corner at the Athenaeum, he could still hear from the first-floor windows the party enlivening the night air, and could have sworn he heard Mungo laugh.

*

Flemyng knew as he walked alone across Downing Street, with the letter in his inside pocket, that it fitted with everything else that he had been discussing in Paul's office since the first strained meeting on Thursday. Some connections still eluded him, but he was confident that he would find them by the time the evening was over. Paul's summons was unusually abrupt: Flemyng suspected a development that couldn't wait.

Paul's office was still a place of shadows. Two standard lamps cast pools of light in opposite corners and his green desk light was dimmed. As Flemyng arrived Paul rose and, for almost the first time since the affair began, took his hand. 'Thank you, Will. I think we're nearly there.'

There was no Gwilym.

Paul began with his own feeling of frustration. Manson's death was a drug-induced accident, it was clear, but no one could establish his movements in London, his reason for visiting parliament and whether or not he was successful in contacting anyone in government. And if he was, what conversations he then had.

'But I have something for you,' said Flemyng, interrupting and patting his pocket.

The effect on Paul seemed disturbing rather than consoling, as if he had been hoping that the last awkwardness was passing away. He raised his eyebrows, but didn't smile. The unspoken instruction to Flemyng was to wait.

Back at his desk, he opened a red file and took out a single sheet of paper. 'Friend Osterley has done us a good turn. You'll remember that he found a desk clerk who'd spoken to Manson as he left the hotel on Wednesday evening. Well, Osterley's people checked the lines from the public phone boxes nearby. We have access to certain information about such lines, as you well know. The basics, no more. One was out of order, and Osterley established that no calls had been made from it for more than a week. The other, however, was clear as a bell, relatively speaking. Special Branch have identified all the numbers that were called from that phone on Wednesday evening. There weren't many.'

Flemyng waited as Paul's gaze settled on the sheet of paper in his hand, as if to make sure for a second or third time that he was not making a mistake.

'We have checked the numbers. Two of them are of interest. Only two.' Then, a statement that he tried to deliver with lightness: 'Yours is not one of them.'

Flemyng smiled, and his rush of relief was obvious.

'One is Sorley's. Dialled first, and the connection lasted for just about four minutes. So, time to talk.' Paul paused and allowed his eyes to meet Flemyng's.

'The other, to which the public phone box was connected for barely a minute, was Jonathan Ruskin's. Very short.'

Flemyng sensed a flow of adrenalin, a sharpening of his senses. 'Four minutes with Sorley? A proper conversation.'

'Yes,' said Paul. 'I haven't spoken to Harry yet, nor to Jonathan. He's coming back from Oxford after his speech about now, I gather. But it's obvious that we have to talk to them both. They're the only people we know who may have spoken to Manson, apart from his embassy friend. We assume he didn't try to ring you, and as yet there's no suggestion connecting him directly to Forbes. We'll speak to him, of course, but I propose to ask Harry and Jonathan to come here tomorrow morning. Tom Brieve we'll talk to again, though he's now in France. I'd like to sleep on it, and I'm sure you would.'

Flemyng put his hand in his inside pocket. Strengthened by the events of the past hour, he spoke confidently and without any hint of hesitation.

'Paul, I have something that you need to see. I've been keeping it back, but events have made it clear that it's part of this story in some way. I had once thought it separate, one element in a random collision of events. I should have known better from the start.

'I've never believed in coincidence in politics. And this is so disturbing that I can't separate it from our crisis. I've learned, I think, that this whole affair is driven by the heart.' Paul puckered his brow.

'Think of it as an exercise in fragility.'

As Flemyng placed the envelope on the desk, he reached for something else in the pocket of his blue suit. He pulled out a handkerchief, shook it, and from it tumbled the small piece of marble that he had picked up in the room where Joe Manson's body was discovered for the first time.

'And this is intriguing. I suggest you keep it in your desk. I'll explain tomorrow.'

He gestured to the envelope. 'Read what's inside.'

Like Lucy, Paul bent over the page, pressing it flat on his desk, and read slowly with concentration, seeming to cover each paragraph twice. After he'd finished, he stared at the letter without saying a word.

'Any thoughts?' said Flemyng.

'God Almighty,' Paul said. He looked up, then down again. 'I wonder which of them is more in need of help.'

'I agree.' Flemyng's face was a picture of relief.

'Who is this?' said Paul. 'I can't work anything out from the style and there's not a mark on the thing. You know, don't you?'

'Not for certain, but maybe. Forgive me, but I'll wait, because I must.'

Paul sat back in his chair and sighed, covering his eyes with his hands. 'This place should be run by psychiatrists, not civil servants. What am I supposed to think? People give up half their lives trying to get into public life, fighting elections till they drop, then spend the rest of their time enjoying the destruction they've visited on themselves. I'm not sure I can take this.'

Flemyng shook his head. 'We have to. I got a hint from Lucy that you're wondering why I've been preoccupied. Well, here's your answer. Madness is such a hateful word, but it haunts me. Because in these corridors – balanced and rational though we believe ourselves to be – there's madness on the loose. I knew it the moment I saw this letter, waiting to be signed and delivered. My guess is that it's one of many, probably sent to the same person, and they take us into the dark.

'Paul, we have to face the fact that he speaks here about being killed by this. Killed.'

'I share your alarm,' said Paul quickly.

'You asked me to think. I've come to one conclusion – that this is at the heart of things. How and why I don't know, but I've decided it must be. I'll be honest and say that this is instinctive rather than rational on my part, but I'm going with it.' Flemyng asked Paul to put the letter in his desk, and said they should turn to the Manson calls. Paul said the morning conversations would take place in his office, Sorley first, at ten, then Ruskin an hour later.

'We must realize that we could be dealing with a number of different stories here. A misunderstanding, an old friendship, an innocent request, a dead end. You name it. And let's not forget that you are still *Friend Flemyng* in the notebook, the man who knows something. But what does it mean?'

Flemyng laughed. 'We're used to that, aren't we? What's politics for, if it doesn't teach you to look both ways at once?'

They were more sombre as they shook hands, and parted. Flemyng watched Paul turn back to his desk, his shoulders dropping as if weighed down by an unseen burden. His last words were, 'Leave Forbes and Brieve to me.' His burdens alone.

*

Abel's next message to Maria was, for him, unusually long. He didn't send it until after midnight on the evening of the Travellers' party, when Flemyng was already in bed beside Francesca and Paul's office was dark, and the dispatch of the coded request and his account of the day's business, received by Maria with Fat Zak Annan squatting in his chair by her side, was the first act of the last day.

Wherry had been helpful. Communication was his trade, he said cheerily, and he stayed while Abel made his calls and composed his message securely without fear of disturbance. He took his time. Maria told him in a phone call that Barney Eustace had gone to New York the previous evening, as Abel had requested, and after she had spent a nervy few hours, had reported success. She would be waiting for Abel's full account of the London developments, but it was his show and he had as much time as he needed.

So he laid it out in careful paragraphs that said enough but not too much – his confidence that the proper connections were now being made, his brother's place at the centre of the affair, and his belief that in a few hours all the pieces would be in place because of his private visit that morning. Before sending his message, he made two short phone calls, speaking to an old friend to postpone a dinner he'd arranged for the next evening. He then placed a brief call to Poughkeepsie, New York. He saw no reason to alter his careful text as a consequence, and off it went to Maria by the secure means provided by Wherry, leaving Abel tired but ready for the exertions of the day ahead.

'Nightcap?' said Wherry, with a beaker of scotch at the ready.

'I will,' said Abel. They toasted the morrow, knowing that the reckoning had come at last.

TUESDAY

TWENTY-THREE

Flemyng slept, and dreamed of home. He was fishing on a boat tossed wildly on the loch, then running on the drove road so fast that he seemed to twist in a spiral across the eastern landscape. By contrast, at the same moment, he was watching the orrery move so slowly that it seemed as if the earth was refusing to spin. A kaleidoscope of colours from the woods and the hills sparkled and flashed in his eyes until he imagined himself blinking in pain. The house was bending to the wind, and the burn turned into a rushing river, spume rising from the rocks and water spreading across the land. Papers had been cast on the surface – files, letters, telegrams and torn pages – all swept along in a torrent until they disappeared in a whirlpool that seemed to draw him down. His eyes opened with a start, and he found himself in a sweat. He had been trembling, and took a few moments to find calm.

Did he wake or dream? He could see his mother in her studio, the muddle of easels turning it into an obstacle course of canvas and wood, her brushes scattered on the floor and her still-life arrangements giving the place the air of a deserted theatrical set. He watched her, big-boned and dark, long fingers working with the oils, her eyes alert for any change in the light.

As consciousness came, so memories crowded into his mind. He'd sometimes sit with her for an hour or more, and she'd speak of New England and the whole family that he knew from their summer laughs and adventures there, the rickety cabin on the lake that he remembered from the early days, why she had always loved the Atlantic breakers more than the silent woods, where she'd learned to paint, how she wanted the boys to share among themselves all her books and American things, and treasure them after she was gone. She'd read Lowell and Frost to him, and he still held them close.

She would stop painting for a few minutes, stand by the window, then come slowly back to the stool where she perched while she worked. Sometimes she'd sing quietly to herself, and Flemyng remembered days which he knew moved all three of her boys in different ways. Each kept his set of secrets, hidden as if they were locked away in jewelled boxes and placed in private corners of the house.

The light was coming, and he became aware of time. After a few minutes he was able to recall the shape of the day that was planned. His confidence had returned. Francesca breathed quietly alongside him, dead tired. He knew she was bearing the burden of his anxiety, and he promised himself that he would make amends. Quietly, he rose and prepared for the office.

He heard her ask softly if he was OK, then go back to sleep. He moved steadily through the house. Within fifteen minutes he was ready, his mind clear.

Sitting at his desk, he took a blank sheet of parliamentary notepaper, crested with the green portcullis. From outside, the dawn chorus was an accompaniment to his thoughts. He tried to write two lists of questions, one for himself and one for the meetings in Paul's office.

He had wrestled in the night with the search for the last link, and it eluded him still. He pictured the pieces of paper lying in

Paul's office – the travelogues, the newspaper and magazine cuttings, the timings of the phone calls, the letter itself. They made different patterns in his head, one springing to the fore and then another. He thought of the piece of marble, which had helped him, and from his pocket he pulled Archie Chester's card, placing it in front of him. Then for long minutes, he thought of his night-time phone conversation with an old friend to whom he had once thought he might never talk again.

For nearly half an hour, he tried to construct a list of questions on the notepaper. In the end, he had put a line through each of them, except one.

'*Whose pride?*' He underlined it.

Underneath, he wrote Sam's phrase, '*a surfeit of allies*'.

He reviewed his knowledge and realized again, with a twinge of guilt, that he had produced little new for Paul and that his own enlightenment had come from others. His instruction, however, had been to think. He stepped gently downstairs, opened the door from the kitchen and went outside. He sat on the swinging chair. The sun was rising over the house and his energy began to flow.

He considered the pieces of paper again, and Paul's concern, Lucy's advice about the letter, and his own gradual understanding of the importance of Archie Chester. He had to find an entry point, the chess player's line through the enemy ranks. He rose and paced the garden, turning at the back wall and retracing his steps in a straight line, then turning again. He made a symmetrical pattern on the grass. At its centre was Francesca and her reminder about his family, the revelation that Mungo had found unexpected meaning in his mother's double life – a justification, and a benefit.

Then, as if clouds were lifting slowly, a path opened up in front of him and led him on. He followed it, imagined Sam by his side, and thought of the emotional life of his trade, its importance and its violence. The frailty hidden in every public face.

For several minutes, he turned his thoughts upside down and back again. The pattern fell apart, then put itself together, each time in the same way. He must be right.

Slowly, enjoying his relief, he went inside and rang Paul, who'd be in the office, although it was not yet half-past six. He wouldn't be expecting the request, but Flemyng knew it would be accepted, eventually.

'Abel should be with us,' he said.

Paul hesitated at the other end of the line. 'You may be right, but spell it out. I need to be sure.'

Flemyng said that he wasn't suggesting that Abel should sit through the opening of the conversations that would start at ten, because Sorley and Ruskin would be justified in objecting. They were accused of nothing, and couldn't be subjected to questioning by a foreign official without decent warning, if at all. But there was another way, he said. If Abel could situate himself in the ante-room, in the domain of one of Paul's secretaries, he would be available if required. Flemyng said it might prove a useful addition to their armoury. He deliberately put it no higher. 'You never know,' he said. 'An extra hand to the pump, that's all.'

Agreed.

He rang Abel's hotel from the kitchen phone, knowing that his brother would be up and about. 'Today's the day, just like you said last night. We're going to do it the way I want, you and I together. Ready?'

They arranged to meet for breakfast.

*

They met in a café near the Abbey, Abel having taken the opportunity for a random stroll through Westminster, enjoying the knowledge that no one in the early crowds knew who he might be, why he was there, nor the troubles that had brought him into their midst. He enjoyed a peal of bells, the first noisy coughing of the rush hour, the promise of a clear, hot day with the clouds high. Buying two newspapers on the corner of Parliament Square, he walked towards the park. More cricket on the front pages than politics. Heatwave talk. Good.

Turning back to the square, he stopped at the Lincoln statue. Abel wondered if Joe had come that way, whether he had found what he was looking for, and what led to his desperate plunge at his moment of success, if that was how he'd seen it. He watched an official car appearing from New Palace Yard under Big Ben, then turned away. Five minutes later he was in a hole-in-the-corner café in Great Peter Street, squashed at a corner table with his brother at right angles to him and two strong teas in front of them.

Their conversation would have been inconsequential to any listener but it established, for them, the shape of the day. They looked beyond the morning encounter with Flemyng's colleagues – two and a half hours away – to more time with Mungo, and another trip home together. 'I dreamed about it,' Flemyng said, his face brightening. 'An escape mechanism, and a useful one.' Some of his fear had dispersed.

'I'm not surprised,' said Abel. 'You have to find a way of putting this out of your mind for a few hours. I couldn't. I spoke twice to Maria in the night. God knows what they're thinking at the hotel switchboard. She's antsy, as you'd expect.'

Flemyng said, 'Fill me in. When I knew her in Paris she was tough. Irresistible, but a bit scary. Always a step ahead.'

Abel spoke without hesitation about his dependence. 'She's a rock. I'll explain more later, maybe when we're home, but it all comes back to her. I need Maria – plenty people do – and she's got to be protected.' For the first time since they had sat down, Flemyng was aware of the weight on Abel's back. 'This means everything.'

When they left the café after thirty minutes or so, and set a course for Whitehall, they had the chance for some quiet, serious words. 'You always knew that this wasn't about an ambassador, didn't you?' said Abel.

'I assumed from the start that it was bigger.'

Abel said, 'You're right, and painfully so.'

Flemyng looked at him. 'I know our pride's involved. Yours too?'

After a pause, Abel said, 'And how. You know how we are… same as you but worse. You'll find out why. But you've got to get there on your own.'

Then they had to split up. The crowds were swelling on the pavements. Abel said he'd like to walk, clear his head. 'But I've got a suggestion about somewhere we might visit over lunchtime if our timetable holds.' When he explained where and why, his brother smiled and thanked him. 'Of course. I wouldn't have thought of it. Thanks.' Abel clasped his hands in a signal of satisfaction, raising them in a boxer's salute. First, Flemyng would spend an hour or so in his office, getting rid of as much paper as he could. They'd meet at the door to the cabinet office in Whitehall at a quarter to ten. Sorley would come first, and then Ruskin. Neither of them would know why.

'First time we've done this together, right?' said Abel.

'That hadn't occurred to me,' said his brother.

They exchanged a smile. For a few minutes they spoke of

how it might be done, played a few tactical games. Then, without warning, Abel turned into the crowd and was gone.

Flemyng walked through the courtyard to the corner door, and took the stairway up to his office. He asked Lucy to come in, and to shut the door behind her.

She spoke first. 'Please tell me more. Where is this leading?'

And for the first time in the crisis, he seemed to Lucy to deny her a glimpse into his thoughts. 'I can't, no. But it will soon be over. That's all.'

Turning away from her towards the window, and missing her expression of pain, he spoke as if to himself.

'Something struck me out there,' he said. 'I was in the square, then in Whitehall and the crowds. But nobody out there – not a single soul – has the slightest notion of what we've been living through. They haven't heard a whisper. It's odd, because this may turn out to be the most important day I've had in politics. Who knows?'

Lucy watched him from the back, said nothing.

'Here we are, with all this stuff.' He gestured to the towers of paper on his desk, the two red boxes on the floor with the files slipping out, the tray with the heap of telegrams, the phones that could connect him to anyone, anywhere. 'The people in the office. Our tower of Babel.

'And it's such a very private life.'

TWENTY-FOUR

Their preparations were nervous. Paul was groping for an anchor of normality. Having been introduced to Abel, he spoke with exaggerated formality as if he were trying to persuade the brothers that he was convening a meeting about budgets or appointments, not death.

'Let us remember,' he began, 'that we are dealing here with a demise brought on by a man's own weakness, and that it is a tragedy. Our concern for the other events with which Joe Manson found himself connected must not wipe that fact from our minds. We simply need to know whom he met, and why. We shall then know why he came, whether the story I have been given about a serious personal accusation is true, and whether or not it has any public implications or significance for us beyond the fact that it has occurred. There, our remit ends.'

Flemyng, sitting in the chair by the window which had become so familiar to him in recent days, knew that Paul feared he might no longer be able to keep order in an office where it was everything. As a consequence, he was desperate to set limits. Flemyng understood the alarm and felt its grip, but it was not unwelcome to him. Part of him had come to love the fear.

Abel, across the room, carried the air of sober relaxation that served him so well. Flemyng understood that his brother had knowledge that was denied to him and to Paul, and wondered whether it would emerge in the next few minutes. He watched Paul, whose eyes were on Abel, and tried to organize in his mind the questions that might take them to the next stage.

He found as he did so that in his mind's eye he could see Lucy reading the letter for the first time, hear her quiet in-breaths of astonishment. Several times in the past few days he had felt anger rising inside him at the cruelty he'd seen on the page; at this climactic moment he was able to keep it down. Panic would put everything at risk.

One of Paul's phones rang.

'This is a surprise,' they heard him say. He chewed a lip and fidgeted in his chair. 'How bad?' Abel glanced at his brother.

Paul was pulling at his neck, shaking his head. 'It's not good, but I suppose there's nothing we can do. Say I'll be in touch later today.' He dropped the phone into its cradle, seeming to resist at the last moment a temptation to slam it down.

'Sorley's office. Apparently he's in a desperate state. His wife has rung in, worried to death. Hasn't slept, she's given him some pills and refused to let him leave the house. We thought we'd managed the public climbdown on his bill pretty well – exceptionally so, I'd say, and he's bloody lucky – but it's hit him hard. So he's off parade this morning. I'll insist on seeing him this afternoon instead.'

Meanwhile, there was Ruskin in an hour. Paul said that while they waited he could pass on some more detail on the last sightings of Manson.

'We've been sweating the police who were on duty in the parliamentary precincts on Wednesday and Thursday and I have learned two things. The trouble is that security is such a shambles… You'd think with the bomb threats and so on they'd have got the point – security cameras or something. Maybe one day. But we do have some information.'

Abel was closer to him than Flemyng, and Paul chose to look him in the eye.

'Manson got into the building twice, once on Wednesday night, and again early on Thursday. He was seen by a duty officer at St Stephen's entrance who noticed the jeans, assumed he was a tourist and directed him to central lobby. The previous night he went through Westminster Hall – told the officer he was interested in the history of the place – and he could have ended up anywhere if he had his wits about him. He didn't mention an appointment, just ambled down the steps into the hall and wandered off.'

'Twice?' said Flemyng.

'Definitely,' Paul said. 'It was him. We got a picture from the embassy – after a bit of pressure, and a little trouble – and the officers identified him.'

Abel spoke briefly, and they broke up, allowing Paul to make some phone calls. 'You wouldn't believe that business goes on as usual, but it does. Treasury taking advantage of the heat again, and getting the Home Office into a state.'

When they came together again the clock was sounding eleven. 'Are we ready?' said Paul. 'Jonathan will be in the waiting room by now.' The brothers rose and Abel left with Flemyng to take up position in the outer office. Paul pressed an intercom button and asked his secretary to show Ruskin in through the other door.

As he came in, Paul stood to greet him quite formally, and that was enough to establish the atmosphere.

'Jonathan, please sit down. I'm sorry for the urgency but we do need to talk. It's a matter that we'll discuss with several others, too, in the coming days. You're the first, that's all. On hand as ever, and we're very grateful.'

'Sure. Always ready.' Ruskin was smiling, shrugging, his long body loose and relaxed. Then he said, 'We?'

Paul ignored the question. Ruskin had placed his briefcase on the floor, and loosened his green woollen tie, turning away for a moment to hang his light grey suit jacket on the coatstand beside the bookshelves.

'What's up?' he said, folding himself into the chair facing the desk. 'Need some help?' He rested his hands firmly on its arms and leaned forward in his listening pose, body inclined slightly to one side. He wore a dazzling white shirt, and his hair was shining and perfectly groomed.

Paul used words designed to hit him amidships, because he had to see how he reacted. Any other way and he might be lost. 'Jonathan, this is personal.' For a public man, the dread phrase.

It was a test, but there was no sign of fear.

Paul was measured and gave no sign of agitation, although before the questions began he had reminded himself of the weakness of his position. They knew of a short phone call to Ruskin, nothing more: no evidence that he had spoken to Manson or met him, nothing that suggested contact had been made. There was nothing from fingerprints at the scene where the body had first been discovered. Osterley had confirmed as much, having taken a set from the desk in Ruskin's office on Sunday evening. He had done the same operation in the offices of Brieve, Forbes, Sorley and Flemyng, with Paul's reluctant blessing and without their knowledge. Nothing. They might as well have been on different continents when Joe Manson laid his last tracks on the earth. Yet this was bound to have the flavour of an interrogation.

Paul was flying half blind, with no vision of what lay behind the next bend. He knew for all but a certainty that Manson had phoned Ruskin's number from a box near the Lorimer and that the call had lasted for only a minute or so. No more. Paul was full of jitters, but showed nothing.

He said that he was going to ask a simple question, the significance of which would have to be taken on trust. Ruskin nodded, but his candid blue eyes conveyed mystification. 'Carry on.'

'Did you meet an American called Manson last week? Thursday, perhaps. He may have used another name. McKinley.'

Ruskin smiled, and put one hand straight out towards Paul, palm upwards, expressing surprise and also giving the impression of being the bearer of a gift. 'D'you know, that's just about the last question I was expecting.'

He unfolded himself from the chair and went over to the window, saying over his shoulder? 'May I have some water?'

Paul poured a glass.

'We know he rang you,' he said, and added softly, 'I'm sorry.'

Ruskin spun round. 'Sorry?' His voice had tightened. 'Paul, have I been watched or something? Get it out. What's going on?' The first sign of anger.

But, to Paul's astonishment, his rising irritation was controlled in an instant, and Ruskin slipped back into his customary fluency as if his anger hadn't shown. The music was back in his voice. Walking from the window towards Paul, he said, 'I did meet him, as a matter of fact. It was very strange, and unpleasant. He was an odd man, and I'll tell you the whole story. But why do you ask? And what's with the business of the two names? Not a spy – please!'

Paul held up a hand to stop him. 'No. I'm doing this another way. Sorry, Jonathan, but it's been a bad weekend. One of the worst. I've asked Will Flemyng to help sort it out, for reasons you will know.'

Ruskin nodded, discomfort beginning to take hold. He was standing with both hands clasped behind him.

Paul glanced towards the door to the outer office through which Flemyng now came, leaving it ajar. Abel remained out of sight, perched on the corner of a desk in the adjoining room, close by.

'Will,' said Ruskin, smiling despite the awkwardness of the scene. 'Ready for a holiday?'

Paul intervened. 'I'm going to leave you two old friends alone now. Believe me, this will be better.'

Flemyng could see the abrupt handover had left Ruskin a little shaken, despite his smile. His face was beginning to turn white and there was sweat on his forehad that hadn't been there when he arrived. The long body was tensed up in the chair. Flemying's mind skipped away. Francesca was right, he thought, he does have Sinatra eyes. Ruskin's mouth was turning downwards, and he patted his fair hair in place several times in the course of the time that it took for them to arrange themselves opposite each other at the desk. 'Bloody hot,' he said, although Flemyng looked cool and comfortable.

He had considered beginning with an apology for the strangeness of the encounter, but decided against. It was the wrong moment to let go.

'Jonathan, we go back years. There's trust between us despite the business we're in. I think that's why Paul has asked me to...' he appeared to struggle for a moment '... take this on.'

He explained that there was an interlocking series of problems facing them, of which very few people were aware, but with which Manson might have some connection, as yet unknown. He was careful to use the present tense. Anything Ruskin could give them would be useful. That was all. He was one of the few who had spoken to Manson in London, it seemed, and might be able to help.

Ruskin chose first to address Flemyng's role in helping Paul, and said that, from his vantage point, in an office quite close to where they were sitting, he was aware of the many sensitivities that never surfaced in cabinet papers. Flemyng realized Ruskin was trying to seize control of the conversation – and took his cue. 'Sensitivities?'

'They've brought you in, so it will be a big one. I know my Will.' Ruskin leaned back, and his voice rose a little so that he made his next sentence a declaration, making a characteristic spring, up and over the bar.

'Let me try Berlin.' His blue eyes were glinting, and his smile widened with a hint of triumph.

'No. That means very little to me,' Flemyng replied in a monotone, his face showing nothing. 'Out of my reach nowadays,' giving Ruskin his expected victory.

'Well,' he said, 'you probably know enough to realize that in Berlin at this very moment there's a festival of sensitivity.' Flemyng had always admired his happy way with words, and realized that the wizard was at it again.

'I get the odd glimpse behind the veil.' Ruskin was grinning now and his colour was back. He said that sometimes he was able to enjoy forbidden fruits that ordinary mortals never tasted. 'I exclude you from that, Will, of course. We both know your past, and I'm reminded time and again by some serious friends in offices not far from here how much they cherish your memory.' Patronizing bastard, Flemyng thought. 'Even if they don't keep you in the loop any more.'

Flemyng turned his back and took a moment to walk to the

window, not responding. It took him a few seconds to compose himself.

Ruskin was getting up to speed. 'If we're going to get this awkwardness with the Americans fixed to our mutual advantage – I hope I'm not speaking out of turn, or recklessly, God help me – I realize that we have to find a generosity of spirit. We have to be grown-up, however hard it may be. Agreed?'

'I wouldn't know, Jonathan. Not on my radar, as I said.'

And Ruskin smiled again. Their exchange had relaxed him.

'I suppose I'm lucky to have free rein, able to poke around. It's a pity your boss is so tight with everything, playing it by the book. He should have brought you in, especially with your track record in the field. In so many dangerous places.'

It was a mistake. Flemyng felt his gorge rising and almost rushed back to the desk, although he managed to exert control and take the few steps slowly.

He stopped. In that moment, his decision was made. 'I'm afraid there is something else that we have to discuss.'

Ruskin laughed. 'What, about your boss? Changes at the top? Probably about time.'

'Please stop it, Jonathan. I'm not taking the bait.'

Flemyng spoke steadily and refused to look away. He held Ruskin's eyes. 'Sorry, but it's time to begin.'

TWENTY-FIVE

The old friends faced each other across the desk. Ruskin had not been silenced by Flemyng's announcement that he was turning to new and maybe serious business, and spoke now of secrets that were his alone. Whispers, fragments for his store. Bravado led him on, into territory that at this moment probably surprised even him. 'When we started down this path, you and I, who'd ever have thought I might some day know more than you?' he said. Then he laughed, acknowledging the crudity of his boast. But Flemyng, who'd bridled at the first arrogant thrust, had decided to resist the urge to fight. Instead, he waited. Ruskin's mood had lifted in the few minutes since Paul's departure, and now words were tumbling out of him. 'Who knows? It may be you who gets to the top. I can see it in you. We're the best, you and I – that much I do know.'

Aware that the other man would quickly run his course, because something wild was now at work in his conversation and he was bound to lose control, Flemyng said nothing. Ruskin found that he had no sounding board and his voice began to falter.

'Will, is there something wrong?' The question was weak and revealing. A cry. It was his turn to wait. Finally, Flemyng spoke.

'I'm sorry to show you this, but I must.' He opened the drawer of Paul's desk and took out the sheet of paper. 'I'd like your opinion, Jonathan.' As if it might make a difference, he added, 'I found it by accident, I promise you that,' and with the apology turned the knife for the first time. He slid the letter across the desk.

Ruskin took the photocopy, flicked an eye over it and stared. A line from a favourite poem came to Flemyng's mind: *And in an instant, all was dark.*

Ruskin coloured, and his hand seemed to try to find a grip on the desk, fingers scratching at the leather.

His eyes were suddenly alive, as if lit from behind, and his whole demeanour was transformed. Drops of sweat appeared on his jowls and his lips trembled. He gave way to fury and stamped one foot on the floor. After the uncertainty of the last few minutes, he was a man caught in the grip of terrible knowledge.

Flemyng, still and contained, said nothing more, but waited, watching every movement.

'I supppose you think I'm mad?' Ruskin said. It was close to a scream.

Flemyng had expected some preliminaries, so Ruskin's move was bold enough to make him play for a little time, and prepare himself.

'Why do you ask?'

Flemyng heard the ticking of Paul's clock at the fireplace behind him, registered the long shafts of sunlight that crossed the room. Paused just long enough.

He repeated the question, 'Why do you ask?'

Ruskin couldn't hold back. The waters broke. All of a sudden, rage poured out of him.

'Where the hell did you get this? I know the answer – bastard! Snooping around. Bloody photocopiers.' He squared up to Flemyng and shouted, 'Have you any notion what I've been through? Any idea at all?'

Flemyng refused to react, but reeled him in, slow and steady. He was trying to force a rhythm on their exchanges, and made a reply that refused to pick up Ruskin's pace. Dragged him back. 'I didn't say you had written it,' he said. 'But Jonathan, the time has come to talk.'

And Ruskin was forced to tell the story from the start.

He flopped down into the chair before the desk, his head sinking low on his chest. 'Of course I wrote it. You know that. Don't play games.'

Flemyng's next words cut through him. 'You asked me if I knew what you'd been through. What about the person who received this? I've an idea what he must have been through. How long have you been tormenting him? Maybe you saw him cry, heard his agony. Did you? Does his shame excite you?'

Softly, he added, 'Rivals don't just win or lose. They sometimes destroy each other.'

He went on without a pause, 'You're a cruel man, Jonathan, and let me answer your previous question. I don't know what mad means, not really. But I think you've passed into a world I don't understand. Do you?'

They were both motionless, as if waiting for a signal. Flemyng caught a glimpse of Paul's face in the doorway, scarred with sadness. Ruskin, looking straight ahead across the desk, didn't see him. Flemyng went on, 'Anyone reading this for the first time might think it was the person receiving this letter who'd been behaving irrationally, madly, and tearing you apart deliberately. The writer is the victim, tortured and maybe betrayed. In need of help.' He watched, but there was no fight left in Ruskin, who had slumped until his head was nearly level with the desk.

'But that would be wrong,' Flemyng said. 'These words,' he searched for the right phrase as he tapped a finger on the letter, 'are a disguise. It's the person who wrote this who's lost his balance and maybe his mind. I'm sure you sign all the letters – there's nothing anonymous here. You've created a relationship that destroys, maybe kills.'

Flemyng leaned back. 'And it won't be the letters alone. Bad advice, offered in confidence. Little stratagems to undermine him. Gossip in the right places. Manipulation, then an offer of help in his troubles, and a story of your own betrayal to turn the knife. Is that how it's been? A relationship that's so close it's deadly.'

All at once Ruskin began to weep. He banged one hand down on the letter in front of him. 'Mad, yes. So, victory for you, I suppose.'

He made an explosive noise that on another day would have been a laugh. 'But this is all true – every bloody word down here! I haven't made anything up. I've been driven to it by all this.' He waved one hand, then both of them.

'Us. This damned world we're in love with, that torments us all the same.' He added, 'So cruelly.'

Then, pleading. 'That's something you know as well as I do, isn't it? We're carried along on our hidden troubles.

'Back they come, again and again, like the sea – always there, day and night, rolling on. The tide of our lives. I used to love whatever it brought me, waited for it to come in. Now I think I'm drowning. Have you ever drowned, Will?'

His voice dropped, and Flemyng recognized the signs. He'd been trained to watch for them. With confession there often came a last deception.

For a brief moment Flemyng was not the bastard who had snooped on him, but Jonathan Ruskin's old friend again. One scene was over and they cut to another in the blink of an eye. Ruskin was wiping the tears away as he spoke.

'I'm going to tell you something I'd hoped I would never have to reveal. Please, Will, listen. As a friend, can I say that?

'I'm ill. I can't handle this life, however it may look. I've been on... stuff. Drugs, all kinds of things, and for a long time... this.' He gestured to the letter. 'I've found myself writing things, saying things, I can't understand the next morning. An hour later. I pull myself together for while. Then...'

He looked up and his eyes changed again, dimming as if a light source had been switched off.

'Did I just call you my friend? In this world? We have no friends. I've always known it. Haven't you? You were born to make it look easy. Sometimes I've hated you too, even when we've been close, having fun. Can you imagine what that's like?'

Then Ruskin spoke more quietly, his voice diminished. 'You never turn from your course, never falter. Do you? Must be cold as ice inside.'

He was veering from rage to self-pity and back again, lurching to and fro. Flemyng watched him rip the letter apart with one angry lunge, and then, in horror, saw him try to bring the two fragments back together on the desk, sliding them with his long fingers, one towards the other. For a moment he was a child at play.

The blue eyes came up to meet Flemyng's. 'Have you ever wanted to destroy a person? Crush someone?'

Flemyng sat forward and said, 'Jonathan, I think I know who received this letter, or was meant to.' And then, looking at the twisting, ruined face before him, he drew back and offered Ruskin the chance of an easier confession. 'Are you seeing anyone about this? Your state of mind?'

Ruskin expelled a deep sigh. Relief. 'Yes.'

Flemyng had been prepared for the admission. 'I know. Did you see me in the street in Mansfield Mews on Thursday, from the second-floor window? You went there after cabinet, didn't you?' Ruskin stared at him, his eyes dull for a moment, but before he could say anything, Flemyng changed tack again. He spoke in a measured tone, as if all the emotion of the moment had evaporated.

'I want to talk about the American, Manson. That's why we're here – not for that piece of paper, which is yours.' He gestured to the letter.

Ruskin was pleading with him now, all pretence gone. 'Do you know what the American asked me? Told me?' His voice rose again. 'Blackmail, as clear as day.'

'Jonathan, tell me everything, from the beginning.'

'I will.'

He shifted back in the chair, stretched out his long legs, almost looked as if he was trying to find a way of being comfortable.

Behind the door, in the ante-room, Abel moved a little closer, standing at Paul's shoulder. He could hear Ruskin's voice dropping again.

'It wasn't Thursday, like Paul said. It was Wednesday night.' Flemyng admired his ability to hold the details in his head while his composure deserted him. 'The American rang me, told me what he knew, straight out. I panicked; didn't argue. Told him to come to the House, just like that. What else could I do? It was so quick.

'When he came, he asked me about… my son.' Flemyng nodded, as if he had known all along, and gave no sign that he was hearing Ruskin's story for the first time. With that gesture of encouragement Ruskin accepted one more blow: that it was his secret no more. Gone, carried away on the tide.

'Rape? How dare the bastard! I tell you, Will' – Flemyng knew that he was floundering now – 'she's madder than I am. Vicious. Awful.' He was telling the story from the middle outwards, betraying his assumption that his questioner was ahead of him, and had heard it before.

With Abel listening carefully at the door, Flemyng asked for one important piece of information. For Abel, at Maria's prompting. He told Ruskin that travel records had been examined – didn't reveal by whom, or whence they came – and that he didn't appear to have visited America at what he called the relevant time. How did Ruskin know the boy in Georgetown was his son?

He snorted. 'America? Wrong, Will. Don't get ahead of yourself.' He shifted violently in the chair.

'It was in Oxford. We were together for a few days, no more.' He sounded weary now. 'I could tell you the college. The date of the stupid bloody conference and the number of the room, for fuck's sake. I've been sending money all these years. You doubt me?'

A last flare of pride, not quite extinguished.

'It wasn't over there, it was here. Did she tell your people that? Liar, as ever. Or did you just make a half-arsed assumption?' His instinct for combat resurfaced, even at the moment of collapse.

With Ruskin squirming before him, shrunken and trembling, Flemyng knew it was the moment to strike. 'I want you to meet a friend and colleague of Manson's, Jonathan. We need to know why it was so important for him to confront you. This is about him, not you. Here's his friend.'

Abel walked in. 'Hello, Minister, my name is Grauber.' Flemyng smiled and sat back, the baton passed. Ruskin greeted him inaudibly, seemed unable to rise to shake his hand.

'I'm afraid I have some bad news,' said Abel, without preamble, to give the follow-up punch its full weight.

Ruskin was now almost gasping for breath as he said, 'Bad news?'

Flemyng and Abel were watching every twitch of the face, every flap of the hand.

'Yes,' said Abel. 'Joe Manson is dead. That's why I'm here. This has nothing to do with your son. He is of no concern to us, and we wish him no ill. Nor you, if you can believe that.'

Ruskin sprang to his feet and loomed over them both. 'Dead?' He put both hands on the desk, and turned his head towards Flemyng. 'How?'

'Drugs,' said Abel. 'That's how it was always going to end for him. But I have to tell you that he worked in a sensitive part of our government. You won't have known it, but he did. The consequence is that we need to know what he was doing when he died, because he was in the possession of information that was precious to us.' He added, 'I realize that you understand these things, given your own involvement in sensitive matters.'

Without pausing, making no concession to the figure in a state of near collapse at the desk, he said, as if reconsidering Ruskin's first reaction, 'My question is simple. Did you know that he had died?'

Ruskin's poise came back in ragged fashion at the last, and he staged a rally. Flemyng admired the effort. 'Dead? What are you talking about? All I know is he was as high as a kite – I can tell it when I see it, as Will is aware.' He glared at Abel. 'You're a friend, after all, you know his problem. When he challenged me – insulted me, threatened me – I left him on the terrace at the House. He'd phoned me and I'd agreed to meet him for a drink… because of what he said he knew. Stupid. Said he had the whole story, and that it might all come out. I told him to go away and never come back and that was the last I saw of him. I went to my room in the House and locked myself in, raged for a while.' He sagged back into the chair.

The brothers watched him. They had rehearsed the last piece of choreography, and Flemyng took the lead.

'Jonathan, this has been unpleasant for all of us. You've been frank, and nobody envies you the experience of having a troubling piece of your past thrown at you without warning. We all have something tucked away. But you'll realize with this death – it's very private by the way – that you will need to be spoken to, because you met Manson. He worked for his government, came here under cover, and is dead. We have to know why. The investigating officer is called Osterley, from Special Branch, and he'll contact you. You'll have to lay it all out for him. When you met Manson, where you saw him, every word that was spoken. The lot.'

Ruskin's china blue eyes were wide.

'It will be today. You know what it's like, trying to keep a lid on these things. We need to move fast. He'll listen to your story. Tell him everything, and then it's over.

'He will be particularly interested in the hour of Manson's confrontation with you, because he died on Thursday, not Wednesday.'

Ruskin tried to smile. 'Something must have happened after I saw him then. He was obviously on drugs. I've been there and I've looked over the edge.' With a physical effort that was obvious to everyone, he said, 'I'm so sorry. He was a sad man.'

Flemyng could see that Paul was watching through the crack in the door behind Ruskin, still wearing an expression of horror. He seemed not to have moved for several minutes.

'It was sad indeed,' said Flemyng. 'And violent too, I think, at the end.' He slid back Paul's desk drawer and took out his own blue handkerchief. From it he extracted the short sliver of marble he had picked from the floor of the store-room and placed it on the table. 'Violent enough for a big bust of Gladstone to be split almost in two. I think the crash may have been the last thing Joe Manson heard.

'Poor Manson, mad enough at the end to have a fight with a statue.'

There was silence.

Then Abel said, 'I'd like to thank you, Minister – Jonathan, if I may? It's a difficult moment, especially for those of us who knew Joe. Please tell the police everything you can. No doubt we'll meet again.'

A twitch appeared on Ruskin's face that Flemyng had never seen before, and he sighed. 'I will,' he said as he walked – stumbled, to Abel's eyes – towards the door.

Abel matched his brother's timing with his last shot, Paul watching from the adjacent room.

'There is one particular difficulty that Osterley may ask you to help with. Just so you know.'

Ruskin turned to face Abel. As he did so, he caught sight of Paul. But the fight had gone from him.

'It looks as if Joe died from drugs that were injected. There was a syringe nearby. But we know he'd never used one in his life. Any light you can cast...'

Ruskin gazed at them both in turn, shook his head towards Paul, gave a kind of bow and closed the door behind him.

TWENTY-SIX

The clock struck the half-hour and broke the silence that Ruskin had left in his wake. Paul was back at his desk, with Flemyng opposite him and Abel standing by the window, looking towards the park. 'I need to send a message,' he said. Paul gestured to the outer office, and he left without another word. Flemyng had never seen Paul silenced so quickly, and watched him grapple with feelings that had robbed him, for the moment, of all authority.

Abel closed the door gently behind him and Flemyng waited for Paul, giving him the chance to regain command. After a few moments his grey eyes came up, and met Flemyng's. 'The most terrible scene I've ever witnessed. I had no idea... The agony. How has he hidden it?'

'Necessity,' said Flemyng without obvious emotion, and pressed on.

'Was it you who sent him to see Archie Chester?' Now that he had opened himself up to the questions that must follow, Paul didn't pause to ask Flemyng how he knew. Instead, he let it flow.

'Yes, but not for this kind of thing.' He waved to the door, as if the shadow of Ruskin were still there, refusing to fade in the light.

'Tell me,' said Flemyng.

'We've often used Chester for people in difficulty. Top man, and more discreet than some of these characters. Your old friends have a good relationship with him and he's sorted out a few of their walking wounded, one way or another. You must know that.' Flemyng gave no response. 'Ruskin came to me months ago with a story about troubles he was having at home – maybe true for all I know – and said he needed help. His wife has always hated this life, as you know. Did I know anyone? Naturally I mentioned Archie. I had no idea there was a drugs thing going on. Well, I know now. My God.'

Flemyng said, 'He's dangerous of course, knowing what he does. He sees so many of the papers, wanders the byways, knows where the bodies are buried.' He shook his head at the phrase. 'I'm sorry.'

Paul slapped his hand on the desk. 'Exactly. You know what he's like – ear cocked for any gossip. I couldn't believe it when he mentioned Berlin. I knew then that he'd flipped. Will, that's as deep as it goes.'

He got up and stretched. 'I'm sorry, I found that a physical trial.' He went to the window, and spoke with his back to Flemyng. 'I'm going to fill you in a little more, because I think after the last half-hour you deserve that at least. You're cleared for most of this kind of thing obviously, but we've had to keep this so dark you'd hardly believe it.'

He walked to a side table where his secretary had laid out four china cups and saucers on a wooden tray, even the biscuits that she knew Ruskin liked. The pot of coffee was untouched. No one had noticed it. Paul stood there, the host embarrassed by having forgotten his duties.

Flemyng took up the reins. 'I can help you, Paul. On Berlin, I should tell you that I've discovered enough to give me an outline, and in my head I've been colouring in the picture. Let me try it out, and see how we go. You don't need to say anything.'

Paul made a gesture of relief.

'I have a few facts and I've been thinking about the gaps,' Flemyng said. 'This probably sounds strange, because you think you get it all in this office, but I think for just about the first time in this whole bloody saga I may be able to assist you. Let some light in.'

Paul stayed absolutely still but his shoulders had relaxed.

Flemyng began. 'The way I took your request for help was that you needed me to think for you – to try and understand the connections between people that weren't immediately obvious, and watch how they behaved. My old game. I don't imagine for a moment this is what you wanted me to unravel, but I was drawn to it. Of course I was, like a trout to the fly.

'First of all, I made the assumption that your alarm about Berlin – I know Sassi mentioned it at the opera – must involve a sensitive source. Nothing else produces this kind of panic. It's familiar enough to me from days gone by, and I learned enough from an old friend to set me on my way. But there was a problem I couldn't unlock. More than one, as it turned out.

'A surfeit of allies.' Flemyng echoed Sam's words. 'A phrase I picked up recently, and it won't go away.'

He closed his eyes in a natural effort at concentration. When he resumed he had turned away instinctively to avoid distractions and as he began to spin his story, in a measured, soft tone, he and Paul had their backs towards each other as if neither wanted to acknowledge what lay between them.

'To begin at the beginning, I went back in time. Two decades, Europe in the deep freeze, Hungarians on our conscience, the sixties still over the horizon. You remember it – a grey world. Starting out – Berlin, then Vienna – I was aware of a

357

trickle of gold dust that came through a crack, treasure so precious that it was hardly spoken about, even among friends. I was junior, a boy and not much more on my second posting, but I was lucky enough to see it shine. I know others who spend a half a lifetime and never get the chance, but I was taken into the game, played my part and grew up in a hurry. I was in on it, and I loved the dark, Paul.'

He took a few steps and put his hands on the desk. Paul was still turned away.

'I was blessed. I ran errands to our source, and steadied him in the storm. We spoke, started a friendship, played a little. Berlin, twice in Vienna much later. One or two other places. I was the messenger who turned into something more – an ally, you might say. I brought him comfort, courtesy of London, and held his hand. Prepared him for the years ahead. It was the making of me, as well as him.'

Neither of them had smiled much in the course of the morning, and as Paul swivelled to face him, he saw Flemyng's long face still serious. But there was confidence in his bearing, his hands loose and his voice strong.

'He was mine, Paul.'

Flemyng spoke of the prize he'd been given. 'I was young, new on the street. By chance I fitted the part, that's all. And I think you know this, Paul – our friend wasn't on the other side, in the enemy camp. He was on our side of the wall. But just as precious as if he'd been in Moscow, so we thought. His isn't a story that happens over there. He's in the west.

'And now in the middle of all this.'

Paul, grey and serious, said, 'Go on. You tell it.'

Flemyng was fluent, the story clear in his mind. 'Here's a speculation. After my time, our man prospered. We played him long, and it worked. No name, you and I know the rules.

But year by year, he gave more. And we've learned from him a great deal about how another ally – the big one, our best friend across the pond – is operating on our continent, sometimes on its own and sometimes with others, and not always in our interest. That story is gold dust, for sure. Everything we've always wanted. He was the source we have dreamed about so often, looking east and west, laying Europe bare and preparing us for the time when we're all in from the cold, and we'll start all over again. When he'll still be ours.'

Paul said, 'What was your phrase? A surfeit of allies. How true.'

'And you'll understand how I made the connection,' Flemyng said. 'There was something particular about this asset, our man with the bag of gold dust. A promise that he made me give from the start: that he was ours and not anyone else's. His help was for us alone. And now I hear of a request for access from Washington that has got this whole place pitching and yawing like a ship in a storm. It's too much of a coincidence. I see all the signs – and they smell to me like a mixture of pride and something else. Guilt. I don't think it can be anyone else.'

Paul laughed for the first time. 'When I asked you to think for me, this wasn't what it was about, you know. I needed help with the Manson business because I wanted to know why he was here. That was all. You've raced off on your own. I should have known.'

Flemyng's voice had softened. 'They're inseparable, Joe Manson and Berlin. He was a danger to the whole deal. And I think I know why.'

Paul said nothing. Waited.

Flemyng picked up. 'I decided there must be two operations at risk. One of ours, and one of theirs, coiled up in a knot. Let me try this one out on you.'

He laid Sam's precious fragment before Paul, like the jewel that it was. 'Assume that the Americans discovered they had an ugly problem of their own in Berlin, that normally they wouldn't share, even with us. A leak, operations gone wrong – all the tell-tale signs that one of their own might have wandered off the reservation and gone bad. Embarrassing, but they needed help and turned to us.

'Did you ever hear of an operation called Empress?' Paul stared at him. 'We used an ally to do some of our own dirty business, years ago, on our own doorstep. Inside government. I'm told Operation Empress is a clue, and I think I may know why.'

It's what allies were for in time of need, he said. 'The Americans had heard a whisper about our prize asset so they hatched a plan. Maybe they didn't have the name, but they knew enough. Get us to use our source to identify their leak. Plant information, send some signals and follow them, track him everywhere… that kind of thing. The same kind of help that we got in Empress – an ally called in to muck out the stables.'

He thought of Sam, his excitement at retelling the tale, then his admission that he'd come to a dead end. 'I think I've worked out the next chapter.

'We gave the Americans a dusty answer. We were reluctant, backed away. Unusual, to say the least. So I asked myself why. Sure, they had rumbled the existence of our super-source and we were piqued, appalled if the truth be told, but allies are supposed to help each other out.' He paused, and Paul gestured with one hand: keep going.

'It leaves me facing one conclusion, which may explain why Sassi and my brother and, for all I know, half a dozen other people are crawling round this town with cloaks pulled round them, looking like death.'

He stepped towards Paul as he turned from the window at last.

'I can think of one good reason why their request should provoke so much reluctance on our part, and fear.' They were face to face now.

'*Their* man, their bad egg, is one of ours. Turned by my old friends, bless them, and for all I know just as useful to us as the seam of gold that we've been trying to protect, and keep from the Americans. And we worried that this operation would break him.'

Paul's eyes were in shadow, the sun coming through the window behind him giving his profile a soft halo of light. 'Go on.'

Flemyng said, 'Our closest ally, the special one, has rumbled our game. What we've been doing to them in Berlin, and it hurts us both. The nightmare of nightmares.'

Paul spoke. 'If Gwilym were here, he'd call it a bugger's muddle.'

'Quite,' said Flemyng.

He said he assumed Maria Cooney had worked it out first. 'She understood why we were stalling, why we had something to hide and what it might be. Miles ahead of the game as usual, which is why she's still running her own show.

'She put the squeeze on us. They knew we'd turned one of theirs, and they played hardball. Wanted double rations. All the stuff we'd got from their guy who's been working for us – everything we've had from him and others of his ilk, for all I know – and on top of that, access to our prized source, inside the European government that's going to be the most important of all some day. Our German benefactor.

'And what if we said no?

'The worst threat of all. My guess is that they've threatened to blow our asset so that we end up covered in horseshit.

Humiliated with one European ally – and at the same time denied the stuff from Washington that we depend on, day by day, just to keep our peckers up. The prospect has had a lot of people in this town wetting themselves.

'All for refusing to behave like a good ally.' Flemyng laughed.

'So here was the American deal. Give them access to our source, let them dig our seam of gold, and at the same time open the books on all the material we've had from their guy whom we turned. In return they promise to protect our Big Person, and lift their skirts for us in some difficult places here and there where we need to know things we can't get for ourselves. Trust us, they said: a nice payback. Otherwise, no deal and a long, cold winter.' Flemyng was aware that he was beginning to sound like Sam.

'Then Joe Manson stepped into the middle of it all, doing his girlfriend's business.' Flemyng shook his head.

'He explains the panic. He was the guy who knew too much and might talk. Three allies, at least, would be screaming at each other, and, just for once, so loudly that people out there' – he gestured to the window – 'might hear. The thing we dread more than anything.'

Paul sighed. 'You're there, more or less. We have to buy the deal, because there's no other choice. They have us by our private parts, and they're twisting hard. So here's our problem.

'How can we persuade our big source that everything from him is shared with Washington? He's not that way inclined, as I now know you learned an age ago. Quite the reverse. And he's in a position to know if we start to share it – believe me, he sees everything these days. Why do you think we've got such good stuff on the Americans from that source over the years? As well as goings-on over the wall, I may say. So we've had to be open with him about what the Americans want. Everyone has his pride.

'It's been our game for a long time and we don't want to change the rules. We've had to work to persuade our brave helper, who's been on our side through long, difficult years, that it's better to do what Washington wants than to go down in flames. Very hard when we're having to admit to our American friends at the same time that we've got one of theirs.'

No win, but no choice. Fortunes of war.

'Sassi knows, and he's been good – given us some time. Helped with oiling wheels. We may be able to get what Washington wants, and still keep some of our pride. There I must stop. Almost nobody knows all this. But Ruskin, and this is what's scaring me rigid, knows more than he should and he's worked out much of the rest for himself. Just how much, I can't say, because I'm frightened to ask, and that's the truth.'

Massaging his cheek with nervousness, he added, 'You're so similar, you know. Peas in a pod when it comes to this kind of thing.

'If he knew nothing, it would be a crisis that was more… normal. As it is, we can't know what he might do.' Serious again. 'And what else did Manson tell him?'

Flemyng thought for a moment. 'Was Ruskin going to the Washington embassy?'

'Might have been, God help us,' said Paul. 'But not for sure. He's got his supporters.' He looked down at Ruskin's letter which still lay on his desk, torn apart. 'But it could have been Forbes. Even you, although that would have been over Forbes's dead body. Sorry, inappropriate.'

So Forbes had been poisoning the well. 'That's why I'm "the bastard Flemyng",' he said, and Paul's eyes creased at the corners. 'Forbes rang me on Sunday morning at home – I'd been on the hill, in the early light – and said he wanted to pass on something as a friend. Said he was worried about Ruskin's balance; alarmed that he might get Washington. Could I help? Crap, of course. He didn't know what we do about Jonathan. Jay playing his own game, as ever, trying to tie the rest of us in knots.'

Paul said, 'We were going to sort it out this week, after Paris. Putting somebody big there was going to be part of the repair job after Berlin. A peace envoy. We'll be back to square one now. My guess is that Dennis can pack his tennis racquets, but that hardly matters.'

Flemyng knew he was thinking of Joe Manson's body in its icebox, and counting how many people knew something of the story, wondering what Ruskin might do next.

'Think for me, Will. Keep going.'

Flemyng said, 'I will. I'm going to talk to Abel in a minute. He'll be telling Maria everything, and I'll get his version of events. We've had a few good days together. Maria knows me, too: there were a couple of ploys, way back when. Today should see it done. Let's regroup later. And, Paul, I have more.

'There's another door to unlock, and I may have the key.'

Paul walked towards him, said nothing, neither smiled nor frowned. His face seemed empty. 'More?'

'I'm having dinner with Abel and Mungo tonight,' said Flemyng. 'The three of us, at the club, a kind of celebration. In the midst of this, we've had a real coming together. Join us at about nine if you can. I'll have a good idea how the land lies by then. It would be good if you could be there.'

'I shall be,' said Paul. 'But tell me more about the call from Forbes. I need to know.'

Flemyng smiled. 'Apart from what he said about Ruskin? Said he wanted to help me if I wanted the embassy. Could put a word in where it might help. I asked him why it was so bloody sensitive.'

Paul asked how Forbes had responded.

'That he had no idea. Relations better than ever, he said. Nothing on the horizon. Which, I guess, is about as far from the truth as you can get. As he well knows, because he's in the middle of it. Don't you love our game?'

Paul raised his hands. 'I'm not really in it.' He shook his head. 'You do the politics. We carry on.'

But Flemyng had more. 'Let me ask you straight. Did you know that our super-source was once mine?'

Paul shook his head. 'No. But when Osterly gave me that line from Manson's notebook – *Friend Flemyng knows* – I wondered why he was treating you separately from the others. You were on a different page. I decided that what you knew was something different from the others. Yours alone.'

Flemyng turned away before he spoke. 'You were right, and you weren't the only one to work it out. It wasn't the rape I might know about, but something else.'

Paul said that he felt sympathy for the source, a friend who'd helped London through difficult times and who'd remembered the guarantee that Flemyng had been the first to give him, when they were youthful recruits on the battlefield. 'This could break him,' said Paul.

'I know,' said Flemyng. 'I spoke to him last night.'

TWENTY-SEVEN

Flemyng hailed a cab in Whitehall. 'When were you last there?' Abel asked him as they climbed in.

'Ages ago,' he said.

When Abel had suggested after their breakfast together the visit they were about to make it had startled Flemyng because it was unexpected, but then struck him as obvious. He thought of the small, light dining room where he'd passed happy times with friends, the bar where he'd told his share of tales, the photographs that lined the walls and stairwell like the filmstar trophies of a proud maître d'. But these were faces that would mean nothing to outsiders, their fame a matter of private pride. Members knew the building simply as Our Place because it was where they could mingle with their own kind, and let the rest of the world pass by.

They were not far from the Lorimer, in a crescent of mansion flats, and stopped the cab so that they could walk the last two hundred yards. There was no brass plate at the door, only a bell. But the door opened as they came up the steps and a dapper, grey-haired figure, ramrod-straight and without a crease on his suit or his military tie, beckoned them in. 'The club is delighted to welcome you both. Let me take you to the secretary's office.'

Flemyng was greeted quietly by two men climbing the stairs together, on their way to lunch, and an elderly woman in a

high-backed chair in the corner of the lobby gave him a warm
smile. She'd been a fixture in the office library where he used
to retreat for solace and thinking time, and he got a little wave
from her. But it was the habit in the club not to interrupt conversations, and she let the brothers pass without a word. They
heard laughter from the bar. When the secretary closed the
door of his office behind them, he welcomed them both and
addressed Abel.

'We're delighted to help, Mr Grauber, and I've looked out
one or two things for you. I'll leave you for a few minutes. I
know you're both busy and can't spend much time here today,
but perhaps we may dine one evening. I should be able to help
you further.' With a brisk nod of his head, he left them alone.

On the table were two brown leather folders, recovered
from the informal club archive in the basement. Abel opened
the first, and they looked together at an album of photographs.
They both thought of the picture Mungo had produced at
Altnabuie, of the Bletchley hut on a sunny day. These showed
the house at the centre of the park, three different huts, a group
of departing passengers at the local station – arrayed like the
survivors of an arduous school trip – and a selection of individual shots. One had been removed from its cellophane folder.
It showed their mother sitting at a desk, a sheaf of papers in
front of her and, on her dress, a brooch which they knew well.
It was still in a drawer in the sitting room at home, and it
always brought her to mind.

'I think there are more,' said Abel. 'And this.' He flipped
open the second folder and they looked at the carbon copy of
a typed report. Flemyng began to read. It was a brief memoir,
written by his mother, beginning in January 1944. 'I'm told we
can't take it away,' Abel said. 'But it's here for us any time we
want it. Today isn't the day, but I suggest we both come back

sometime. OK?' Flemyng nodded, looked again at the picture, and closed both the folders.

They thanked the secretary who materialized in the lobby the moment they'd left his office. And promised to return. Flemyng spoke with obvious emotion. 'Those years made my mother, in all kinds of ways. I think they still teach us a great deal. Thank you.'

'My pleasure. Good afternoon, Mr Grauber. Mr Flemyng. Until the next time.'

Outside, they walked in silence for several minutes and took the tube to Embankment, where they walked along the river.

*

At times they were still feeling each other out, as if, despite everything, they were at the start of a relationship. Yet warmth welled up and brought them by degrees to a closeness that was all the better for having taken time, and been worked at back and forth. Each felt it deepening, minute by minute, although they didn't address the feeling directly. Patience, for both of them, was a way of life. They visited a gallery, then walked without a plan, letting instinct be their guide. By late after-noon they were back at the riverside, Abel with a bag of second-hand books swinging by his side. Only then did they begin to talk of the family and their hopes for the future. 'My energy is coming back,' said Flemyng. 'Does it take a crisis?'

'Probably,' said Abel. 'That's my general rule. When this is over, I hope we'll both take something away from it.' Then, changing pace to speak more slowly, he delivered what he had planned to say.

'And, more to the point, leave something behind.'

He put a hand on his brother's shoulder as he spoke, and squeezed, forcing Flemyng to stand still.

He was silent for a moment, and didn't move. Then all the tumblers in the lock rolled over, and he was in at last, all the way, through the last door. A thrill of revelation ran through him. He said nothing. All at once, he knew how it must be.

He started to walk again with Abel slightly behind him, and a few minutes passed before their conversation resumed. For the first time since they'd spoken in Paul's office, after Ruskin's departure, they turned to Maria. Her message to Abel had suggested that the last pieces were falling into place, and Flemyng said he'd like to see her again, away from the battlefield.

'After this, she's all yours,' said Abel.

Flemyng was caught in the embrace of his own emotions. He recovered by reverting to practicalities. 'What happens with Ruskin? His state of mind, what he knows?'

'If you were Paul you'd have to advise – insist – that they try to keep him in his job, on the condition that he agrees to get straightened out immediately, and is watched right the way through. Keep one more secret in the box and nail the lid down. He'd be a nightmare on the loose.'

They parted as the heat of the day was subsiding, Flemyng leaving Abel at the Lorimer and taking a taxi home, reassured by a feeling of satisfaction greater than he had known for weeks. Two hours with Francesca, then he would come back into town for dinner at his own club, and the end of it all.

*

They dined well, Flemyng having booked the private room where they sat at a perfectly round table, with the lights down low. There were candles on a sideboard and the brothers revelled in the warmth of their soft light. They told old stories, spoke about Altnabuie, and agreed that they would travel north the next day. Flemyng could escape with them for forty-eight hours. Mungo had sent Babble on ahead, and they thought of him preparing happily for the night sleeper and savouring the thought of highland air, hip flask in hand. They spoke of the family investigations that Mungo and Flemyng must begin, and Abel found himself humbled by the relish with which they spoke of the research that lay ahead. 'I'm a schoolboy,' Mungo said. 'Starting again. And do you know,' he continued, raising a glass to toast the family, 'all will be well. For you, too, Will.' At another time, sententious; at that moment, perfect.

Paul arrived on the stroke of nine and greeted Mungo warmly. After a few minutes small talk was suspended. Abel spoke first. 'Mungo, you'll have to excuse us for a few minutes.' He and Paul left the room, closing the door behind them.

'I can tell you that our end is fixed,' Abel said as they sat together on a bench in the empty cloakroom corridor. They had their backs against the panelled wall, and a straw hat hung on a member's peg just above Paul's head; a dangling pink-and-green ribbon touched his shoulder and gave him a splash of colour.

Abel was going through an invisible contract, clause by clause. 'I've spoken to Maria. She knows what your imprimatur means. Paul, she and I understand how difficult this is for your people. But I can tell you that there will be benefits. You're giving us something important, so there will be payback in the future. Generous payback. That's the deal Sassi has done, and your guys know it. He's determined to acknowledge what you've persuaded everyone to do at your end, and he will help. He's seen the cables – a good selection, let's put it like that –

and knows the thing from both ends. Been through it backwards in the last week.'

Paul said, 'I know. It's done.'

Abel continued. 'To be clear, I've told Maria that your asset will be open to us, that it is understood on both sides and everything will be confirmed in a letter, hand-delivered to Washington this week by a trusted emissary known personally to both parties. It will be read at the highest level – the very highest – with only three people present, in an office I need not name. Correct?'

Paul confirmed London's acceptance. In truth, he said, he knew of only two such occasions in his time, but a private letter – bypassing the Washington embassy – was sometimes the only way. It would be written the next day, when the Paris party returned, and carried to Washington immediately. Afterwards, it would be brought home to London where it would rest in the deepest dungeon.

He said, 'We both know how important it is to put this behind us. Believe me, it will happen.'

Their to-and-fro pledges piled up. Paul was authorized to say that certain operations in the past using an American official would be disclosed. The books would be opened, and bygones would be bygones. Each of them knew that things were never so simple, but the promise had to be made.

The smoke could clear, and some of the embarrassment with it.

Abel said that the file would be closed at that moment, and added that there were bound to be some matters in London, and other places too, which could be shared in times to come as recompense. Some, by which they both knew they did not mean all, not by a long stretch. He raised an eyebrow and smiled. 'We never know what we don't know, do we?' he said.

'And it will all be over,' said Paul. 'Until next time.'

Abel looked at the floor. 'Yeah.'

He said that a notice was going out to all American embassies the following week, routine circulation. It would intimate that after a distinguished career in the foreign service, Mr William K. Bendo II, late political attaché and liaison for the Berlin military mission and the embassy in Bonn, was retiring to take a job in the private sector, based in London, carrying the thanks of his colleagues with him.

Abel said, 'We'll be talking to him at some length, as you know, to go all the way back. Starting in a few days. I'm on leave from New York until it's done.'

He went on, 'In the end he was relieved. Profoundly, I think. Always the way. Couldn't talk about it, though. Wouldn't let the last veil drop, even for me.'

Abel recalled the beginning. 'I was just the hound who followed the scent.' It was Maria who first sniffed out the trouble. Poor Bendo.'

'When?' said Paul, being one for timetables. Abel shook his head.

No one wanted blood. As the affair came to its end, each was aware that some day the story might come to life again, but for them it was winding down. Abel's heavy eyes lifted towards Paul's, carrying a hint of amusement. They smiled together in the shadows, and heard a gust of laughter coming from the dining room as a waiter opened the door.

Each reflected on the truth of his different life, that restoration was their common watchword. Keep it running, make it work. They spoke of Maria, and how it had been managed.

'My worry was always that it would get out of control after Manson died, without anyone trying to make that happen,' said Paul. 'We couldn't know what he'd said, who he'd met, whether he'd been trying to unpick the whole thing. We knew nothing of his motives, and that terrified us. And it turned out to be sex, as usual. Ruskin and a bloody one night stand.'

Abel said, 'And we worried that it would foul up everything we were trying to get you guys to do for us in Berlin; that some minister's personal crap would make you batten down the hatches and call it all off. Because it turns out that Ruskin knows too much about Berlin, doesn't he? Without that we wouldn't have had any of this trouble.

'Strangely enough, we've been saved by his collapse. After this morning, that terrible scene, he'll have to pull back. He can't face ruin. You've got him in a job here where he can be controlled, offered help. You can force him through. He's scared to death.' Paul said, 'I know that now.'

Abel continued. 'Maria held it together. Kept her nerve. And all the time I worried about Will, because I couldn't tell him. You realize that. It would break the rules that keep us together. To be brothers, we need some secrets.'

He then surprised Paul. 'I did find out about that message about Will, you know. From Wherry. Who else? *Friend Flemyng knows*, in Joe's notebook. I assumed it was from her. You too?' Paul said nothing. 'She knew of Ruskin's political friends, because she's watched them down the years – fascinated by the whole gang – and told Joe to try to get to Will, thinking he'd know all about it. Knew nothing of the complicated closeness between Will and Ruskin. Had Will's number from me – years ago, for emergency use – and I've wondered why he didn't use it first thing he got here. Any ideas?'

Paul shook his head.

Abel said he'd come to the conclusion that it was something else that Flemyng was meant to know, a story from Berlin. 'I don't think that message came from Joe's woman at all – I think he'd picked it up in Germany on his own. And I've no doubt it came from Bendo. There wasn't much he didn't know about your operations over there, and he was panicking. We know how it is with guys who're near the end. I'll soon find out – we're taking him in to start his debriefing. Might even let your boys know.' He laughed.

There was nothing more to say. They got up, turned the corner back to the dining room, where the other brothers were deep in conversation and claret. On their return, Flemyng went to the lobby to ring Francesca. She told him to contact Lucy, urgently.

He rang, sounding unsure. 'What is it?'

She said there was no trouble of an official kind, for once. But did he remember that on Sunday night – there was an awkward pause – she had mentioned that she was writing something personal. Yes. Well, it had come to pass. She'd been offered her next posting, and had made her decision. 'I was going to say no, but I've changed my mind. I wanted you to be the first to know.' Flemyng was embarrassed to feel relief, but he did. 'Where?'

'Washington, in October.'

He found himself laughing. 'Well, I'll see you there from time to time, no doubt.' He congratulated her, and strode back inside feeling an inner glow that he hadn't known for many days.

It lasted for a few minutes. They shared a glass or two, Abel left to speak to Maria, and Mungo spoke to Paul about Altnabuie, and how the brothers would soon be together on the hill and the loch. He described the world that he'd always known, the place that sustained him. Paul's expression of envy was genuine. He could almost hear the burn tumbling through the woods, the dogs racing for the hill.

The moments stretched out happily. Abel came back. Then

Paul was summoned by a porter's knock on the door and a quiet word. He was gone for nearly ten minutes. When he returned he stood in the corner of the room, and became an outline in the shadows with a tableau of pictures behind him, standing away from a wall light that cast a soft spotlight beside him, and watched over by an Edwardian actor dressed as a Shakespearean king. Flemyng saw that his shoulders were drooping. He straightened a little, and his head went back. Then he turned, a hand at one cheek.

'It's not over. There's a last act.'

TWENTY-EIGHT

During the days that followed, Mungo confessed to his brothers that he wondered when he heard that announcement whether he could hold his emotions in check. As a man whose carefully balanced life had been disturbed by the eruption of family secrets, he was vulnerable to the rising temperature that he felt around him, the flow of events bringing on a fever that he thought of as a proxy for his brother's distress. At Paul's words, he said he found it difficult to breathe, then turned light-headed, thinking himself liable at any moment to let his distress show, even to collapse. It was almost too much to feel another turn of the screw. Flemyng saw him stiffen with great effort when Paul spoke. Abel was quite still, arms at his side. Everyone in the room would later conclude that somewhere in the happy confusion and the heat of that climactic gathering they knew what Paul was about to say.

'Ruskin is dead.'

'Mungo, please,' said Flemyng, breaking the quiet that had fallen. 'If you don't mind.' His brother rose and left the room a little unsteadily, closing the door behind him with a benign gesture. They heard his footsteps cross the hall.

'Overdose,' said Paul.

'That was his driver on the phone, patched straight through by the switchboard,' Paul explained. 'He was due to pick

376

Jonathan up for the airport. He'd planned it, so it seems. Left the door open so that he would be found. As he has been.'

All colour had left Paul's face. 'I'm afraid there's a note. It has your name on it, Will. They're bringing it here now.' There was agony in his expression. 'God save us. This is probably the best way for it to end, and that's the most horrible truth of all.' Abel took the news as if he had been waiting for it, and Flemyng said quietly, 'He was once a friend, and often a good one.'

Twenty minutes dragged. Mungo stayed away. He must have found somewhere where he could sit quietly, probably alone. A messenger arrived, and a letter was put on the table, Flemyng's name underlined on the envelope in Ruskin's green ink. Together they heard his confession.

It was jumpy and nerve-ridden. Flemyng read it quickly and again more slowly in silence, and then gave them some passages aloud. He opened by saying that his colleague's style, Ruskin's care with words, had deserted him at the end, a snake's skin discarded at the last.

'You now know that I was a man in perpetual panic. Total torment. Went to a shrink. Chester tried, and failed. Did you know that? He'll talk now. I couldn't break it.'

There was a pathetic addendum. 'I did try.'

'You'll have guessed what happened with the American. When did you know? He rang me on Wednesday and he was cunning. Didn't get into personal stuff on the phone, it was very quick, but dropped a name that he thought would hook me. He was right, of course. Bill Bendo, our own American.'

Flemyng stopped for a few seconds. He heard Abel sigh.

'I'm assuming you didn't know, Will, but I did – the biggest secret I'd ever learned. Got it by accident and treasured it. I was proud of the trophy on my mantelpiece that no one else was allowed to see. Do you think that's sad? I do, now.'

At this point, Flemyng stopped again, as if to let the horror sink in, and watched Abel. Nothing. He didn't ask about Bendo. Back to the letter.

'*The American came to the House – it must have been nearly eleven o'clock – and changed tack. Dropped Bendo like a stone, poor sod. He knew something of me, and revealed what he'd got from his woman, about the past. I agreed to take him to the terrace, and we went to the far end where we could be alone in the dark. He confronted me – told me what she might do, spoke of my son. I told you that.*'

Flemyng paused at this point and looked around. No one met his eye.

'*Will, my life dissolved in that instant.*'

The intimacy cut through his concentration, and touched the frailty they shared. Flemyng's voice was low as he spoke to Paul. 'Remember – we were there, on the terrace, you and I, soon afterwards. An hour earlier and we'd have seen them together.' Back to the letter.

'*That was our first time, on Wednesday evening. I told the truth about leaving him after that awful drink on the terrace. But he rang again the next morning, very early. I was on my exercise bike.*'

Flemyng was pained by a flashing image, rich in pathos, of the long thin legs pedalling fast, trying to carry him through the crisis and away.

'*I'd had a very bad night. It's when the demons come. I picked him up in the central lobby when he arrived, and while we were walking down the back stairs from the corridor near the library he started making threats. He was jumpy as hell, staring at me. I was taking him that way to go outside; the terrace is the best place in the mornings, as you know. I couldn't believe that we were having this conversation in public. Sparger passed us on the stairs. I* was panicking. *The American said he knew I was bound for Washington, warned me off. Said I'd be ruined if I went. She'd go public and make me the scandal of the decade. Me! But I'd decided I wanted the embassy. A different field of glory. Thought it was mine, and would have it this week. Snapped.*

'*I pushed him against the wall. He pushed back and kicked me away. We were wrestling on the stairs like kids, and more or less fell into that damned cupboard. We shut the door. He went straight for me; no messing about.*

'*I should tell you something about myself on top of today's confessions. I use a syringe. Need it, and more often than anybody realizes. He was full of stuff from the night before – I could almost see it swilling around behind his eyes – even told me all about it, because he'd found out that I was one of Archie's boys. I don't know how he knew that.*'

At this, Flemyng looked at Abel, who shook his head.

'*He thought that was his triumph; but it was the end of him. I was angry. . . cornered. I lost all control. Please understand.*' The tone of the letter was childlike now.

'*I wept. I went mad. Violent. The bloody statue fell over. You showed me that broken bit of marble, and that's when I knew that you might work it out.*'

Flemyng said, 'I could see that it had split off recently. All it told me was that there had probably been a struggle, and therefore it was likely that Manson hadn't been alone in there. It pointed the way.'

Back to the letter.

'*The American was so fragile, still quivering from the night before. A sad sight. I must so often have looked like that. Did I? I've always tried so hard to hide it.*

'*I had thought I might need some stuff and I had the syringe primed. It was heavy stuff, and of course I knew where to put it.*

More than enough. And the worst kind. Twice, three times. . . I don't know, I was holding him down. He passed out and I filled it up and did it again, I suppose to finish him off. Mad. Wiped the syringe, and the door handles and everything afterwards. Put his hand round the thing, quickly. Did it work? But I cried afterwards. Do you believe that? I hope so.'

Flemyng paused. He had nearly come to the end.

'I went to cabinet at ten. Paul saw me there, and I can take some pride from the fact that I showed nothing in the whole hour and a half. Even spoke, tried to be kind to Sorley about his bloody bill. I suppose that was an achievement of sorts. I wonder now how I managed. Most of all what I thought it was worth.

'Then today you had me in Paul's office. I couldn't hold it together when I saw what you had. I copied the letter – don't ask me why – like all the others. All my scribbles. Had to keep the words. They're part of me, my other self. I sometimes read them aloud. You'll find them all in the flat, in one of my old red boxes. I've left it unlocked. It terrified me that they were there, but I needed the danger, more and more. You'll understand.

'Everything's there. The other letters, a terrible diary that I'd like you to read and then destroy. Please, Will, for me. I'm remembering our old friendship now. I've been looking at some of the letters again. It's as if they were written by someone else, but you'll understand. A rival has destroyed me without know-ing it. I used him to kill myself. Say sorry to him. You'll know who he is.'

He gave no name.

Paul waited, and Flemyng said, 'Brieve, of course. Jonathan couldn't bear his own freedom to roam being challenged, cur-tailed. He wanted it all, and it drove him over the edge.'

He didn't wait for an invitation to go on, being ready to tell his story. 'I came to believe – though I was slow to get there – that somewhere in the middle of this were wild emotions that had been let loose. The letter told me that, and I was scared. But who? If I'd been quicker I'd have seen the light on Thursday. Ruskin told Francesca at the opera that he knew I'd been seeing an old friend, gave a name. I won't say who it was, but I'd seen him that morning for the first time for a long time. A panic call. We were outside a psychiatrist's office, and I had a suspicion I was seen. So it was Ruskin who was inside.

'Everything follows from that, doesn't it?'

He shook his head. 'Poor Joe Manson. Two governments worrying about what he knew about Berlin – but that didn't kill him. It was Ruskin's secret that finished him off, not ours.'

He said that after he'd concluded that Ruskin was consumed by jealousy and fear, guessed that he was visiting Archie Chester, he'd realized who the object of his rage must be, who must be the target of the letter. The man who was stalking Ruskin on his own territory, treading the same paths with his own favours to sell, maybe getting ahead of him. Threatening his rise. 'I felt sorry for Tom Brieve for the first time. He must have cried, had long dark nights.'

He described his surprise summons from Brieve on Thursday, and their stilted conversation in the cellar bar before the opera. Wondered aloud if events would have taken a different course if he'd given Brieve time, and some encouragement. But he had denied him that chance. 'Might it have saved Jonathan's life?' he said into the silence. 'Forget Manson, I shouldn't push that question away and I won't forget it.'

Paul shook his head. 'No. It was a collision of events that was unstoppable. The simplest of emotions, let loose in one man, and powerful enough to affect us all, nearly bring us down. And to kill Jonathan.'

Flemyng said there were other references in the letter to his own relationship with Ruskin which, if they didn't mind, he would not read out. 'That would be a kindness to him. I should just say that they are warm, apologetic, sad.'

He looked at the last page. He had reached the end.

'I am so very sorry that it is over.'

Then the wobbly signature, touchingly formal – *'Jonathan Ruskin'*.

Everyone stayed quiet.

After a while, Paul said, 'It will be handled discreetly. A personal tragedy, which, of course, it is.' He looked around for reassurance.

'There will be obsequies, and proper mourning. Maybe even' – his mouth twitched – 'a burst of sympathy for the government. And no more deaths.' It might have been an order.

'Then,' he said, 'it will truly be over.'

The room was silent. Each of them would remember afterwards the feeling of release at the moment of death, and the atmosphere infected them all. Ruskin might be gone, but family troubles were being calmed and, with Paul's command and his announcement that the denouement had come, they began the slow settling of accounts.

Abel leaned back in his chair as if to speak, but gazed ahead. Flemyng saw in his mind the scenes from six days flickering before him, with the faces of Ruskin and Forbes, Joe, Osterly, Sam and Chester, and behind them Maria, dark and tall and wearing a wide smile, appearing before his eyes as a chorus line of ghoulish clowns. They were out of control, disappearing in turn and materializing again, leaping up and zooming towards him like the chaos of another dream. Painted in lurid colours, their faces dazzled him for a few seconds, almost made him cry out. Then the images faded, as if the lights had gone out, and there was blankness. He heard Francesca's voice. Shaking himself, he felt as if he had known a seizure and survived.

He spoke to Abel. 'Could you join Mungo for a minute or two? Sorry. I need to talk to Paul alone. You understand.' His brother looked darker than ever as he rose, the shadows shrouding him and his eyes losing their light. 'Of course,' Abel said. 'Your game.'

*

All was still except for the candlelight playing on the club silver, and flickering over an incongruous snuff horn shaped as a bulbous ram's head. There was no ticking from the clock on the mantelpiece. They were alone. Flemyng got up and began to walk slowly round the table, as if performing a ritual dance to bring things to a close, moving in and out of the patches of light cast towards the table. 'I said earlier there was another secret to unlock. As one of my old friends says, there's always one more.'

Paul waited.

'I'm sorry that it must be now, with blood flowing around. I thought this might have been in Ruskin's letter but it seems Joe Manson didn't tell him what the Americans feared he might, the secret they've been trying to protect all along. Thanks, Joe.'

His hands were clasped together in front of him. 'I've been puzzled from the start by Washington's panic over Manson. Why did they think he could screw everything up? It would obviously be awkward with Ruskin, or whoever it turned out to be, if he were named ambassador and Manson blundered in. But it wouldn't destroy their Berlin operation, because that was no-win for us – we were stuck and couldn't pull out of the deal without a backlash. They knew about Bendo, and they wanted their pound of flesh in the form of our prize asset. Or else they'd blow him: and probably told us how they'd do it, in excruciating detail. We had no choice.

'But there was something else, and they didn't want us to know it.

'I think I know what it was.'

Paul stood up to join in Flemyng's stately progress round the table. They speeded up gently as they went, getting energy from each other.

'Abel avoided an important question that I put to him in your office today when we were alone after Ruskin left. When did they start to suspect that Bendo was ours?'

Flemyng was surprised when Paul smiled, despite everything, and said, 'I asked him the same thing, out there a moment ago. He just shook his head.'

'Think it through,' said Flemyng. 'There's a good reason. Manson made several trips to Europe in the last two years – Abel let that slip – and I'm willing to bet we could find his tracks all over Berlin. They've known about Bendo for longer than we think. Much longer. Manson was doing Maria's business there.'

'And…' said Paul, softly and encouragingly.

'They'd turned Bendo back to work against us,' said Flemyng. 'My guess is that they used him to poison the well without his knowing the whole story. It's the only explanation. For a long time he's been laying false trails, an agent we thought was our own. I'd say he was all over the place, didn't know who was really running him, panicking. I've seen it before, believe me. A fish struggling in the net. But it's we who've been played for suckers in Berlin.

'And now they've got formal access to the best source we've ever had there – and for all I know on the whole sodding continent of Europe since the beginning of time – all because we've had to admit that we recruited Bendo, which it turns out they knew. Nice one, Maria. A corker.'

'Maria?' said Paul. 'She keeps popping up. We must meet.' He managed a laugh.

'It's beautiful.' Flemyng was powering on, his eyes closing as he laid it out, piece by piece. 'And Manson threatened to wreck it. Maria knew he was going a little nuts and understood far too much. She was terrified about him blurting out to Ruskin – or me, or Forbes or Brieve or anybody – that Bendo was being used to send us off in a hundred different directions, a conduit for disinformation. Their hold on us would be broken; we'd have held out to keep our super-source to ourselves. Difficult for her, far worse than our embarrassment in admitting what we did with Bendo in the first place. That was the worry. She didn't care about a randy ambassador. Who does? It wouldn't be the first time.

'That's why Manson was so dangerous with his loose tongue. He could have made us all look stupid, and screwed up the American plan. Politics would have gone haywire – here, in Berlin and Bonn, in Washington, other places where we have to be careful with the Yanks. Not out there' – a wave to the street – 'but where it matters.'

Paul sat swirling a glass of claret.

'Do we tell Abel that we know?' he said. Practical to the end.

Flemyng sat down beside him and picked up his own glass. 'Leave that to me. The answer is no, for now. There's no advantage to it. The deal goes ahead because there is no way back now, the letter is read and approved in Washington, the channel to our source is opened up. Bendo disappears. What's done is done.

'Nothing will look different, although everything will change.'

He timed it perfectly, taking a long sip of wine, allowing a few seconds to pass, and resuming with gusto to lighten the atmosphere.

'And change for us too,' he said, smiling, eyes searching for confirmation that Paul might already be there. He was happy to do this together.

Paul put both hands on the table, and leaned forward. Flemyng was certain now that he knew, and shared the tingle of expectancy that had returned. Journey's end.

'You realize, don't you, that there is a big prize in this for us, despite everything?' Flemyng said. 'I was slow. It only came to me when I was with Abel this afternoon. He said he would be leaving something behind.'

Paul waited, allowing him the honour of moving the last piece on the board, getting them home.

Flemyng picked up. 'We both know that there was a moment when this whole business turned inside out. Someone came to your office and told you about the rape accusation. We put it together with Manson, knew why he'd come to London and – maybe – why he was killed. You and I both understood then that in the middle of this puzzle was raw emotion. Manson's and someone else's. Not politics. Pure passion.

'Everything flowed from that visitor's message, and it's why we're here now. The word was passed on, but I think it contained a second warning that we were meant to work out for ourselves, of which the messenger had to be unaware, because it touched on him and his role in our lives. What he's been up to. We'd understand who had sent him, and what it implied about their relationship – know why he was chosen for the task and what it revealed about him. That second message was, I think, even more important than the first.

'Who?' Flemyng said.

Paul was smiling. 'When we spoke about my visitor at the time, I said "a colleague", didn't I?'

'You certainly did.'

'Can you guess?'

'Forbes.'

Their eyes locked. A few beats of silence followed.

Paul made a gesture of acquiescence. 'After he told me his story, I drew my own conclusion about his source, knowing that Abel was in town and might want to get information to us, somehow, and without using you because that's off limits. Forbes told me that he had been passed the story deliberately; it was no casual discovery, something overheard. He stopped short, for once, of boasting about his sources. You and I can see why. He didn't know who Manson was, nor that he was in London, let alone that he was dead, so he couldn't know the significance of the story and its danger for him – what it would tell us about him and his connections, what he's been doing, maybe for a long time. Who he's worked for. His loyalties, if I can put it like that. And I assume he still doesn't know, which is important.'

Flemyng said, 'The other part he doesn't know is just as important. Abel and me. We'll keep it like that, shall we?'

Paul smiled. 'You can be sure of that from my end. You know, I think he's the first… of his kind… that we've been able to nail properly. Rumours a few years ago about someone – not far from your office – but nothing solid. Plenty of small stuff from time to time, loose talk, lots of people a little too free and easy with sensitive stuff when they're in Washington. But Forbes tilts the scales in a big way. We're lucky, I suppose, though it's going to be hell to handle.

'You told me, Will, that you'd picked up hints of a security panic. I knew nothing of it. But after Forbes came to see me,

I talked to your old friends. Sure enough, there had been talk. It's very tight, they've kept this one to themselves, but they've had an eye on him for a little time, feeding things and waiting for them to be regurgitated in Washington. A black entertainment.

'But they had no proof. Until now.'

Flemyng could see Sam in his mind's eye, the friend who'd wanted to warn him, his arms flying and his story speeding up. A minister… an alarm… surveillance. Except that it wasn't the bastard Flemyng, but the bastard Forbes. He smiled and thought of Abel and Maria, their decision, their offering.

'Let's call it a brother's gift,' he said, and, because they had to set the seal on it somehow, they shook hands in a solid grip. 'We can deal with him, now that it's over. Ruin, but no one will know why. I think we know that it was from him they learned about our source in Germany, maybe Bendo too. And after that, his work was done.' Paul shook his head.

'A painful journey, and through a storm, but you can help. You've been here before.'

*

The six days in July were over. Together they spoke of days of freedom ahead, and Paul confessed his weariness. 'We've both aged,' he said. 'Has this changed you?'

Flemyng tuned in to his more intimate tone. 'No. Just confirmed me in my thoughts.'

Ruskin's confession had hit Flemyng hard, made him review friendships and times of trust, and the tragedies of Ruskin and Forbes had forced him to walk again the boundary between loyalty and deceit that years ago he'd been trained to recognize and navigate. 'Sounds strange, but I'm restored. A friend behaves badly, lets people down, threatens a colleague's sanity, then he kills. There's more betrayal, and I feel the flames burning at my feet. But it's the life I've chosen, and for good. Maybe I've thought all this inevitable, and I feel justified in seeing it all played out.'

After a moment or two, Paul said, very quietly, 'I know.' Then his voice rose. 'I think I should tell you this. Mungo rang me yesterday, and he's never done that before. He's been worried about you. I said you needed this life. He said he's come to understand that, and I think he wanted reassurance that he was right. So he got it.'

Flemyng's head was down, and his words to Paul were spoken softly, as if he were alone. 'I love the life, want the wheel to keep turning. The price is too high, but I know I'll always pay it. I just have to accept that with the good there's a touch of the terrible. Madness, too, and nearer the surface than we think. That's the truth I've learned.'

His hands were locked together. 'I can tell the wild emotions are there, almost feel them.'

'And Abel?' said Paul.

'Balancing loyalties, of which I'm one. But this business has given us energy and we're closer. He feels alive. We know we've been keeping things back, and always will, but we can cope with that because it's our choice from long ago. Trust and deceit, lifelong companions. I used to think I'd accepted that.'

He stood up, and Paul recognized his impulse to find a place to be alone. Excusing himself, Flemyng said he'd go outside for a few minutes. When he went down the steps he found it busy in the warm darkness, theatre crowds heading homeward and a string of orange lights stretching from nose to tail of a winding crocodile of taxis that filled the length of the street. He dodged the rattling traffic and took cover in the dog-leg of the cobbled lane that led to the opera house, where Francesca would be managing a post-performance party. On a quiet corner, half in shadow, he seemed a man apart. He was the only person standing still in the late-night flow, looking forward to a deeper darkness and the silence of the early hours. A passer-by felt a stab of recognition at his profile and nodded a friendly greeting. Flemyng raised an arm, but no words passed between them. On the opposite corner, a jumble of young men tumbled out of a pub, and he heard the bell behind the bar ringing for time. As Paul had known, he was searching for a place of solitude to think of friends – one dead, one facing the end of his career – and had found it in the anonymity of the street, where no one knew anything. An observer asked to describe Flemyng in these minutes, framed in the brick arch of a darkened doorway, would have noted that his head was up and his shoulders back. Confidence was coming back – there was strength in a moment of loneliness, even refreshment.

The consolation that he got from solitude had a physical effect. He recovered his balance in those few minutes, leaning back against the arch without the tautness that Abel had felt in his shoulders, crossing one foot over the other as if posing for a picture and showing off his ease. The night was a veil for the transformation that was required and that he had known would come, even as he prepared for the fall of his friends. His expression didn't change, the dark clefts on his cheeks framing a serious face, and his eyes were down. But when he did stir from his seclusion his tread was decisive and his head was up.

When he retraced his steps and climbed the steps of the club, he saw Mungo crossing the hall to return to their private room. Catching up with him from behind, Flemyng placed a hand on his shoulder. 'I'm sorry that this celebration has been touched by a tragedy.' They paused at the door, and he whispered, 'We'll survive.'

Paul and Abel were sitting together, leaning back from the table, displaying relaxation at a melancholy moment. They were both smiling, and Flemyng saw that Paul had removed Ruskin's letter, wiping away the bloodstain. Mungo exploited his status as outsider to officialdom and briefly assumed the role of host. 'We're going home tomorrow,' he said, raising a glass. 'To a new day.'

Paul joined the toast and then, standing up, prepared to leave for his office and the management of another death. 'I'm afraid this one has to be horribly public,' he said. 'But easier, despite everything. No one out there will know why. They so seldom do.'

He raised both arms and dipped his head in a gesture of farewell, recovering his natural balance. 'I must away.' In the corner, he pulled tight the buckles on his briefcase, patted his pockets and looked over the table, taking in the scene at the moment of farewell.

Flemyng was standing to one side, against the wall. He was keeping his thoughts close, and remained apart. On his face there was a trace of relief that had been absent for days – some of the dark lines were softening now – and it was obvious to his brothers, watching him from the table, that he had recovered some of the physical confidence that had seemed to be threatened in the rush of events. But still, he decided for the moment to stand alone, and said nothing.

Abel rose, and he and Paul touched hands to say goodbye as if a pulse were being transmitted between them. 'We kept the show on the road,' Paul said, in a serious tone. 'Thank you.' Abel put out his hand, as a gesture to accept the compliment. Flemyng watched his eyes. They were warm, and understanding. As his brother turned, he caught Flemyng's own look and smiled. Then he sat down, knowing it was not a time for words.

Paul turned away and the door clicked shut behind him. Abel moved to Mungo's side and put an arm across his shoulder. Their glasses touched, and Mungo's eyes glistened.

No sound disturbed the stillness of the moment. They kept silence in the half light, and treasured the quiet they had recovered at the end of the day.

Flemyng's thoughts were far away, by the woods and the water. Tomorrow, at least, no more madness.